The Novel Map

THE NOVEL MAP

Space and Subjectivity in Nineteenth-Century French Fiction

PATRICK M. BRAY

NORTHWESTERN UNIVERSITY PRESS
EVANSTON, ILLINOIS

Northwestern University Press
www.nupress.northwestern.edu

Printed in the United States of America

10 9 8 7 6 5 4 3 2 1

Library of Congress Cataloging-in-Publication Data

Bray, Patrick M. (Patrick Maxwell)
The novel map : space and subjectivity in nineteenth-century French fiction / Patrick M. Bray.
p. cm.
Revised and expanded version of the author's dissertation—Harvard, 2005, under the title: Novel selves: mapping the subject in Stendhal, Nerval and Proust.
Includes bibliographical references and index.
ISBN 978-0-8101-2866-8 (pbk. : alk. paper)
1. French fiction—19th century—History and criticism. 2. Space and time in literature. 3. Subjectivity in literature. I. Title.
PQ653.B73 2013
843.709384—dc23

2012020393

∞ The paper used in this publication meets the minimum requirements of the American National Standard for Information Sciences—Permanence of Paper for Printed Library Materials, ANSI Z39.48-1992.

CONTENTS

ILLUSTRATIONS

ACKNOWLEDGMENTS

This book attests to my enduring fascination with spaces and places. While writing this book over the years, I have had the good fortune of hiking above an ocean of fog in Big Sur, sneaking into the catacombs of Paris at night, walking through an inhabited cemetery in Cairo, and contemplating an unending sea of cornfields in Champaign. But a book is made of more than nostalgic atmospheres. Innumerable friends and colleagues have nourished this project with their time and insight. Nearly every sentence bears the trace of a conversation (real or imagined) with a dear friend, to the extent that rereading my text is like traveling across a virtual space of memory. Textual time travel is all the more important when it becomes the only way to communicate with those who have passed away.

This book began life as a dissertation at Harvard, the idea for which came from seminars on authorship and literary theory taught by Abby Zanger and Naomi Schor. My advisor, Janet Beizer, and my readers, Tom Conley and Christie McDonald, offered not only a wealth of knowledge and insight, but have followed the project through all its stages. I am grateful for their mentoring and remain awed by their scholarship. Nelly Furman has been a friend and mentor from the beginning; her enthusiasm inspired me to become a *dix-neuvièmiste*. Lawrence Kritzman, through his devotion to the study of literature and the warmth of his friendship, has taught me the value of an intellectual community.

The Bibliothèque municipale de Grenoble graciously allowed me to consult the manuscript of Stendhal's *Vie de Henry Brulard*, which proved invaluable to the first two chapters. Stanley Hoffman and Michel Zinc facilitated my entry into the Bibliothèque de l'Institut de France, where I was able to scrutinize firsthand Gérard de Nerval's "Généalogie fantastique." I owe thanks to the Sablé Center at the University of Toronto for allowing me to consult their materials on Zola's dossiers for the *Rougon-Macquart*. I have benefited from the financial support of several institutions whose help was crucial to the realization of this project and for which I am duly grateful. I received a dissertation completion fellowship granted by the Mrs. Giles Whiting Foundation, a summer faculty fellowship from Indiana University, a Hewlett international research travel grant, and a humanities released time grant as well as a publication subvention from the University of Illinois. I would also like to thank Jonathan Strauss, Emily Apter, and Lawrence Kritzman for generously inviting me to speak at their institutions; the Zola chapters of the book have greatly benefited from the discussions that ensued.

Significant portions of the book were read at different stages by Lia Brozgal, Ross Chambers, Elisabeth Hodges, Natasha Lee, Richard Regosin, Philip Usher, Armine Mortimer, and Lawrence Schehr. I thank all of them for their encouragement, their careful reading, and especially for their patience in correcting my myriad typographical whims and rhetorical flights of fancy. My editor, Henry Carrigan Jr., deserves special thanks for believing in the project from an early stage and shepherding it through the review process. I would like to thank Andrea Goulet and David Bell, whose comments enriched the final manuscript.

The support, friendship, and dynamic energy from three intellectual communities have sustained me during the project. At both the Nineteenth-Century French Studies and the Twentieth- and Twenty-First Century French and Francophone Studies Colloquia, an incredible group of friends and scholars meets once a year and inspires me throughout the year: Bettina Lerner, Ari Blatt, Sara Pappas, Jonathan Strauss, Marina van Zuylen, Deborah Jenson, Maurie Samuels, Dorian Bell, Lauren Fortner, Alison James, Steve Spaulding, Alison Rice, Jeff Fort, Joseph Mai, and countless others. At Indiana University, I particularly appreciated the intellectual camaraderie of Sonya Stephens, Oana Panaïté, Margot Gray, Caroline Strobbe, Gil Chaitin, and Jérôme Brillaud. At the University of Illinois, I would like to express my gratitude to everyone in the French Department for their warm welcome and continued support: Jean-Philippe Mathy, Armine Mortimer, Karen Fresco, Margaret C. Flinn, Alain Fresco, Laurence Mall, Adlai Murdoch, Peter Golato, Zsuzsanna Fagyal, Marcus Keller, Annie Tremblay, and Émile Talbot. Larry Schehr's critical insight, humor, and friendship cannot be replaced. Students in my graduate seminars on literary and spatial theory engaged in exciting discussions with me and helped to refine my arguments. I am particularly indebted to Jenelle Grant, Elizabeth Black, and Audrey Évrard. Other colleagues at Illinois have expanded my intellectual horizons and have created an incredibly rich community of friends and scholars (in no particular order, and with apologies to anyone unintentionally left out): Jim Hansen, Renée Trilling, Justine Murison, Derek Riddle, Rob Rushing, Lilya Kaganovsky, Caroline Szylowicz, Jane Kuntz, Richard Powers, David O'Brien, Jennifer Greenhill, Irene Small, Masumi Iriye, Lauren Goodlad, Michael Rothberg, Eleanor Courtemanche, and Ted Underwood.

Jean-Louis Jeannelle, Louis-Georges Tin, Estelle Castro, Julien Artero, Pauline Perrignon, Julien Meyer, and Catherine Meyer have all provided friendship, thrilling conversation, editorial advice, lodging, and numerous lessons on how to be a French intellectual. Maj-Britt Eagle first brought me to literature, philosophy, and critical theory, and inadvertently saved me from medical school. I am deeply grateful to my parents, Pamela Bray and David Rydland, for instilling in me a love of books and an understanding of the vital importance of beautiful landscapes. I owe an unpayable debt to my late grandparents, Gordon and Luella Dague, for their countless sacrifices and unwavering support.

I dedicate this book to my wife Maggie and to my son Sebastian—may we continue to build beautiful things together.

AUTHOR'S NOTE

All translations are mine, unless otherwise cited. An earlier version of chapter 4 appeared as an article in *French Forum* under the title "Lost in the Fold: Space and Subjectivity in Gérard de Nerval's 'Généalogie' and *Sylvie*," *French Forum* 31, no. 2 (Spring 2006): 35–51. I would like to thank the editors of that journal for their kind permission to reprint the article.

The Novel Map

INTRODUCTION

Here and There: The Subject in Space and Text

Talisman and Map

Toward the end of October 1830, an unnamed young man, having bet and lost his last coin on cards at the Palais Royal, enters a curiosity shop on the Left Bank to while away the hours until the evening, when he can throw himself in the Seine under cover of darkness. To his mild surprise, the dejected youth finds before him four galleries of astonishing antiquities encompassing all regions of the world and reaching back to the beginning of time. In a state of confusion between waking and dreaming, he practices a Cartesian philosophical doubt ("le doute philosophique recommandé par Descartes") concerning these fantastic visions, reminding himself that magic does not happen in the Paris of the nineteenth century. Suddenly, there appears in the shop an ancient man, the antiquarian proprietor, who resembles either Moses or Mephistopheles. Mocking what he supposes to be the trivial torments afflicting the young man, he offers him both a general law of human nature and a Faustian bargain. The antiquarian's philosophy juxtaposes on the one hand the two words Will ("VOULOIR") and Power ("POUVOIR") that sap the force out of life, and on the other Knowledge ("SAVOIR"), which lulls the mind into a perpetual calm. Between the deadening stillness of scholarly detachment and the fatal pursuit of sensual gratification, the old man encourages him to choose knowledge, as it affords the vicarious, "intuitive" pleasure of seeing. If the youth rejects his sage advice, a shagreen ("chagrin") or talisman made from a wild ass's skin will confer on its contractual owner the power to effect anything he wills. The talisman bears an inscription in an Eastern language promising to shrink in size with every wish granted, "even as thine own days" and is roughly the dimension of a "geographical map."

So begins Honoré de Balzac's 1831 novel *La Peau de chagrin.*[1] Of course, the unknown young man ("l'inconnu") accepts the bargain with the talisman only to die at the end of the novel, and the reader's knowledge of Parisian society and human nature grows as the magic skin shrinks with every wish fulfilled. I would like to argue that the talisman functions as both text and map of the unknown subject, the "inconnu" whose story, the reader is often reminded, could belong to anyone. He acquires an identity and a name, the impossibly fanciful Raphaël de Valentin, but only after he accepts the contract, when he leaves the shop and encounters some friends on their way to a gala. The morning after, the third-person novel becomes a fictional autobiography as Raphaël recounts in flashback the woes that led him to contemplate suicide. As if in a lucid dream, exactly like the "Cartesian" one he experienced at the start of the novel, Raphaël can see, not all of human history and geography as he did in the shop, but his entire life spread out before him in the distance:

> Je ne sais en vérité s'il ne faut pas attribuer aux fumées du vin et du punch l'espèce de lucidité qui me permet d'embrasser en un instant toute ma vie comme un même tableau où les figures, les couleurs, les ombres, les lumières, les demi-teintes sont fidèlement rendues. . . . Vue à distance, ma vie est comme rétrécie par un phénomène moral.[2] (120)

Instead of the wine or a "moral phenomenon," Raphaël might attribute his heightened awareness, his ability to see his whole life framed in the space of a painting or contracted in the distance, to his new "skin" that is from now on bound to his fate. The talisman, later in the novel explicitly compared to a map, is a simple atlas that represents time spatially; Raphaël counts with horror the dwindling years, days, and minutes remaining in his life by carefully tracing the skin on the wall and accurately measuring the gap between the line and the talisman that expands with every desire realized. Just as Raphaël and the magic skin share a mysterious and inextricable bond as geography to map, their contractual union is inscribed as text into flesh: inspecting the talisman in the shop, Raphaël attempts to cut away a slice of the magic skin to see how the text was engraved, but the lettering reappears, as if materializing Jean-Jacques Rousseau's words in his *Confessions, intus et in cute* ("inside and under the skin").

Balzac's *La Peau de chagrin* allegorizes the transubstantiation by which any subject can be inscribed in the space of a text. Like Descartes, whose anonymous doubter must first doubt his own material existence before proclaiming the metaphysical and universal "cogito," and like Marcel

Proust's nameless narrator, who floats amid various bedrooms of his past before landing in the bedroom of the present and the beginning of his narrative, Balzac's unknown young man, on the verge of suicide, finds himself outside of space and time ready to abandon himself to the unknown of a text. His suicide by drowning exchanged for the certain death of the self in a text, his initial anonymity replaced by the universal "I" of a narrative that refers to anyone, Raphaël de Valentin signs a contract of dubious value. To write oneself as text, to enter into narrative language is to lose the connection with the material world. Fighting for his life, attempting to abolish all desires from his mind, Raphaël imposes an absolute, prescribed order on his new mansion, where he no longer has to engage with the world. He reserves his concern only for the magic skin, the map of his life, which shrinks in inverse proportion to the expanding novel recording the details of his agony. After the analeptic, autobiographical middle section of the novel, Raphaël's story returns to the third person; the slow contraction of the skin, the world surrounding him, and his life can only be witnessed from the outside. The allure of the talisman lies here, in the illusion of a text upon which can be engraved an image of one's entire life from birth to death.

The question of the subject's relation to space and text has been at the center of French thought for at least the last several hundred years. From Renaissance cosmography to poststructural critiques of cyberspace, French thinkers conceive of power in spatial terms. The constructions and contradictions of the modern subject were formed before the Enlightenment and the French Revolution. The founding text of the Cartesian moment and of the modern conception of subjectivity, the *Discours de la méthode* takes the ambiguous form of a spiritual journey of a man who discovers a scientific method and epistemology but who eventually does away with the spiritual in favor of the rational—the mirror image of the journey taken by Raphaël de Valentin. René Descartes's project is purposefully oxymoronic: an anonymous autobiography that creates a universal model for subjectivity. The narrating *je* ("I") is divided into at least two modes; the first *je,* autobiographical and personal, prepares the way for the second *je,* which is metaphysical and universal. The care taken in the employment of the two rhetorical voices is designed to guide and control the understanding of the reading public. The autobiographical voice announces itself as if it were writing a fictional text: "[Je ne propose] cet écrit que comme une histoire, ou, si vous l'aimez mieux que comme une fable" (*Discours,* 49–50) ("[I only propose] this text as a story, or, if you prefer, as a fable"). This is the "fable" of a man who searches for truth in all of the traditional methods: letters, science, travel, and war. But instead of finding a certainty for truth in any of these ways of learning, instead of finding his own Being, he fears losing himself in illusion (after one has traveled too long "on devient enfin étranger en son propre pays"—"one becomes in the end a stranger in one's own homeland"; *Discours,* 52). The autobiographical voice prepares the way for the metaphysical voice by demonstrating its own incapacity for finding the truth and establishing the negation of knowledge not derived from reason. The autobiographical voice creates an itinerary of salvation, a pilgrim's progress, where the self can be lost; the metaphysical voice draws a perspectival map for the foundation of subjectivity.

Descartes recounts in the first four sections of his *Discours* the studies of his youth, his travels, his doubts concerning scholasticism, and finally the fateful night when he feigns that he has no past, no body, no perceptions. All that remains is the fact that he doubts and thinks. The moment of doubt, and the creation of a universal subject, is a moment of fiction that depends upon the feigned negation of time (both past and future) and of body:

> Je pensais qu'il fallait que . . . je rejetasse comme absolument faux tout ce en quoi je pourrais imaginer le moindre doute . . . je voulus supposer qu'il n'y avait aucune chose qui fut telle qu'ils nous la font imaginer . . . je me résolus de feindre que toutes choses qui m'étaient jamais entrées en l'esprit n'étaient non plus vraies que les illusions de mes songes . . . que je n'avais aucun corps et qu'il n'y avait aucun monde ni aucun lieu où je fusse. . . .[3] (*Discours,* 98–101)

From the moment of doubt, which is a moment of fiction, he establishes consciousness, then being, and finally God in an ontological proof in the tradition of Saint Anselm. He constantly moves between the use of fiction and the counterfactual mode (indicated by the imperfect subjunctive) and a condemnation of imagination and the unconscious. Descartes incessantly worries throughout the text about publication, about losing possession of his theory, of his self. He claims that no one has ever understood or ever will understand his method, but he wants the *Discours* to provide a model: his discovery is unique and personal, but reveals the centrality of reason and its universal effect. The paradox of an inimitable yet rational model pervades the *Discours* through the mapping of textual space. In *The Self-Made Map,* Tom Conley has argued that Descartes's is a cartographic text. Descartes's famous affirmation of planned cities by rational engineers and architects also applies to the planned writing of the text and more generally to the planned invention of subjectivity (Conley, 289–91). The single, mathematical perspective of the architect configures the city in the same way that the authority of the author configures the text and its future readers:

> The cartographic subtext implies that the space that the author is describing is available to anyone and everyone, like a regional projection, but that a regional projection is also conceived according to the laws of monocular perspective. An all-powerful author needs to be placed at the vanishing point of a city-view redesigned by mechanical or artificial means. (Conley, 291–92)

In the unsigned and anonymous *Discours,* Descartes inscribes himself at the vanishing point of his cartographic text (Conley, 298). He is a new subject reborn from maps, "René Descartes." Cartesian metaphysics relies on a suspension between an autobiographical and a fictive mode in order to present a theory of a unified, universal subject, which is nonetheless dependent upon the perspective of an author mapped onto the spaces of a text. Descartes's vision of a universally applicable method and a rational subject relies on the fiction of a "novel map," a textual projection fusing the subject with its object of study.

As if in response to Descartes's intuition that his universal experience of the cogito may not be repeatable, Jean-Jacques Rousseau, at the other end of the Enlightenment, developed in his *Confessions* a theory and praxis of an intensely personal autobiography, of a unique style and character. The originality of Rousseau's enterprise is that it places at the center of hundreds of pages of text the history of one individual—it makes the self into a subject worthy of investigation. Previous forms of autobiography, memoirs, journals, and conversion stories sought to elucidate a truth beyond a single person, whereas autobiography since Rousseau shifts the emphasis of discourse to the uniqueness of the individual (Lejeune, *L'Autobiographie en France,* 15–16).

Rousseau can place himself at the center of the *Confessions,* as the subject of significant attention, because he believes himself to be unique and different from others. He affirms that he is not better or worse, simply different. He does not even claim that he knows all of the truth about his past. What matters is not the subject's privileged perspective with regard to an absolute objective truth (as in Descartes), but rather the sincerity of feeling, the affirmation of individuality, what makes one subject different from another. As opposed to Descartes's universalizing cogito of negation and thought, Rousseau creates a personal cogito of sentiment

("Je sentis avant de penser: c'est le sort commun de l'humanité"—"I felt before thinking: this is the common fate of humanity," *Les Confessions,* 36). Rousseau's project exceeds a simple avowal of his own originality, for he offers his autobiography as a tool for others to know themselves. The *Confessions* will not just create Rousseau as a textual subject open to the scrutiny of readers, but will transform its readers into individuals, into subjects of the study of feeling. If Descartes attempted to mold his readers into rational practitioners of the method for which he is the only model, Rousseau proposes to make his autobiography the basis for any subsequent understanding of the self by means of antirational feeling.

Rousseau's argument that his innate difference (his individuality) and original enterprise (his autobiographical text) constitute the basis for any future knowledge of the self relies on the assertion that his autobiography provides the reader with adequate knowledge of Rousseau through an accurate representation of himself. The text that presents such a unique subject must itself be unique. In the *Confessions,* Rousseau conflates his book with himself even further, ultimately revealing the autobiographical simulacrum that equates the autobiographical subject with the textual subject: "Si la nature a bien ou mal fait de briser le moule dans lequel elle m'a jeté, c'est ce dont on ne peut juger qu'après m'avoir lu" (*Les Confessions,* 33) ("If nature was right or wrong to break the mold in which she formed me, only after having read me can one judge"). To read the *Confessions* is to read Rousseau, and yet if nature broke the mold used to cast Jean-Jacques, the text can only be a forged copy of the original. Rousseau's autobiographical subject simultaneously follows at least two textual models, that of a religious confession in the style of Augustine, and that of Rousseau's own previous novels and *discours.* Jean-Jacques is the man of nature who received the kind of education that he would later promote in *Émile* and yet who was later corrupted by society. The well-known "conversion" scene in book 8 (structurally similar to Augustine's conversion scene) reveals the stakes of textuality when Rousseau reads the subject for the Académie de Dijon prize and enters the world of letters. His decision to write and enter the public sphere is both a fall from the state of nature and the revelation of the positive and transformative power of writing. Rousseau's conversion as a born-again man of letters, and by extension his rebirth as text in the *Confessions,* risks corrupting his nature, erasing his original difference, through the contamination of (inter)texutality. But once the "fall" has happened, the only cure, the only way to correct one's ways, is to control the power of textuality by using it to serve the individual.

While Descartes and Rousseau provide the models for a theoretical and textual subjectivity, the historically determined discourses of space and time in the nineteenth and early twentieth centuries influenced the experience of subjectivity and served as catalysts for the transformation of the subject. Rousseau's focus on the individual subject was adopted by the universalizing and centralizing project of the French Revolution. As Michel Foucault has famously theorized in *Surveiller et punir,* starting in the late eighteenth and early nineteenth centuries the state and other institutions assumed the role of producing and controlling individuals through education, discipline, and surveillance. The promise of freedom gained through self-consciousness dreamt by the Enlightenment was now transformed into a method of normalizing, classifying, and organizing the subjects of the State. The overarching metaphor for the new surveillance society, according to Foucault, was Jeremy Bentham's late eighteenth-century invention, the panopticon: a mechanism that organizes human beings into individuals who interiorize the power of surveillance, each one of whom becomes "le principe de son propre assujettissement" ("the principle or beginning of his own subjection"; *Surveiller et punir,* 236). The exterior space of surveillance is now converted into the interior space of the subject.

At the turn of the last century, Henri Bergson in *Matière et mémoire* and *L'Évolution créatrice* criticized the spatialization of thought, of time, which sought to measure time as if it were space. Spatial time, present in the spatial metaphors of language and in the idea of homogenous time, prevents us from perceiving time's true nature as duration, as well as the creative processes of life or "l'élan vital." But Bergson's rejection of spatial quantity over temporal quality tended to neglect art forms, such as cinema and even literature, that combine the spatial and the temporal to visualize an image of time emerging from space. Rebelling against the sway held over French thought by Bergson at the beginning of the twentieth century, phenomenological thinkers from the middle of the twentieth century such as Gaston Bachelard (*La Poétique de l'espace*) or Georges Poulet (*L'Espace proustien*) sought to describe the effects of space on a conscious mind, as revealed most clearly in literary works. Whereas Bergson insisted on the role of intuition over analysis, Bachelard proposes a "topo-analysis" in which the intrinsic qualities of specific types of places (essentially interior spaces such as houses) are analyzed in relation to their power to create poetic images (both representations of the real and unreal inventions). Bachelard's treatment of the transformation of space as image in a literary text risks simplifying the ever-changing relation between writing subject and textual space to a series of recurring topoi.

With structuralism and what became known as poststructuralism in the United States, space became not just the object of thought but its subject; space can be conceived of as what structures thought and subjectivity once philosophy turns its attention away from consciousness. Claude Lévi-Strauss's rearrangeable "mythèmes," Pierre Bourdieu's "habitus," and Foucault's "panopticon" describe social phenomena in spatial terms even as their own thought relies on spatial metaphors. What might distinguish poststructuralists from structuralists is a certain self-awareness of the (spatial) patterns of thought. The philosopher turned writer of texts, in drawing a diagram of power relations at a given time, also invents alternative structures of thought and action: as Gilles Deleuze writes, ventriloquizing Foucault, "écrire, c'est lutter, résister; écrire, c'est devenir; écrire, c'est cartographier, 'je suis un cartographe . . .'" (Deleuze, *Foucault,* 51) ("to write is to fight, to resist; to write is to become; to write is to draw up maps, 'I am a cartographer . . .'").

While structures express a subjectivity determined by space, the origin of the structure along with its blind spots and internal breaks cannot be known. The obsession with spatial structures inevitably leads to the search for an image beyond space where new spaces and new subjects can emerge: either the negation of space, utopias (Louis Marin's *Utopiques*) and nonspaces (Marc Augé's *Non-lieux*), or the invention of other places, Foucault's "heterotopias" or Michel de Certeau's subversive (narrative) practice of space. Reality itself becomes a "simulacrum" for Jean Baudrillard, and for Paul Virilio the increased speed of information and transportation shrinks space faster than Raphaël de Valentin's shagreen, to the point where all movement stops.

To paraphrase Jacques Derrida in "Le Signe, la structure, et le jeu dans le discours des sciences humaines," the subject of space at the center of French thought blocks the play it opens up and makes possible (*L'Écriture et la différence,* 409). Whether the subject is completely determined by spatial structures or it is an ideological burden to be discarded, scientifically quantifiable or an Enlightenment illusion, theories of subjectivity either dissolve or normalize the relationship between the subject's constituent parts—self and nonself. On either extreme, theoretical formulations of subjectivity tend to obscure possibilities for individual transformation through a restructuring of subjectivity.

Just as theories of subjectivity provide an important but limited understanding of the spatial subject in literature, in a similar way, the empirical discipline of geography, or geographical information science (GIS), can offer tools that illuminate a particular real place at different specific moments in history, which may usefully be compared to the places represented in a text. As Stanley Fish suggests in his *New York Times* review of the collected volume *GeoHumanities* (edited by the geographers Michael Dear, Jim Ketchum, and Douglas Richardson and the English professor Sarah Luria), a hybrid, interdisciplinary approach such as "geohumanities" represents the breakdown of the distinction between empirical and interpretive discourses. But if Fish can assert that "interpretive methods and perspectives are necessary to the practice of geography" and that the humanities "have been busily moving into, even colonizing" geography and other disciplines, the converse must be approached with caution, since geography as an empirical, quantitative discipline necessarily reduces time to space. As Edward L. Ayers writes in one of the volume's central articles, "Mapping Time," the metaphor of the layering function so crucial to the mapped time of GIS "is a useful fiction, since it reminds us of the structural depth of time and experience" (Dear, *GeoHumanities*, 223). Mapped time is a fiction useful for geographers to understand their own interpretive strategies, but the literary scholar, already dealing with fictional maps and texts, must not conflate the metaphors used by empirical disciplines with actual quantifiable evidence. Whether the current interest in digital humanities, the sociological approach of Pierre Bourdieu's mapping of the character Frédéric Moreau in *Les Règles de l'art*, or Franco Moretti's call for a textless literary criticism in *Graphs, Maps, Trees*, quantifiable approaches supplement and supplant the fictional maps of the text with maps of the critic's own invention. One empirically based fiction, that of a contemporary scholar, covers that of another, the literary text.

While theoretical concepts provide insights on particular strategies deployed to write the self in the space of a text and empirical analysis can offer a glimpse of how space changes across time, literature alone conveys the experience of abandonment to language from the inside, the defiance of an individual who realigns spatial boundaries to imagine a new world and new subjects.

The Novel Map

The literary and cultural contexts in nineteenth-century France reconfigured both the ways literature could represent subjects and also the ways subjects related to space. This period saw the emergence of autobiography in the wake of Jean-Jacques Rousseau's *Confessions* and the rise of the novel as the dominant literary genre. First-person works occupying the space between the two genres of autobiography and novel show that the act of writing the self unsettles the linguistic and representational stability of the subject while also providing the self with the freedom to redefine the subject.

At the same time as the literary field was transforming itself, the physical space of nineteenth-century France was radically altered. The Revolution of 1789 rationalized the division of national space, drawing up *départements* around natural landmarks. The Cassini and États-Majors maps from the beginning of the nineteenth century gave the most detailed representation of geographical space available in the world. Space itself was both "compressed" by the rapid development of transportation technologies such as the railroad and homogenized and abstracted by the state's centralization, as David Harvey has argued.[4] The "production of space" by capitalism, according to Henri Lefebvre, disrupts the subject's relationship to space when space becomes "pulverized" as it is parceled out and sold.[5] This pulverized and commodified space destroys the connection not only between places but also between subject and place, connections that can be repaired through the fictional maps found in first-person texts.

The division and abstraction of space for the production of homogenous subjects requires the concomitant division and abstraction of time. The nineteenth century was obsessed with theories of history, genealogy, evolution, and progress, all of which are various ways to measure and analyze the course of time. Alongside this theoretical abstraction of time, the nineteenth century witnessed the progressive introduction of standardized time through rail schedules, optical and electrical telegraphs, and the eventual adoption at the end of the century of Greenwich Mean Time (Kern, *The Culture of Time and Space,* 11–15). Chronological, homogenous time has the same effect on the subject as pulverized, homogenous space: a shock experience that alienates the subject from the past and prevents the assimilation of time into lived experience.[6] Personal time and memories become isolated from the march of standard time and history. The romantic notion of being born too late, the decadent belief in the end of civilization and the degeneration of the race, and even Taine's critical trio of "race, milieu, moment" all attest to the experience of being subject to a time outside of the subject's control. The dominant literary movements of the second half of the nineteenth century (from the decadents to the naturalists) incorporated the shock of time and the acceptance of fatalism into their aesthetic. The bulk of scientific thinking before Einstein accepted the atomistic nature of time (Kern, 20–21).

The double context, literary and cultural, in which the novel map emerged necessitates a reading that is attuned both to the specific literariness of the text (the subject as represented by language) and the text's materiality as a map. By looking at the maps drawn in the manuscripts of Stendhal's *Vie de Henry Brulard* (1835), Nerval's "Généalogie fantastique" (1843), *Sylvie* (1853), and *Aurélia* (1855), and Zola's *dossiers préparatoires* for his *Rougon-Macquart* series (1871–93), I argue that the maps present in these works serve as emblems that indicate the subject's unstable position between a visual and concrete representation in a map and a readable and abstract representation in narrative. Similarly, in Sand's novel *Nanon* (1871) and in Proust's *À la recherche du temps perdu* (1913–27), I show how the novel and the narrating self are structured around maps outside of the text: Nanon learns to read and memorize the complex Cassini maps to navigate the routes of France, while Marcel intuits the geographical and social space of Combray and Paris as a function of his family walks on "Swann's Way" and "the Guermantes Way."

From Stendhal's illustrations of the events in Grenoble during the French Revolution to Sand's tale of a young peasant girl whose explorations through revolutionary France allow her to cross the social and economic boundaries of her humble origins, from Zola's detailed account of Haussmann's transformation of Paris to Proust's description of the society circles during the Dreyfus Affair, the mapping of space in the nineteenth-century novel sets the parameters of political action and defines the limits of interaction between subjects.

Far from being a death sentence (magic shagreens notwithstanding, an inevitable fate for us all), Raphaël's talisman affords new possibilities of conceptualizing the self in time and space—as a subject of space. The talisman is a "novel map," a term I use in this book to refer to any device in a narrative text that simulates a holistic image of the self occupying multiple times and multiple spaces. The novel map inscribes the writing subject in the spaces of the text, placing the subject simultaneously in the fictional world of the narrative, in the material world of the reader as a graphic representation on a page, and in the real-world spaces, such as Paris, referred to in the map-novel. For the geographer and historian of cartography Christian Jacob, all maps present the contradiction of materiality and representation: "[La carte] est un mélange problématique, où la transparence de l'illusion référentielle coexiste avec l'opacité d'un support qui matérialise cette image" (*L'Empire des cartes,* 41) ("[A map] is a problematic mixture, where the transparency of a referential illusion coexists with the opacity of a medium that materializes this image"). The "referential illusion"—the idea that the "here" of a map is identical to a distant "there" of another space—must coexist with the graphic representation of space, a simple X which stands in for a singular place. Like the cartographic simulacrum which maintains the "referential illusion," the autobiographical simulacrum, as defined by Louis Marin, simulates the (present) presence of the author in a past narrative creating the seamless illusion of an autobiographical subject.[7] Yet just as the different types of textual spaces coexist without ever becoming strictly identical, the subject of these spaces is always only represented and never present. The multiplicity of spatial representations of the self, both readable and visible, that attempt to situate the subject in the text only serve to emphasize its absence. The novel map, a simulacrum representing an imaginary totality beyond time and space, can only exist in a work of fiction; Raphaël's talisman works by magic.

In what follows, I show how the novel map, this fictional representation of the self as subject of space, structures first-person narratives in nineteenth-century French fiction. Taking as exemplary the works of Stendhal, Gérard de Nerval, George Sand, Émile Zola, and Marcel Proust, I study how the inscription of a subject into a fictional text occurs through a superposition of the visual representations of space found in maps with the linguistic representations of space in written narrative; the resulting textual play intensifies the experience of space and unsettles the boundaries between subjects and places.

I broadly define the subject as a construct that determines the interactions between a conscious self and its others (the world, the body, the past, or other subjects). There is, however, an uncertainty principle of subjectivity, since the only way to comprehend or measure the subject (that is, from the perspective of a conscious self or from that of its objective other) modifies the relationship between the self and its outside, and so any attempt to grasp subjectivity consequently changes its very nature. The narrative subject that emerges from the human subject's transcription into text constitutes a new web of connections (between author and text) that both reproduces the original structure of the subject (conscious self and other) and complicates this original structure exponentially. The writing act is inherently transformative, as the writer produces both a reflection of the self and an object that is other than this self. The text creates simultaneously the author as subject and a textual subject that is different from the author. The authorial subject and the textual or novel subject become superimposed and, at times, indistinguishable from one another. The literary work that results is a hybrid text caught between the contradictory genres of truthful autobiography and fictional novel. The play of these contradictions, the textuality of the literary text, allows the subject to alternate between a state of dissolution in the text (where the novel subject is lost in the plurality of meaning) and one of actualization outside the text (where a new, "real" autobiographical subject is constructed).

Textuality creates the possibility for the subject's self-transformation. The novel maps the subject and thereby draws the boundaries between self and nonself. As the lines that delineate the subject shift, they alter the relation the self has with its other. The textual space reconfigures the subject's place in society, erasing social barriers and redistributing what Jacques Rancière calls the "partage du sensible"[8] ("distribution of the perceptible"). The interior space of disciplinary surveillance is folded outward and projected onto the exterior, mapped space of the text. These mapped spaces of the text contribute to the suspension of form and matter found in all art, since maps represent both the space outside the text and also participate in the text's system of signs. The novel map ensures that the texts cannot be read definitively as either autobiographies or as novels, since either mode of reading would privilege only one aspect of the dual nature of cartography as material object and representational construct.

The Subject of Space

In the first part of my book, "Stendhal's Privilege," I show how Stendhal, in his ambiguous work *Vie de Henry Brulard,* lays the theoretical foundation for the novel map along with an exaggerated anxiety of the loss of the self to the play of the text. The first chapter reads Stendhal's text as a work that combines novel, autobiography, and cartography. Through a variety of techniques, especially the use of maps, emblems, and drawings, Stendhal's text plays with the differences between the author (whose real name was Henri Beyle), the narrator, and the character (Henry Brulard). The second chapter returns to the first image of Stendhal's text, where he introduces another cartographic representation, a bird's-eye view of Rome, which allows him to see his own past, present, and future in a novel map. Nevertheless, the narrator professes that the act of writing and of drawing erases memory and being, which leads him abruptly to terminate the narrative only eighteen years into the "life" of Brulard. I contend that Beyle/Brulard prematurely closes the narrative in order to maintain the suspension between Beyle and Brulard, authorial and novel subject.

In the second part, "Nerval Beyond Narrative," the work of Gérard de Nerval breaches the border so ardently defended by Stendhal between author and subject, real and textual space, leading inevitably to madness. Nerval's novel maps provide the cure to his narrative illness. In chapter 3, I demonstrate how Gérard de Nerval's writing of a travel narrative, the *Voyage en Orient,* creates simultaneously the space of the "Orient" as text and the textual subject that travels through it. Nerval's desire to restart his literary career, to rewrite himself as sane, leads him to orient himself through his inscription in Oriental space. Nerval's narrator is able to pass himself off as "oriental" by the appropriation of foreign languages and customs, and by the introduction of three rewritten oriental myths. Chapter 4 analyzes Nerval's "Généalogie fantastique," *Sylvie,* and *Aurélia* to show how the spatial metaphor of the fold, as theorized by Gilles Deleuze in *Le Pli,* inscribes the subject in the world. In *Sylvie* space folds in on itself, isolating the narrator in his own illusions; in *Aurélia* space is opened up and now contains multiple times and perspectives which allow the narrator to embrace others and the flux of time.

The third part, "Sand's Utopian Subjects," examines George Sand's first signed novel, *Indiana* (1832), and one of her last novels, *Nanon* (1871). Sand's novels, I argue, figure the double bind of women's textual subjectivity, since their fictional works were received by critics as inevitably autobiographical and their autobiographical works as inherently distorted. The play between truthful fiction and a fantasized autobiography along with the inscription of real places into the language of a text did not offer women a liberating escape from the traditional structure of subjectivity, since they did not enjoy the same status of subject as their male counterparts. Instead, Sand places novel maps, utopias of her literary imagination, into her realistic texts, inventing a new world out of the old. In Sand's first signed novel *Indiana* (chapter 5), the unstable movement of meaning in a text and of places in the city pose a mortal danger to the eponymous character's sense of self. Only the improbable utopian ending in the Île Bourbon renews identity and language for both Indiana and the male narrator. *Nanon* (chapter 6), Sand's last great novel, is a first-person account of the French Revolution by a peasant woman who learns to read the Cassini maps of France as she builds her own agrarian utopia in the center of France. In the blank spaces of history, Sand writes the story of a young woman who builds her own community in the blank spaces of a map.

Part IV, "Branching Off: Genealogy and Map in the *Rougon-Macquart,*" reads the preparatory notes for Émile Zola's *The Rougon-Macquart,* a novel series that studies the moral and genetic decadence of Napoleon III's Second Empire by following the trajectories of two branches of one family. Zola displaces traditional representation, especially the visual, in the form of the preparatory notes for his novels. The thousands of pages of Zola's notes contain countless sketches, diagrams, maps, and lists of observations that attempt to convey a one-to-one correspondence between objects and linguistic representation. Focusing on the hand-drawn map of the "Aire Saint-Mittre" which opens the preparatory notes for the *Fortune des Rougon* and serves as the site for the origin of the novel series, I show in chapter 7 how in the passage from note to novel, visual representation and authorial autonomy are sacrificed in favor of the freedom of verbal expression. In chapter 8, I analyze the "archive fever" present throughout the novel series as a symptom of anxiety about the origins of the novel in the dossiers manifested in the novels' narrative. Zola's novel map, the Rougon-Macquart genealogical tree, hides and supplants the missing origin, serving as both the beginning and the ending of the novel cycle.

The final part, "Proust's Double Text," argues that Marcel Proust's monumental novel *À la recherche du temps perdu* at the beginning of the twentieth century incorporates the nineteenth-century novel maps of his predecessors as the very structure of his novel. The novel subject, Proust's anonymous narrator, exists only at the confluence of two differing texts, the novel about space written by Proust and the novel of time announced by the narrator. Chapter 9 describes how the division of space in Proust's novel into two "Ways" imposes a law of place and a law of immutable signs. As the narrator wanders through the places of the text, he slowly learns how to decipher signs and eventually discovers the arbitrary nature of the text's cartographic system, just as the reader perceives the text's semiotic system. Chapter 10 reads Proust's novel as if it were the book about time its narrator claims to write at the end of the text since time, as duration, is represented within the novel about space by means of metaphor, movement, and the cycle of narration itself.

PART I
Stendhal's Privilege

> Il est, dans l'histoire littéraire, des personnages qui déroutent les procédés ordinaires de la critique et qu'on se sent envie de traiter comme des personnages de roman.*
>
> —Léon Blum, *Stendhal et le beylisme*

Stendhal, Dominique, Henry Brulard, M.B.A.A. (Monsieur Beyle, Ancien Auditeur), and Mr. Myself are some of the many names and pseudonyms that testify to the multiplicity of the subject Henri Beyle. In his writings, Beyle contradicts the mystification of identity, the will to hide behind an encoded pseudonym, by a nearly constant impulse toward self-exposure in the form of autobiography. Henri Beyle felt the need to write, and in particular, to write about himself, from a relatively early age. What is perhaps more remarkable is that he was able to do so almost continuously from the age of eighteen until his death. There exist texts of autobiographical content that cover nearly every period of his life forming a more or less uniform autobiographical project.[1]

The *Vie de Henry Brulard* in its structure, unity, and scope is unlike Stendhal's other autobiographical writings.[2] By way of an analysis of the progression of Stendhal's autobiographical works, the *Vie de Henry Brulard* can be differentiated from the oeuvre and made autonomous (made to have its own name, the difference between Henri/y Beyle/rulard). The *Vie de Henry Brulard* transcends the earlier autobiographical writing with the creation of a novel subject, Henry Brulard.

*There are in literary history personages that throw off the ordinary processes of criticism and which one wants to treat like characters in a novel.

The earliest autobiographical writings were a collection of various personal diaries published posthumously as the *Journal,* and begin with the young Beyle's arrival in Milan with Napoleon's army in 1800, tapering off only in 1823. From 1800 to 1814, he regularly made an entry every night, after which time the publication of other works (*Histoire de la peinture en Italie, Vies de Haydn, de Mozart, et de Métastase,* and *Rome, Naples, et Florence* where the pseudonym Stendhal makes its first appearance) seems to have satisfied some of the writing impulse (Martineau, "Avertissement," in Stendhal's *Oeuvres intimes*, 7). Indeed, the subject matter of the journals is often closer to that of his nonfiction publications than to a sentimental diary. At various moments, Beyle makes it clear that the journals are intended only for him, or at best for the Henri Beyle of the future. These are private literary journals, where every play seen and book read is carefully recorded, dated, and picked apart. Especially in the early journals (1800–1805), Beyle's main interest is in his future as a playwright; details concerning his travels, his life as a sous-lieutenant, the women he loves, are secondary and seem to be presented only for their possible connection to future literary endeavors. Gradually, however, the journal itself becomes the site of stylistic experimentation, the entries become longer, descriptions are more detailed.

The object of study eventually returns to Beyle himself: "Faire incessamment (le 13 octobre, jour anniversaire de mon départ de Paris) l'examen de ma conscience" (*Oeuvres intimes,* 895) ("Incessantly examine (October 13th, anniversary of my departure from Paris) my consciousness"). By studying himself, he can arrive at a perfection of his character and profession (as writer). The creation of an aesthetic leads to the creation of an identity. The methods of self-examination vary widely and anticipate one of Stendhal's principal literary inventions, what Georges Blin calls the "restrictions de champ," where the narrative field is restricted to the perceptions of one character (*Stendhal et les problèmes du roman*). Moreover Beyle rereads the journal from earlier years to discern what his thought process had been; he often describes himself in the third person with the help of an ironic narrator.

The end of the *Journal* coincides with the appearance of short (1–4 page) autobiographical essays, "notices autobiographiques," that Yves Ansel has called "fiches d'état civil," or an administrative curriculum vitae (Ansel, 2). Often in the third person, they summarize the life and anticipate the death of Henri Beyle, in the form more of a fictionalized auto-eulogy than an autobiography. Yet they represent a necessary step toward autobiography (and beyond), by separating it from an "exercice de style," and preparing the story of his life as a public and no longer private matter.

In 1832 Beyle began a more ambitious project, the *Souvenirs d'égotisme*, in which he envisioned recounting the "space of nine years" (1821–30) that he spent in "exile" in Paris, banished by the Austrian government from Milan. For the first time he recounts a part of the past, and not the immediate present. It is a much more personal text than the "auto-eulogies" which precede it. Writing has become a way to know himself, and to be known by others in the future: "J'avoue que le courage d'écrire me manquerait si je n'avais pas l'idée qu'un jour ces feuilles paraîtront imprimées et seront lues par quelque âme que j'aime . . . Quel homme suis-je? Ai-je du bon sens, ai-je du bon sens avec profondeur?" (*Oeuvres intimes,* 1427) ("I admit that I would lack the courage to write if I didn't have the idea that one day these pages would be printed and would be read by some soul whom I love . . . What type of man am I? Do I have good sense, good sense with depth?"). He continually expresses reluctance to write and doubts as to the possibility of drafting a memoir which is not "boring" or vain; the only remedy to this doubt is absolute sincerity and a minute study of the individual, a quality he terms "l'égotisme": "[Si ce livre] n'ennuie pas, on verra que l'égotisme, *mais sincère,* est une façon de peindre ce coeur humain" (*Oeuvres intimes,* 1482) ("[If this book] doesn't bore, the reader will see that egotism, *the sincere kind,* is a way to paint this human heart"). And yet Stendhal's *Souvenirs d'égotisme* is left unfinished, barely twelve days after it was begun; instead of the space of nine and a half years, he only finished three. The failure of the *Souvenirs d'égotisme* lies, perhaps, in its very sincerity. Stendhal only writes what he already knows is true about himself, and therefore is unable to discover the motives for his actions. By recounting the recent past, the author cannot take sufficient distance from himself or the events in his life.

Three years later, in November 1835, he took up the same themes again in the *Vie de Henry Brulard,* but instead of writing about a relatively recent period of his life, he began with the beginning. In the *Souvenirs d'égotisme* he states only half in jest that he was (morally and intellectually) twenty years old in 1821 (*Oeuvres intimes,* 1487), placing his "birth" at the beginning of the *Journal,* with his arrival in Italy and his first steps to becoming a writer. By placing this new "Life" (the usual page heading he gives to the manuscript) anterior to his "birth" as a writer, by changing the character's name to Brulard (he had first written Beyle), the text has made a shift from autobiography toward the novel. The frequent protests that he does not wish to "fall into the novel" only help to accentuate the precariousness of the text. The desire to find the truth about himself, to be sincere, is even more present in the *Vie de Henry Brulard* than in the *Souvenirs;* the concern that "on peut connaître tout, excepté soi-même" ("one can know everything, except one's self") which appeared in *Souvenirs d'égotisme* (*Oeuvres intimes,* 1482), becomes "quel oeil peut se voir soi-même?" ("what I can see itself?"), in the manuscript, "soi=même" (*Oeuvres intimes,* 41). By looking into the past, by changing the subject into an object of study, Beyle (or perhaps from now on the writer Stendhal) can successfully become other to himself. He can become *roman*ticized.[3] It is commonly recognized by Stendhal experts that the *Vie de Henry Brulard* is an unfinished work, a draft of something left to be published after his death; Gérard Rannaud, editor of the "Edition diplomatique," the first to include reproductions of all manuscript pages, claims that there is no "established text," but rather an unfinished "editorial manuscript" (Stendhal, *Vie de Henry Brulard écrite par lui-même,* I). I would argue that the *Vie de Henry Brulard* forms a coherent whole (much more so than his other unfinished works, such as *Lucien Leuwen*) that describes the entire childhood of Brulard, from Grenoble to his "escape" to Paris and then to Milan.

The *Vie de Henry Brulard* is then a unique text in Stendhal's oeuvre, suspended between novel and autobiography, deceptive truth and truthful lie, past and present. *Brulard*'s instability, the becoming of the novel subject Brulard, relies on the instability of the text itself. Chapter 1, "The Life and Death of Henry Brulard," analyzes the construction of an autonomous textual subject. The subject of autobiography is converted into narrative and the novel subject is born with the declaration "je vais naître" ("I am going to be born"). This new subject is at once a true representation of Beyle and an abstract, fictional invention, Brulard. The text creates and conceals this dual nature through the autobiographical simulacrum which collapses the differences between narrator, author, and character. The tension between word and image introduced by the presence of countless maps, diagrams, drawings, and engravings in the narrative maintains the distance between autobiographical and novel subject. Maps inscribe another Brulard into textual space that cannot be perfectly assimilated into either the written Brulard of the narrative or the author Beyle.

The second chapter of this section, "The Ghost in the Map," reveals how *Brulard* questions from the outset the very possibility of autobiographical truth and the eventual results of the autobiographical project. The cartographic inscription of the subject occurs through the reduction of the self to language, the transformation of the personal to the universal, the repression of memory through the affirmation of chronological time. The only recourse is to textuality, the control of meaning through the play of signifiers. Another model of cartography, what I call the novel map, is proposed which counters chronological time, layers Brulard's past and present, and embraces the ambiguity of the novel subject.

Chapter One

The Life and Death of Henry Brulard

René

The contradictions of its first two chapters orient the *Vie de Henry Brulard,* as a chaotic autobiographical discourse gives way to a linear narrative. Various styles and perspectives succeed each other as the narrator struggles to define the project and to summarize the "life" of Brulard. After describing the view of Rome in a style reminiscent of Chateaubriand, the narrator wonders, "Je vais avoir cinquante ans, il serait bien temps de me connaître. Qu'ai-je été, que suis-je, en vérité je serais bien embarrassé de le dire" (*Oeuvres intimes,* 38) ("I am going to be fifty years old, it's about time I get to know myself. What have I been, what am I, in truth I would have a hard time saying"). In vain he tries to respond to these questions by evoking the opinion of others, which leads him to stray off the subject. By the middle of the chapter he has lost a unified notion of the subject (himself) and of his narrative. In the rest of the chapter, he attempts to define himself, his character, "without lying," by telling his life thematically but not chronologically; this takes him from 1832 to 1802, to 1880 and to 1935 (the dates he hopes his text will be published and understood), to 1809, and back to 1835 (the present of the narrative).

By the end of the first chapter, the text is almost impossible to follow. The free association of places and people disturbs the habitual chronological progression of autobiography. As the narrator himself admits: "Mais je me laisse emporter, je m'égare, je serai inintelligible si je ne suis pas l'ordre des temps, et d'ailleurs les circonstances ne me reviendront pas si bien" (44); "Mais je m'égare encore . . . Mais je m'égare" (*Oeuvres intimes*, 45) ("But I let myself get carried away, I'm straying off topic, I will be unintelligible if I do not follow the order of events, and moreover circumstances will not come back to me very well"; "But I stray again . . . But I stray"). The incoherency of the writing is evoked through the use of verbs of movement or space ("carry away," "stray," and "come back"), suggesting that the error lies in the spatial component of the analysis. The text calls for a more temporal perspective, one that is less "topical" and more chronological. The narrator is literally "carried away" from one place to another in the text, occupying several different moments at a time. Subjects change over time, in a sense they are because of what they become. A narrative based solely on the association of place would tend to confuse time periods, negating temporal progression. The distinction of subject and object can only occur through the analysis of time; Brulard can only become text through chronological narrative.

In chapter 2, Stendhal changes tactics and tries to order his narrative logically and chronologically (similar to the "notices autobiographiques" that he had written earlier). The methodology employed in this chapter is reminiscent of René Descartes's *Discours de la méthode,* a text that, like *Brulard,* conflates autobiography and fiction in its search for the foundation of subjectivity. The Cartesian method attempts to negotiate the interaction between subject and object through classification and analysis. A problem, here the subject Brulard, must be divided up into distinct parts, numbered, and catalogued in order to understand how the whole functions. For perception and analysis to be clear and free from subjective bias, the basis for subjectivity must be reducible to a universal. Descartes momentarily pretends to be without past and without a body (what Sartre will later call "being-in-itself"), reducing his existence to pure consciousness or thought ("being-for-itself"); Cartesian subjectivity is then a timeless (or perhaps instantaneous) hollowing of the self to the point where the only thing left is consciousness. The pseudo-Cartesian method found in *Brulard*'s second chapter announces a new cogito and the birth of the subject as text. Like Descartes, Brulard/Beyle must momentarily put past and body aside, with the aim of reaching a truthful analysis of the self by rendering it text (other).

In the ten pages of the second chapter, the narrator organizes his life, not without more detours, by four major categories according to temporal order, recalling Descartes's second rule, "diviser chacune des difficultés . . . en autant de parcelles qu'il se pourrait" (*Discours de la méthode*, 49) ("divide each difficulty . . . into as many sections as possible"). The first category is Stendhal's military and public career: "né en 1783, dragon en 1800, étudiant de 1803 à 1806 . . . J'ai été homme d'esprit depuis l'hiver de 1826, auparavant je me taisais par paresse" (*Oeuvres intimes*, 46) ("born in 1783, dragoon in 1800, student from 1803 to 1806 . . . I have been a man of wit since the winter of 1826, before I kept quiet out of laziness"). The subject is too vast to be reduced to simple dates, rank, and social status, with the result that certain details seem incongruous. Most obviously because his careers overlap: his "military" career was little different from his public one, and his diplomatic career coincided with his literary one. How can one suddenly become "a man of wit"? Such declarations ultimately conflict with the narrator's conception of the subject as changing over time.

The narrator must look elsewhere for the essence of his life, leading him to resume his affective "career" by ranking the women he loved: "Pour les considérer le plus philosophiquement possible et tâcher ainsi de les dépouiller de l'auréole qui me fait *aller les yeux*, qui m'éblouit et m'ôte la faculté de voir distinctement, j'*ordonnerai* ces dames (langage mathématique) selon leurs qualités diverses" (*Oeuvres intimes*, 50) ("In order to consider them as philosophically as possible and to try thus to remove the halo that gets *in my eyes*, that dazzles me and impairs my ability to see clearly, I *will arrange in order* these women (mathematical language) according to their individual qualities"). The Cartesian predilection for light as the privileged metaphor for knowledge (especially in the *Monde*) and the edict that one should accept as true only that which is presented clearly and distinctly to the mind are here inverted. The narrator's *cristallisation* of these women has produced too much light, blinding the would-be philosopher. As the narrator states later in *Brulard:* "On ne peut pas apercevoir distinctement la partie du ciel trop voisine du soleil" (*Oeuvres intimes*, 433) ("One cannot perceive distinctly the part of the sky too close to the sun"). But by mathematically placing the women in chronological and social order and numbering their initials, he can remove the sacred halo. The "vanity" of these women, and obviously of himself as well, leads him to contemplate his finances, and then the (dis) loyalty of his friends, the third and fourth categories. Finally, at the end of the chapter, he presents a simple chart which he likens to his friend André de Jussieu's collection of plants: "Enfance et première éducation, de 1786 à 1800. . . . 15 ans, Service militaire de 1800 à 1803. . . . 3 ans, . . . Second service, consul du 15 septembre 1830 au présent quart d'heure. . . . 5 ans" (*Oeuvres intimes*, 54) ("Childhood and first education, from 1786 to 1800. . . . 15 years, Military service from 1800 to 1803. . . . 3 years, . . . Civil service, consul from September 15, 1830, to the present quarter of an hour. . . . 5 years"). This schematic is more convincing than those previous, but only because it is much more vague, completely erasing all but the general trajectory of his life.

Stendhal candidly and almost joyfully declares his newfound distance from himself. His intellectual solitude in Rome, which will later be related to the state he felt in Grenoble, is aggravated by the classification of his relations, creating an even greater distance between himself and all credible outside criteria. The narrator must seek inside himself, far from any sentimentality, for his identity. This new approach is almost certainly the exact opposite of the one employed in the first chapter; here we have, as he himself calls it, a "military" or "mathematical" system of classification, whereas in the first chapter (to be studied later) there was an affective palimpsest of memory that led to opaqueness of vision.

The discourse of this second chapter, with its manifestly objective and objectifying realism, will take precedence over that of the first chapter with its more subjective, personal tone. The goal of knowing the truth about himself, of "seeing" himself as other, results in self-abstraction. And yet the piling up of details and charts prevents the entry of the subject into the narrative, that is, a discourse of the event in the past: "Il faut narrer, et j'écris des *considérations* sur des événements bien petits mais qui précisément à cause de leur *taille* microscopique ont besoin d'être contés très distinctement. Quelle patience il vous faudra, ô mon lecteur!" (*Oeuvres intimes*, 52–53) ("I have to narrate, and I am writing *reflections* about very small events, but which precisely because of their microscopic *size* need to be recounted very distinctly. How much patience you have to have, oh my reader!"). These necessary general considerations mark the presence of the narrator, who is thus independent from, or outside of, the narrative that follows, guaranteeing some measure of objectivity.

In order for this preliminary discourse to be transformed into narrative, there must be a superposition of the present of the narration and the past of the narrative, the "I" of the narrator and the "I" of the narrated subject. Louis Marin evokes Émile Benveniste to show how autobiographical narrative, the combination of discourse and narrative, can only occur through simulacrum ("The Autobiographical Interruption," 600). Narrative, "with its intent on objectivity," is devoid of discourse's enunciative marks: the person "I-you" as opposed to the nonperson "he," the present opposed to the nonpresent of the past (599). A ruse changes the "I" into a "he," present to past, while maintaining the virtual "presence" of the author/narrator. In fact this simulacrum incites the reader to forget the subject of the narrative: "Memory set up as narrative simulates forgetting" (600). The narrator Brulard/Beyle recounts the memory of the child Brulard, forgetting and erasing the difference between the two.

The shift from discourse to narrative takes place at the end of chapter 2 and the beginning of chapter 3. After one last attempt at a totalizing summary (his "beginning in the world" in 1794, the date closest to the events of *Brulard*), the chapter ends with the concise formula, "après tant de considérations générales, je vais naître" (*Oeuvres intimes*, 55) ("after so many general remarks, I am going to be born"). For the narration to begin, everything else must be moved aside, the new "je" must start from nothing, it must be independent of the narrator.

The doubts about the narrator's identity (the "what am I?" of the first chapter) have culminated in a Stendhalian cogito and the birth of a new subject, Brulard. Just as Descartes feigns that he has no body, no past, but exists only in thought, Brulard proclaims that he has renounced the "general remarks" of the past, and exists only in the text. Paradoxically, this move toward universality and logic can only be possible through a mechanism of the imaginary: Descartes "feigns" that he is only thought and Brulard/Beyle must pretend that he can be born again.

Autobiography relies on a slippage between pronouns and between verb tenses, and from the beginning it is already slipping into fiction. The autobiographical subject is at once autonomous from the "authorial subject" (for how else could it be perceived?) and conceived as an ideal (fictional) projection of the "authorial" self. This is made possible because language collapses distinctions, now reduced to metaphor, and the subsequent forgetting of the nature of language as metaphor. The difference between the two subjects (Beyle and Brulard, author and character) is created and then forgotten by the text.

Brulard, "je," the narrator/main character, is born by and in the text. This birth is the goal of autobiography (the perception of the self as object), and yet it also constitutes the inscription of the self into a fictional narrative.[1] Stendhal transforms his "general remarks" into narrative, sacrificing his personal experience in order to become text. The inscription of Brulard into a text, a sort of textual or simulated subject, does not just occur once, but recurs at various moments throughout the narrative. Product of language (a metaphor that is then forgotten), the textual subject reveals itself and the impossibility of its simulacrum (a subject imagined by an "author" to reflect the author) through slips in language, through wordplay. Affirmed and denied in the play of visible/legible markers, thriving in the ambiguity of letters, Brulard masks Beyle.

Even before the declaration that he is "going to be born," the narrator stages a scene of writing and the inscription/encryption of Beyle. Before he classifies the women of his life, he recalls a recent trip to Lake Albano near Rome, when he traced their names in the dust:

> Je trouvai que ma vie pouvait se résumer par les noms que voici, et dont j'écrivais les initiales sur la poussière, comme Zadig, avec ma canne . . .: Virginie /Kubly/, Angela /Pietragrua/, Adèle /Rebuffel/, Mélanie /Guilbert/, Mina /de Griesheim/, Alexandrine /Petit/, Angeline, que je n'ai jamais

> aimée /Bereyter/, Angela /Pietragrua/, Métilde /Dembowski/, Clémentine/, Giulia/. Et enfin, pendant un mois au plus Mme Azur dont j'ai oublié le nom de baptême, et imprudemment, hier, Amalia /B/. La plupart de ces êtres charmants ne m'ont point honoré de leurs bontés; mais elles ont à la lettre occupé toute ma vie. A elles ont succédé mes ouvrages."[2] (47–48)

He includes a sketch of himself by a tree with a cane, the name "Zadig" next to the figure with the cane, and under Zadig, "Astarté" in slightly larger characters and different ink, perhaps as if "drawn" by Zadig. Two pages later the same scene is summarized: "J'écrivais sur la poussière comme Zadig ces initiales: V An_1 Ad M_2 Mi A_1 $Aine_3$ Apg_2 Mde C_4 G_5 Aur (Mme Azur dont j'ai oublié le nom de baptême). Je rêvais profondément à ces noms, et aux étonnantes bêtises et sottises qu'ils m'ont fait faire" (49) ("I wrote on the dust like Zadig these initials, V An_1 Ad M_2 Mi A_1 $Aine_3$ Apg_2 Mde C_4 G_5 Aur (Mme Azur whose given name I have forgottn). I dreamed deeply about these names, and about the astonishing blunders and foolishness that they made me do"). There is a double substitution that occurs in this inscription of initials: the narrator's life can be summed up from A (Astarté/Angela) to Z (Zadig/Azur), reduced to the names (which are further reduced to initials) of his lovers, but the narrator also takes the place of Zadig by his citation and imitation. In the *conte philosophique* by Voltaire, it is Astarté who traces Zadig's name; in the written text her name is not mentioned, but it appears in the sketch ambiguously (is it placed under "Zadig" to indicate that Zadig drew the word "Astarté," or is it a correction of the written text?). Occupying Zadig's position, then, it would be the women whom he loved who would trace *his* name, he would exist through their writing.

To appropriate their names, to "be occupied to the letter" of their initials, he writes the nicknames he gave them (Métilde for Mathilda, Azur for Alberthe de Rubempré), places their family or married names in brackets (perhaps creating a rift between their public and private lives, or their social status), and places a number in subscript to indicate the ones "qu['il a] eu" ("that [he] had"). In a "Testament" (will) giving the manuscript to a publisher, his only condition is that all the women's names be changed to prevent scandals (or perhaps to preserve his own appropriation of them). Angela is always counted twice, since he met her during his first trip to Milan and had an affair with her during the second, eleven years later. A salient detail in the accompanying drawing is a note declaring that this page was written at night, making it illegible. Every sentence of the passage is thus written twice, retraced word for word, as if to

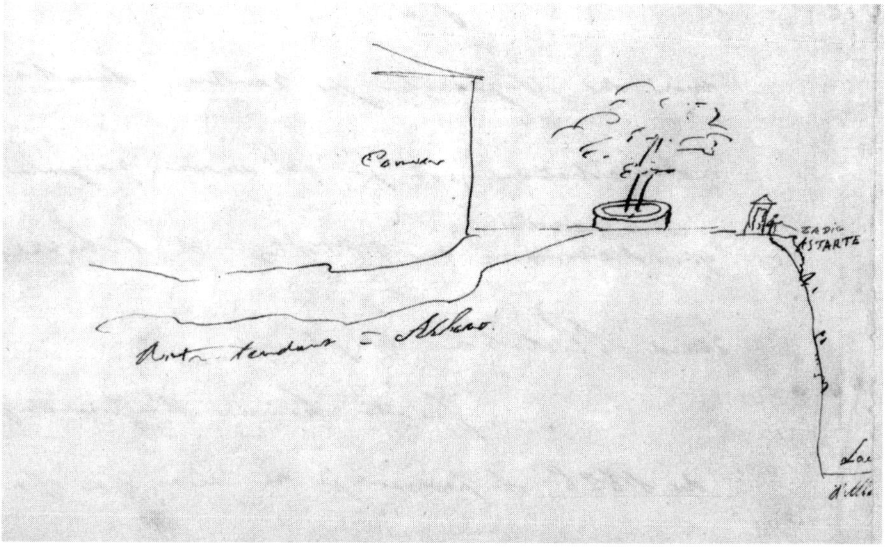

Figure 1.1. The narrator as Zadig. *Vie de Henry Brulard,* R299, vol. 1, no. 113, folio 53v. Courtesy of Bibliothèque municipale de Grenoble.

emphasize the physicality of writing, to take pleasure one more time in the evocation of the names. If one were to murmur the initials quickly, the sound might approach "va maman" (Marin, "Sur un certain regard du sujet"). The unwritable, unspeakable love jumps out of the initials, revealing at once this "initial" love, the one trait that unites the women, and the textual matrix from which Brulard will emerge.

Henry's decision to become a writer and dramaturge, à la Molière, is similarly imbued with shame and secret desire as revealed through the tension of text and image. While his maternal grandfather, Doctor Gagnon, was seeing patients, the young Brulard would sneak into the extensive library to look for the "histoire naturelle de *la femme*" (184) ("the natural history of *woman*"). By good fortune, he moves away from Pliny toward a confused stack of libertine novels belonging to his uncle (marked with an L on the accompanying and subsequent maps): "c'était l'essence de la volupté. . . . La possession d'une maîtresse réelle . . . ne m'eût pas plongé dans un tel torrent de volupté. Dès ce moment ma vocation fut décidée: vivre à Paris en faisant des comédies comme Molière" (185) ("this was the essence of pleasure. . . . The possession of a real mistress . . . would not have plunged me into such a torrent of sensual delight. From this moment on my vocation was decided: to live in Paris whole making comedies like Molière"). All his desires culminate in literature, its production and its consumption, revealing the inextricable link between text and individuation through desire (to write).

His "tyrannical" Aunt Séraphie is portrayed as the principle obstacle to Henry's goal as a writer, and so provides the perfect foil for Henry's individuation. Her religious devotion and deceptively angelic name (like Henry's father Chérubin) hide the ultimate hypocrisy: she is Chérubin's mistress (a phantasm Brulard suspects but cannot prove). Later in the novel, when she is sick and dying, she causes Brulard one last embarrassment:

> Une de ses dernières actions avait été, un soir que je lisais sur la commode de ma tante Élisabeth, au point H [of the accompanying sketch], la *Henriade* ou *Bélisaire* que mon grand-père venait de me prêter, de s'écrier: 'Comment peut-on donner de tels livres à cet enfant! Qui lui a donné ce livre?'[3] (221)

Like Brulard's discovery of his vocation as writer, this scene mixes desire to read (he had implored his grandfather to loan the book to him) with the danger of being rebuked. Henry, "au point H," is drawn as a stick figure at one end of the room, whereas "toute la famille était en rang d'oignons devant le feu au point D" (222) ("the entire family was in a row like a bunch of onions in front of the fire at the spot marked D") at the other end of the room. Why would his religious aunt be angry that Henry read the edifying, moralistic, and relatively dry *Henriade* and *Bélisaire*? Critics have overlooked that inscribed in Voltaire's epic *Henriade* and Marmontel's didactic novel *Bélisaire* is not Henry Brulard, but Henri (-ade) Beyle (-isaire). The repressed identity of the author Henri Beyle is composed of the letters of the books he read as a child. The "true" author, outside of the text, is reconverted to text by his reading.

His aunt serves as a catalyst for the process of individuation by publicly shaming him. Séraphie's rant amounts to an interpellation: Henry/i is separated from the rest of the family and called by his "real" name. This interpellation attempts to fix the identity of the subject, temporarily unraveling the simulacrum that collapses Beyle and Brulard, narrator and character into one. The textual stability is retrieved when Dr. Gagnon dismisses Séraphie, excusing her for being "malade," suggesting that she is mentally ill.

This ambiguity between personal insight and (inter)-textuality maintains and exposes the impossible nature of *Brulard:* a fictional autobiography, Henri Beyle as text. Worrying whether his readers will be able to tolerate four or five volumes "of *I*s and *me*s" the narrator exclaims:

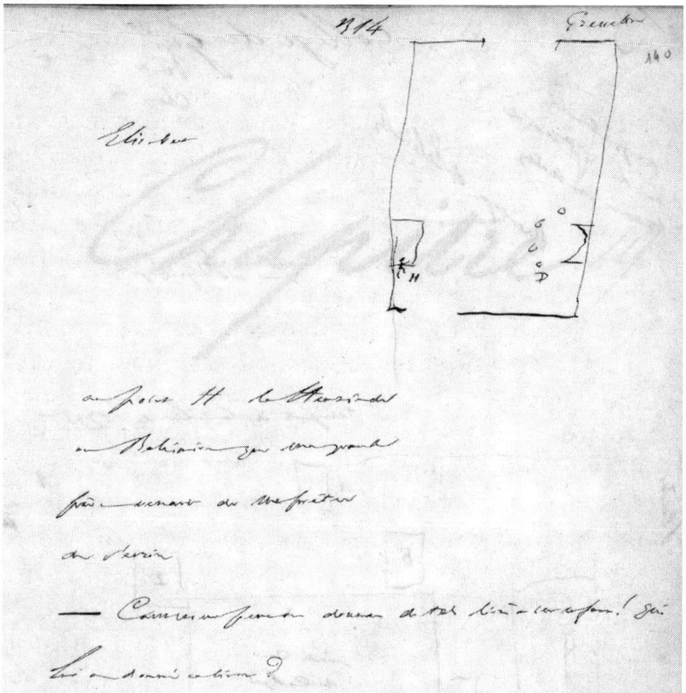

Figure 1.2. Henry in the corner H, the rest of his family in a line at D. *Vie de Henry Brulard,* R299, vol. 2, no. 283, folio 140. Courtesy of Bibliothèque municipale de Grenoble.

> Cependant, ô mon lecteur, tout le mal n'est que dans ces cinq lettres [*sic*]: B, R, U, L, A, R, D, qui forment mon nom, et qui intéressent mon amour-propre. Supposez que j'eusse écrit *Bernard,* ce livre ne serait plus comme le *Vicaire de Wakefield* (son émule en innocence), qu'un roman écrit à la première personne.[4] (284)

Editors have negated the ambiguity of the text, the "unconscious" of Brulard, by "correcting" the manuscript: the "sept lettres" of B, R, U, L, A, R, D. replace in the standard editions the "cinq lettres" of the unwritten (and yet always present) B, E, Y, L, E. The text seems to have already anticipated Philippe Lejeune's *Le Pacte autobiographique* and set out to challenge it. Lejeune defines the autobiographical pact as "l'affirmation dans le texte de cette identité [of the "*nom* auteur-narrateur-personnage"] renvoyant en dernier ressort au *nom* de l'auteur sur la couverture" (Lejeune, *Le Pacte autobiographique,* 26) ("the affirmation in the text of this equivalence [of the *name* author-narrator-character] referring back in the end to the *name* of the author on the cover"). Any slight deviation from this "pact" excludes the work from the category of autobiography, since autobiography, for Lejeune, is "all or nothing" (25).

Yet, in order for Stendhal's autobiography to work according to the logic it proposes in the first two chapters, an ambiguity must prevail, and not an affirmation, regarding the identity of the author/narrator/character. This margin of doubt concerning the identity of the subject creates the necessary distance for self-reflection: the textual "birth" of Brulard allows Beyle to see himself. Moreover, if Beyle, Stendhal, the narrator, and Brulard were all identical, they would not be distinguishable.

Brulard wants to be between autobiography and fiction. Beyle is inscribed in the text, is manifest for the astute reader, a "signature" or guarantee of autobiography; but autobiography is "all or nothing," and the character (Brulard) is not expressly equivalent to the author. The narrator admits to playing with the possibility of writing a novel, changing the name, once again, into "Bernard." Yet he does and does not change the name; it is not Bernard written by Brulard, but Brulard written by Brulard (who is not Brulard, but Stendhal, who is Beyle).

The various title pages only serve to complicate matters: "Vie de Hy Brul[ard] écrite par lui-même. *Life.* Nov. 35."; "Vie de Henry Brulard À M.M. de la Police. Ceci est un roman imité du *Vicaire de Wakefield.* Le héros, Henry Brulard, écrit sa vie, à cinquante-deux ans, après la mort de sa femme, la célèbre Charlotte Corday . . . Moi Henry Brulard j'écrivis ce qui suit à Maro [Roma] de 1832 à 1836" (430–31) ("Life of Henry Brulard. To Messrs. The Police. This is a novel imitated from *The Vicar of Wakefield.* The hero, Henry Brulard, writes his life, at the age of 52, after the death of his wife, the famous Charlotte Corday . . . I, Henry Brulard, wrote what follow in Maro [Roma] from 1832 to 1836"). Any student of Stendhal's novels would know never to trust a title page or a citation (think of how many of the citations of *Le Rouge et le noir* are invented),[5] but *Brulard* presents some revealing paradoxes. Even if one were to discard temporarily the identity real-author/narrator, the assumed author according to the title page would be Henry Brulard, *himself;* leading the reader to believe that the text claims to be an autobiography. But as Miriella Melara has remarked, "the addition of 'imitated novel' . . . is both unexpected and disconcerting. An author who has apparently undertaken the task of writing his own life story admits to having imitated a novelistic paradigm" (249). As with the *Henriade,* the *Bélisaire,* or *Zadig,* Brulard/Beyle is already a repetition, a reinscription of another text. Philippe Lejeune maintains that these titles are not to be taken seriously, in part due to the unpublished nature of the text, since the humorous nature of the titles can only be meant to entertain Stendhal and was not conceived for the final edition (*Le Pacte autobiographique*, 29). Since autobiography is "all or nothing," Lejeune must assume that the title pages are not part of the "text itself" but a camouflage, a ruse to divert unwanted readers. The narrator writes of willing the manuscript to an editor after his death, but there are no indications for what will or will not be included in "*l'édition*," leading the modern critic to accept all of the manuscript or none of it. Once again, *Brulard* is able to have it both ways, all and nothing, autobiography and fiction, the identity and nonidentity of Brulard and Beyle.

The continual rebirth of Brulard as text could be said to conclude with yet another "birth." Near the end of the text, the narrator describes working at the Ministry of War in Paris for his powerful relative Pierre Daru (who will later facilitate his first voyage to Italy), when, in the middle of the passage, he writes: "Je vais naître, comme dit Tristram Shandy, et le lecteur va sortir des enfantillages" (381) ("I am going to be born, as Tristram Shandy says, and the reader will leave this childishness"). The repetition of such a key phrase thirty-seven chapters later marks the time, the space of the text, which separates the two occurrences, and delineates the "Life" of Brulard. Soon after, Henry will leave with the army across the Alps to Milan, the city he will consider his true *patrie* (homeland or "fatherland"), or perhaps *matrie*, for his mother's family claims Italian heritage. Indeed, Beyle's tombstone in Montmartre cemetery is engraved: "Arrigo Beyle, Milanese/ Visse, Scrisse, Amò"—"Henri Beyle from Milan, Lived, Wrote, Loved." Moreover, the text begins in Italy, and so it also ends there. But this "je vais naître" differs greatly from the first. It is a repetition of an earlier moment in the text, and also a citation of another famous literary *égotiste*, Sterne's *Tristram Shandy.*[6] Repetition engenders difference since the second cogito modifies the meaning of the first, confirming the reader's suspicion that Brulard is pure text. The second part of the sentence is playfully ambiguous. If Brulard/Shandy is going to be born, wouldn't the reader *enter* rather than leave these "enfantillages"? Or perhaps, by appropriating the words of (or rather attributed to) Sterne, the narrator trades places, and becomes *himself* the reader, thus becoming able to leave behind his childhood. Instead of a birth, then, this might be a death or a disappearance: "By means of this interruption and uprise, a triple substitution is simultaneously brought about: 'I' and 'he'; reading and writing; life and death. I disappropriate myself by means of the other, I appropriate the other by means of myself" (Marin, "The Autobiographical Interruption," 606). The crystallization of narrator, author, and character, which composed Brulard as text, dissolves as Brulard enters a fictive intertext and the autobiographical "je" claims to be reborn outside of the text as a reader. The fictive narrator would remain to tell the story of Brulard/Shandy. The author turned reader is cut from the text, allowed to read and be read. The death of Henry Brulard as written text coincides temporally (1800) with the birth of the writer, Beyle/Stendhal, of the *Journal.*

Des/Cartes

The questioning of genre, the suspension between Beyle and Brulard, the play between the readable and the visible, are guaranteed by the most unique aspect of the *Vie de Henry Brulard:* the over 170 sketches that are scattered throughout the text.[7] Some drawings depict objects (his one and only childhood toy, a spinning top), others are abstract representations of concepts, but the overwhelming majority are maps: street maps of Grenoble, Paris, and Milan, maps of mountains, maps of houses, the spaces of his youth. According to Béatrice Didier, the sketches are an analytic procedure to distance the author from the emotion of past events, to re-create the past objectively in its entirety.[8] This cartographic impulse is another manifestation of the Cartesian, the "mathematical" and "military" analysis of his life. As such the maps would seem to be a way to spare the narrator from tedious description, another sign of the novel (in *Souvenirs d'égotisme,* Beyle attributes his inability to write novels to the boredom he derives from material descriptions à la Walter Scott [*Oeuvres intimes*, 1454]). However, the maps are rarely "geographic" but rather "topographic" (Marin, "Sur un certain regard du sujet," 226–27); they schematize relations between space and the subjects that occupy it, rather than describing a real surface relation that would produce space.

Maps would then have a narrative function, linked to the subject's relation to space through time. They would not add "a reality effect" but would supplement, sometimes replace or call into question, the written, readable, text. Very often they contain their own legends, with writing over the place represented. These legends do not always correspond to the references in the text or in the map itself. Many of the maps fill an entire manuscript page, thereby literally opening a rift in the text.

This second, visual narrative would also require the presence of the textual subject. The engraving "San Girolamo nel deserto" by Domenichino, separating the phrase "je vais naître" from chapter 3, reinforces the birth of the subject in the text as character (both as printed character or letter and as character). Carol Mossman has suggested that the engraving of Saint Jerome, the translator of the Bible into Latin, could be interpreted as an (ironic?) evocation of the self-sacrifice of the writer for the sanctity of textuality (Mossman, 350). Saint Jerome is, of course, always represented next to a skull, contemplating mortality and his own humility in the face of the greatness of the holy scriptures.

The first engraving of the manuscript, fittingly enough "La Resurrezione di Lazaro," serves as an introduction, a leading into the presence of the image in the text.[9] The actual painting by Garofolo is not present, but only the engraving, that is, an abstraction devoid of color and subtlety. The resurrection of the image occurs through a trace, a poor copy torn out of another book. The image depicts a triumphant Jesus and a weary Lazarus. The resurrection of Lazarus prefigured that of Jesus, and also of Brulard, who twice declares "je vais naître." The witnesses to the resurrection are holding their noses, perhaps referring to the degraded state of Lazarus, or to the degraded state of the painting turned engraving; or perhaps this is an oblique reference to a note on the following page, "Petits faits à placer, 1 mauvaise odeur des gens qui assistaient aux vêpres à la charité" ("Little facts to place, 1 bad odor of those who attend evening mass"). The presence of the engraving of Lazarus opens a space between the readable and the visible which prevents any one interpretation from taking root.

As we have seen in the introduction, Christian Jacob has pointed out the inherently problematic nature of maps. Maps seem more real than written text because there is a material support that appears to coincide with the referent, yet the obligations of perspective (reducing three dimensions to one or two) reveal a referential illusion. However, the presence of a map in a text changes the function of a map or an image; the function is less problematic than it is ambiguous, since the referent is displaced. The place or the object represented might very well exist, but the fictional narrative adds another possibility of signification. Do the maps in *Vie de Henry Brulard* refer to the "real" Grenoble or to the Grenoble in the narrative, or even just to itself as map (questions never fully answered by *Brulard*)? The image stands independent of the text, but participates in the network of meaning.

The first sketch by Beyle presents Zadig/Astarté/Brulard tracing initials in the dust, a visual *mise en abîme;* the narrator draws the narrator drawing the narrator's newly assumed name. "Astarté" in the drawing provides the key to understanding the misquotation of Voltaire, absent in the written text. Brulard is present and absent in the sketch, just as he is and is not already a citation, is and is not the same as the author.

He first appears in a map, on his own, in the chapter following the first "je vais naître," in the first passage about his mother. The text introduces her, describes her vaguely, and then announces her death and his incomprehension of the event. The next page in the manuscript portrays an overhead view of the room they shared: "1. Mon matelas. [My mattress]—2. Moi. [a very crude figure composed of two circles placed on the bed]—3. Lit d'Henriette." ["Henriette's bed," next to a large X or cross instead of a body] (61). The X takes the place of the lost mother, marks the spot of the object of desire. On the following page the text reveals the significance of the map: "Un soir, comme par quelque hasard on m'avait mis coucher dans sa chambre par terre, sur un matelas, cette femme vive et légère comme une biche sauta par-dessus mon matelas pour atteindre plus vite à son lit" (61) ("One night, as by accident I was laid to sleep in her room on the ground, on a mattress, this lively woman, light as a doe, jumped right over my mattress in order to get to her own bed more quickly"). Many commentators have interpreted this leap to be the revelation of sexual difference (notably, Lang, 1083); the text gives away no details, only the possibility of meaning. The very absence of the mother (or the absence of the mother's phallus), marked by the X, creates a lack that can only be filled by the drawings, "a substitute for the missing object of desire" (Mahuzier, 207). Later in the novel he takes drawing lessons, and admits, "ma mère avait eu un rare talent pour le dessin" ("my mother had a rare talent for drawing"); could drawing (and indirectly the presence of maps in the text) be his way of searching for his mother? (Didier, préface to *Vie de Henry Brulard*, 13).[10] The death of the mother gives birth to the narrator: "Elle mourut donc dans sa chambre . . . Là j'étais né . . ." (*Oeuvres intimes*, 63) ("She died in her room . . . There I was born . . ."). The text and the map have condensed time, forcing the death of the mother from complications in childbirth (Henri/y's younger brother) and the birth of Henry to coincide.

Henry, "au point H," H', B, or M, is present in almost all of the maps. This presence is at once a doubling of the textual identity (the subject is visible in the map and readable in the text) and its reduction to an emblem (an initial, a dot, or a stick figure). The narrator is able to refer to himself in the text as image, turning himself as subject into an object. This would seem to be a direct response to the question he asks himself near the end of the first chapter: "Quel oeil peut se voir soi-même?" ("What eye can see itself?") (*Oeuvres intimes,* 31), as well as to the inscription of the Delphic Temple, "Gnoti Saouton" ("know thyself") quoted later in the text (218). As Christian Jacob writes in *L'Empire des cartes,* "l'oeil ne voit pas, il construit, il imagine l'espace. La carte n'est pas un objet, mais une fonction" (29) ("The eye does not see, it constructs, it imagines space.

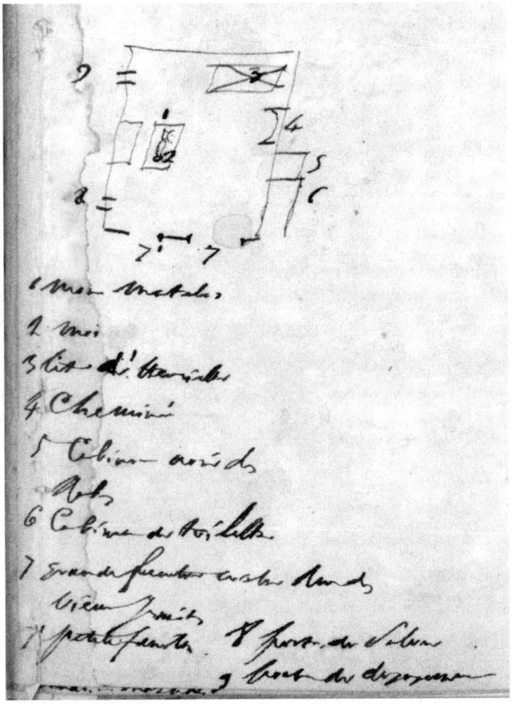

Figure 1.3. Henry in his bedroom. *Vie de Henry Brulard,* R299, vol. 1, no. 211, folio 102. Courtesy of Bibliothèque Municipale de Grenoble.

A map is not an object, but a function"). The function of the cartographic eye in this text would be to imagine the relation of objects in space, at a particular time, in order for the narrator to "see" himself. The double perspective of the narrator, who seems to be both subject and object, is a ruse made possible by both the succession of text and image and the reduction of Henry to a dot and an initial. The space between text and image, their different media, create the distance, the cartographic mirror, for the narrator to "perceive" the Henry on the map, that is, to refer to it. At the same time, H (Henry/i), B (Beyle, Brulard), and M (Moi, which could be anyone), by their ambiguity, can signify either the present of the narration or the past, the author, the narrator or the young Henri/y. This ruse is analogous to that of autobiographical narrative: a simulacrum (here, a map) is needed to incite the reader to forget the dual position of the narrator in the past and the present, in the written text and in the image.

The maps, as supplements to the text, occasionally both give away and maintain the simulacrum, in the same way that the letters of the text give away the presence of Beyle; they guarantee the authenticity of the autobiographical representation and simultaneously call the genre of the text itself into question. Twice, more than one moment of time is explicitly represented in an analytical map, disrupting the relation of Henry "au point H" to the rest of the space represented: in chapter 33, there is a map of Grenoble with a bridge built by his friend Crozet in 1827, though the narration in the map and the text indicate 1800 (314); in chapter 13, there is a new road constructed in 1810, "que je n'ai jamais vue" ("which I have never seen"), and posterior to the narration, which takes place in 1791 (155). If neither the narrator, nor Henry could have seen the road or the bridge, how can the map function coherently as a system of relations?

In one extraordinary series of maps (chapter 33), an element of time and movement creates an alternative narrative to the written text. Henry and his friends plan a "conspiracy" against the "arbre de la Fraternité," a scrawny tree planted symbolically in the main square of Grenoble across from Henry's home during the Revolution. The tree holds a sign with a crown, a scepter, chains, and some uninspiring verse, which constitute an offense to the young Brulard's aesthetic sensibility. The written text recounts the incident with the narrator's usual apology for his lack of memory and the fuzzy details of the representation. The maps, however, are set up like a comic strip, a treatment for a film. The first map is an overhead view, a sort of establishing shot; the legend indicates details not yet relevant to the written narration, but anticipating it: F. the tree, P. the well, C. the house that the Dlles Codé [*sic*] rented. The second map is larger, giving more details; there is now a dotted line, from M to M' for "marche," that indicates the entry of the conspirators and their eventual flight (also not yet mentioned in the text). The third sketch is covered in writing, pointing out all the neighbors that could be watching and who might turn in the youths to the "corps de garde"; the tree itself has disappeared in order to highlight the sign. Then there is a "cut," a change in perspective: the profile of one conspirator is shown firing the pistol (two semicircles indicate the sound or the shot) at the sign on the tree. The last two maps represent the presence of the "corps de garde," followed by the flight of the conspirators (the gun still smoking), now signified by the line FFF ("Fuite"), through the Dlles Codé's living room. As at other points in the text, "l'auteur 'se voit' en H puis en H' sans avoir aucune idée de ce qui s'est passé dans l'intervalle" (Coulont-Henderson, 146) ("the author 'sees himself' at H and then at H' without having any idea what happened between intervals"). In the interval between maps—between cuts—is where movement occurs. The reader, who imagines the movement and fills in the interval, necessarily produces the "action" of this conspiracy. The narration of the written text is not only superfluous, but deficient, unable to provide a credible account of the story.

Certain maps produce memory in the written text instead of being produced by it (which seems to be a reversal of the usual procedure). An event, a place, is drawn in a map even though the accompanying text claims amnesia. A few pages later the text, aided by the visual representation, will "remember" the event or place. One could classify the maps, then, into two groups: those that prolong the text and those that short-circuit it by marking an ellipsis in the writing (Coulont-Henderson, 142). At these moments, the repetition of the same image (such as the grandfather's house which is drawn over a dozen times, from all perspectives) would seem to trigger the writing of the text.

But the inversion of text and image upsets the dual position of the narrator/subject in text and image created by the citation of the map in the text. Instead of the text referring to itself as map, instead of the "I" of the narrator/Brulard existing in the past and present, the written text arises from the map: the text produces itself. The written narrative must refer backward in the space of the text and backward in time for the reader. The production of "memory" by certain maps reverses the chronological order of narrative established in chapter 2. The narrator is now a repetition of the narrated, the past has taken over the present of narration. Instead of the surpassing of time itself, this is an invasion of the (imagined) past that problematizes the textual subject. Unlike the "conspiracy" episode, where the accumulation of individual sketches suggests movement to the reader to the detriment of the written text, these "short-circuiting maps" inspire the text to invent narrative instead of representing the past.[11] Despite, or because of, the analytical "Cartesian" maps, the truthful autobiography has fallen into the novel.

In the *Vie de Henry Brulard,* Stendhal has devised a unique representation of the self through the convergence of autobiography and novel, text and map. The "truthful" autobiographical text would paradoxically be based upon a moment of deception or imagination, where the autobiographical subject gives way to an independent novel subject. The narrator/author imagines or desires the self as other in order to obtain knowledge of the self. The textual ruse would postulate a sort of Holy Trinity, where the author, narrator, and subject are entirely distinct (creating an autobiographical mirror) and yet the same (the reason for the writing of the text). This imagined other, through a new cogito ("after so many general remarks, I am going to be born"), is momentarily stripped of particular details, until it approaches a universal, allowing it to become text. The new textual subject is then recounted by a narrator, whose discourse is impossibly the same as the subject's (a present superimposed onto the past of the subject). The autobiographical simulacrum collapses these distinctions, inciting the reader to overlook the imaginary conception of autobiography.

The textual subject, at least as can be deduced from *Brulard,* exists through a discourse of simulacrum, the ambiguous identities of subject, narrator, and author, and the multiplicity of meaning inherent to textuality. The more ambiguous or even incoherent the representation, the more truthful the image of the subject, since, in Stendhal's logic, a style that is too polished must be lying (which is his principal objection to Rousseau and Chateaubriand). If the (textual) subject is revealed through a pun, then the ultimate text would have to indulge in the free play of language. The abundance of precise "military" and "mathematical" maps draw the limits of the subject, and yet add another level of meaning, often increasing the ambiguity of the text. Maps literalize Brulard's "what eye can see itself" because they encode the self as a sign represented by a letter, a dot, or a stick figure, while becoming, themselves, interpretable text.

However, as I explore in the following chapter, the textuality of the *Vie de Henry Brulard* must be controlled so that any one element (the autobiographical or the novel subject) does not upset the suspension between the elements necessary for the transformation of subjectivity. When the maps create an alternative fiction that oversteps the bounds of the autobiographical simulacrum, an element of censure, in the form of an alternative cartography, emerges that prevents the text from turning definitively to fiction, just as the gaps in the chronological narrative of Beyle/Brulard's life prevent the dominance of the autobiographical mode. Brulard the novel subject must be reined in by Stendhal the writer in order to resemble and yet transcend Beyle the author.

Chapter Two

The Ghost in the Map

The incomplete fusion of autobiography and fiction allows the entry of the subject into text, it promises the only possibility of objective self-knowledge and creative self-definition. The tension between the identities of Beyle and Brulard can only be preserved if the text remains ambiguous: both autobiography and fiction, and neither one nor the other. The narrator constantly worries about the status of the text, on the one hand about the "truth" of the autobiography and on the other about his lack of memory which might lead him to invent narrative. I analyze in this chapter the various mechanisms employed by the narrator to control the excesses of autobiography and fiction in order to preserve a tenuous balance that would sustain Henry Brulard's dual nature as a fictive reflection of a "real" Henri Beyle.

Fiction's threat is that the story of Brulard may no longer reflect that of Beyle, that the author might lose control of the subject (himself). Novelistic paradigms are more or less easily avoidable; the text generally evades suspense, flowery rhetoric, and excessive description that might evoke an artificial realism. The presence of images and maps continually interrupts the narrative and thus impedes the development of a coherent fictional story about Brulard that could compete with Beyle's own life.

But the very conversion of the self into (fictive or not) text, its reduction to the universal subject of the cogito, its representation at a single instant in time, inevitably imperils the integrity and continuity of the author's existence, the uniqueness of personal experience. In order for the reader, for the author himself, to perceive the subject, it has to be inscribed into reductive language and placed into irreversible chronological time. Yet this incessant analysis and universalizing jeopardizes what Beyle treasures most, his own memory.

Caught between the illusory self-knowledge of the analytical maps and the text's invention of memory in ambiguous language, the *Vie de Henry Brulard* falls back once again on the powers of textuality. The text alternates between analytical, chronological descriptions that reduce the subject to discrete and fragmented moments (represented as ichnographic maps or overhead views) and holistic views that temporalize space and reflect the subject's place across time (represented as bird's-eye views). *Brulard*'s playful oscillation between partial concealment and total exposure denounces the harmful effects of writing (chronological narrative erases memory) and yet uses writing, in the form of a novel map, to imagine his entire past and supplement memory.

The first section of this chapter, "Monta(i)gnes," explores a temporal cartography present in the *Vie de Henry Brulard,* what I liken to a bird's-eye view. The first chapter of Beyle's autobiography begins with a view of Rome from on top a mountain, where the narrator/Brulard/Beyle overlooks the Eternal City, his entire life, and time itself. The perception of time and the evocation of memory hallucinate the ghosts of the past, the dismemberment of the self caused by chronological narrative. The bird's-eye view presents layers of time over space and blurs the distinction between text and self. The second section of this chapter, "The Dazling of Memory," traces *Brulard*'s simulated fear of textuality to the fear of the dissolution of the self through language. A mistrust of representation masks, by explaining away, *Brulard*'s own control of textuality.

Monta(i)gnes

The majority of maps in the novel could be described as "military" or "mathematical" according to the text's own precise relations of objects in space at one moment in time. They are almost exclusively ichnographic (overhead or floor plan) views with little "unnecessary" detail; the space is flattened; the only point privileged is an impossible abstract view from above. They seem to correspond to the textual impulse for autobiographical truth and objectivity, while often revealing its limits. Another model of imagining space, however, is present in the *Vie de Henry Brulard* which functions as a counterpoint to the "Cartesian"[1] analytic mapping. At the beginning of the text, the narrator describes a view from a mountain, what could be called a bird's-eye view. This different type of map includes the perspective of the viewer in the map itself; the relation of the viewer to the objects and the space represented is privileged over the relations of the objects to themselves. As one imagines a city from a bird's-eye view, certain buildings eclipse others, as contrasted to a street map. Moreover, a duality or plurality of moments in time is implied: the viewer/reader necessarily scans the map in the present; as his or her viewing position (as well as the distance, and therefore the time, between all objects) is already inscribed in the perspective, one could say that a layer of present time covers the image. At the same time, the map, and what it represents, exists prior to the viewing, a past in wait for the present. This perspectival view differs from the "Cartesian" map already described: in the former (bird's-eye view) there is no simultaneity of subject and object, but rather of past and present; in the latter ("Cartesian"), the "subject" views the "object" from the outside, they can only occupy the same position successively by a deception in the text, a conflation of the written and the visual. The past does not invade the present in the bird's-eye view, but coexists with it, which suggests the overcoming of time itself.

The rather uncharacteristic first chapter begins with just such a view. It is uncharacteristic since it contains no sketches or maps (only an eighth of the chapters do not), and yet it develops one of the key cartographic moments in the text. The narrator finds himself overlooking Rome, high on the Gianicolo Hill ("le mont Janicule"), with a view of the entire city. Marcel Proust, in *La Prisonnière,* accurately summarizes Stendhal's contribution to literature in one sentence: "vous verriez dans Stendhal un certain sentiment de l'altitude se liant à la vie spirituelle" (Proust, *À la recherche du temps perdu III,* 879) ("you will see in Stendhal a certain feeling of altitude tied to spiritual life"). Like one of his fictional characters, Stendhal's narrator is spiritually moved by this view of Rome; so much so that one could say that the entire work flows from the musings inspired by this moment:

> Je me trouvais ce matin, 16 octobre 1832, à San Pietro *in Montorio,* sur le mont Janicule, à Rome, il fesait [*sic*] un soleil magnifique. Un léger vent de sirocco à peine sensible faisait flotter quelques petits nuages blancs au-dessus du mont Albano, une chaleur délicieuse régnait dans l'air, j'étais heureux de vivre. Je distinguais parfaitement Frascati et Castel Gandolfo qui sont à quatre lieues d'ici, la villa Aldobrandini où est cette sublime fresque de Judith du Dominiquin. Je vois parfaitement le mur blanc qui marque les réparations faites en dernier lieu par le prince F[rançois] Borghèse, celui-là même que je vis à Wagram colonel d'un régiment de cuirassiers, le jour où M. de Noue, mon ami, eut la jambe emportée. Bien plus loin, j'aperçois la roche de Palestrina et la maison blanche de Castel San Pietro qui fut autrefois sa forteresse. Au-dessous du mur contre lequel je m'appuie sont les grands orangers du verger des capucins, puis le Tibre et le prieuré de Malte, un peu après sur la droite le tombeau de Cecilia Metella, Saint-Paul et la pyramide de Cestius. En face de moi j'aperçois Sainte-Marie-Majeure et les longues lignes du Palais de Monte Cavallo.

> Toute la Rome ancienne et moderne, depuis l'ancienne voie Appienne avec les ruines de ses tombeaux et de ses aqueducs jusqu'au magnifique jardin de Pincio bâti par les Français, se déploie à la vue.[2] (37–38)

Stendhal's view of Rome in the *Vie de Henry Brulard* is much more than a majestic panorama. The panorama of Rome leads to a reflection on the ancients, on painting, on aging, and finally on subjectivity; it is all of Stendhal's works in miniature. Highly personalized, it contains many autobiographical anecdotes and details. Some of the details are relevant to the narrative that will follow (his presence or nonpresence at the battle of Wagram, and the Lake Albano) others are not (most of the Roman buildings). Many of the best-known sites, though in theory visible from this viewpoint, are not described: the Pantheon, the Santa Trinità del Monte, the Palatine Hill and Forum, the domes of the baroque city center (closer and larger than Santa Maria Maggiore and San Paolo), the Coliseum and the Palazzo Farnese (only mentioned on the following page). The majority of place names correspond to "personal" monuments hardly visible at all. The Vatican is brought up in the text later by reference to the *Transfiguration,* though the Holy See, and the painting it contained, is not visible from San Pietro in Montorio. The relatively faraway hill towns of Frascati, Albano, and Palestrina ("quatre lieues" or 17 km away from Rome) mark the outer limit of the view, and so, even on the clearest day, could hardly provide any visual details; the Villa Aldobrandini above Frascati could barely seem more than a speck on the landscape. Indeed, what is privileged is the narrator's personal relation to place, especially in its capacity to evoke particular events in time. The overall movement of description is first the location of the narrator (San Pietro in Montorio), then the limits of his view (Frascati, Albano, Gandolfolo, and Palestrina), eventually the places closest to him (the orange grove, the Priory of Malta, the Tiber). It is as if all of Rome, "ancient and modern," were approaching him. This initiating map inscribes the narrator's affective perspective on the city, while situating the narrative in the present (1832), as he reminisces about time. "All of Rome, ancient and modern" presents itself to him, as well as, and especially, his own "Life."

This is, of course, Stendhal's Rome and not yet Brulard's Grenoble (Brulard does not live past Milan). As this chapter stands as a preamble to the rest of the novel, *Promenades dans Rome,* written in 1829, is a preamble to *Brulard.* The *Promenades* is a pseudo-travel journal composed of Stendhal's memories of Rome (written in Paris) and his unabashed plagiarism and parody of other popular guides (Crouzet, *Promenades,* VIII); in short, it is a mixture of genre and citation. It is evident that the later

Souvenirs d'égotisme and *Vie de Henry Brulard* would follow the same path as the *Promenades:* a fictional autobiography that tries to balance objective concerns through the fragmentation of the autobiographical genre. More remarkable is the fact that the beginning of the first chapter of *Brulard* is almost a direct citation from the *Promenades:*

> San Pietro in Montorio. J'admire de nouveau la vue; c'est *sans comparaison* la plus belle de Rome: on voit tout admirablement bien et l'on voit le mont Albano et Frascati, Cecilia Metella, etc. Il faut un jour de soleil à nuages chassés par le vent; alors tous les dômes de Rome sont tour à tour dans l'ombre et dans le clair.[3] (*Promenades,* notes, 750–51)

This view is, then, Stendhal's idealized vision of Rome, about which he fantasized ("ce lieu est unique au monde, me disais-je en rêvant"—"this place is unique in the world, I told myself dreaming") in Paris while writing the *Promenades,* and in which he encapsulated, crystallized, the ancient city.

What at first seems to be a view of Rome on a particular day in 1832 is actually a palimpsest composed uniquely of memory and citation. This view of Rome in 1832, an ideal moment, a literary moment for Stendhal, is not a factual detailing of a view, but an aesthetic invention, a novel map. By all accounts he was in Abruzzo, not in Rome, from the 7th to the 20th of October in 1832. The manuscript margins state clearly "*Book* commencé le 23 novembre 1835" (37) ("*Book* started November 23, 1835"); the ink and paper used is the same throughout the first chapter. The "present" of the narrative jumps forward three years to 1835 to coincide with the actual writing. There is hardly a break in narrative voice (and no graphic break in the manuscript), as Stendhal announces, "Je ne continue que le 23 novembre 1835" (40) ("I can only continue November 23, 1835"), as if trying to slip the date past the reader. It is true that earlier that year (June 20 to July 4) he worked on the *Souvenirs d'égotisme,* but Rome is hardly mentioned in that text.

By antedating the text, Stendhal stresses the proximity to his fiftieth birthday (January 23, 1833) and links it to the city of Rome, and in particular to San Pietro in Montorio. The presence, or rather absence, of Raphael's *Transfiguration* in this church for 250 years provides the essential digression: the painting would have, at least symbolically, shared this view; fifty years is the echo of 250 years (Béatrice Didier has emphasized Stendhal's particular number symbolism in relation to death [*Stendhal autobiographe,* 202]). The painting is now "buried" in the Vatican, resurrected in the text of *Brulard.*

Rome is the city of tombs and death: "Quand on arrive de Naples à Rome, on croit entrer dans un tombeau. Il est peu de contrastes aussi douloureux" (*Oeuvres intimes II,* journal entry 1832, 157) ("When you arrive from Naples to Rome, you would think you were entering a tomb. There are few contrasts as painful.") The Castel' San Angelo (formerly Hadrian's tomb), the tomb of Cecilia Metella (made famous by the neo-classicists Winkelman and Piranesi), the pyramid of Cestius (an elaborate tomb designed by an ancient Roman banker), and the tombs along the Appian Way are all spectacular ancient monuments to death cited in the view of Rome. In the *Promenades,* Stendhal recounts the last wish of the poet Tasso, to die on the Gianicolo overlooking Rome: "La vue si étendue et si belle que l'on y a de Rome, cette ville des tombeaux et des souvenirs, doit rendre moins pénible ce dernier pas pour se détacher des choses de la terre, si tant est qu'il soit pénible" (*Promenades,* 376) ("The expansive and beautiful view one has here of Rome, this city of tombs and memories, must make less painful this last step to detach oneself from the things of this earth, if indeed it is painful"). San Pietro in Montorio is, as Stendhal himself writes: "au lieu même où Saint Pierre souffrit le martyre" (*Promenades,* 397) ("the very place where Saint Peter was martyred"). Six of the twenty engravings included in the manuscript have directly or indirectly as subjects Saint Peter (Mossman, 344), thus all referring back to this first paragraph and continually recalling both the church and Saint Peter's martyrdom. Tasso (next to his oak tree) and Raphael (through what nineteenth-century art critics considered his most celebrated painting) both achieved glory through their "transfigurations," their artistic sublimation, on this same hill: "De plus grands que moi sont bien morts!" ("Much greater men than I have died!"). Stendhal anticipates his own transfiguration into the text as Brulard. This "spiritual" moment (as Proust would have it), inspired by a fictional view, allows Stendhal to "play dead," to see his whole life from beginning to end, allowing for the commencement of a complete, and thus fictional, autobiography (but one without an end).

The reflections on mortality are enhanced by the Gianicolo's position in the Roman landscape; it is at the westernmost limit of the city, with only fields behind it. The narrator has his back facing the West (the occident, meaning where the sun dies) and remains until the sun falls behind him, hinting at the end of his own life. As the narrator says midway through *Brulard,* "[il y a] trois ans que m'est venue, sur l'esplanade de *San Pietro in Montorio* (Janicule), l'idée lumineuse que j'allais avoir cinquante ans et qu'il était temps de songer au départ et auparavant de se donner le plaisir de regarder en arrière" (115) ("three years ago came to me, on the esplanade of *San Pietro in Montorio* (Gianicolo), the luminous idea that I was going to be fifty years old and that it was time to think about the final departure and before then to abandon myself to looking backwards"). The name Gianicolo is derived from Janus (January), the two-faced god of doors and liminal spaces. The narrator can thus occupy the threshold between two moments in time, facing the future (the sunset of his life) while looking back at the past (the view of Rome), just as his text will occupy the threshold between autobiography and fiction.

As the tombs of Rome evoke Brulard/Beyle's mortality, its ruins and the memories they recall hallucinate the dismemberment of the body in time. The totality (in time and space) of the view of Rome distorts the subject like a baroque anamorphosis, revealing different moments and facets from different angles. Disturbing the idyllic portrait of Rome is the recurrence of traumatic or sublime images that haunt the text. The "sublime fresco of Judith" recalls, of course the severed head of Holofernes. The innocuous repairs done on a wall summon up François Borghèse, colonel at Wagram, present when Beyle's friend M. de Noue lost his leg. The repairs included in the same sentence as well as M. de Noue's name (de-noue, "dénoue" or "untie") anticipate the loss of his leg. A series of ancient tombs is listed, starting with that of Cecilia Metella, which had inspired Stendhal's acquaintance Byron in his *Childe Harold* and is best known for its bucranium, or ox skull (the medieval name of the tomb was "Capo di bove," "oxen's head"). Next in the list is San Paolo, which marks the spot where Saint Paul was decapitated. Cestius's Pyramid is the tomb of an ancient Roman banker and is adjacent to the Protestant cemetery of Rome, where Keats, Shelley, and others are buried. Finally the Appian Way makes an appearance, with its hundreds of monuments to death. The repetition of death and dismemberment apparent in the bird's-eye view of Rome suggests that the narrator's attempt to grasp the totality of the self and its place in the flow of time has failed, leading to a feeling that he has lost any unity of the self and hallucinates his own dismemberment.

The conflation of the mind and the city is at least as old as the second book of Plato's *Republic,* but in modern times Rome has become the privileged site of the human psyche. Goethe, in the December 20, 1786, entry of his *Italian Journey,* attests to the confusion of exterior and interior he felt in Rome: "It is history, above all, that one reads quite differently here from anywhere else in the world. Everywhere else one starts from the outside and works inward; here it seems to be the other way around" (Goethe, 154). The bird's-eye view also takes as its point of departure the viewer. In *Brulard,* the entire image of Rome is unfurled, unfolded ("se déploie à la vue") in the text from memory, an interior space becoming exterior again through writing. It is literally imagined, transformed into an image to be seen ("je vois," "je distingue," "j'aperçois," "Quelle vue"). There is a reversal of interiority and exteriority, a Möbius strip of consciousness, where Rome reflects Brulard and Brulard Rome. The history of Rome, "ancient and modern," cannot be separated from the narrator's sense of time and memory, past and present: "tous les souvenirs de Tite-Live me revenaient en foule" (38) ("all the memories of Titus-Livy come back to me"). His memories of reading Titus-Livy, or literally the memories of Titus-Livy himself, are present as he gazes at the ancient city.

The conflation of text and memory, of the space of Rome and time itself, of city and subject is eloquently elaborated by Montaigne (one of Stendhal's 3M of French literature, Montaigne, Molière, and Montesquieu, "les trois M donnent du plaisir en français par du noir sur du blanc" [*Oeuvres intimes II,* 165–66]) ("the three M give pleasure in French through black on white") in "De la vanité":

> J'ay veu ailleurs des maisons ruynées, et des statues, et du ciel, et de la terre: ce sont tousjours des hommes. Tout cela est vray; et si pourtant ne sçauroy revoir si souvent le tombeau de cette ville, si grande et si puissante, que je ne l'admire et revere. Le soing des morts nous est en recommendation. Or j'ay esté nourry dès mon enfance avec ceux icy; j'ay eu connoissance des affaires de Romme, long temps avant que je l'aye eue de ceux de ma maison: je sçavois le Capitole et son plant avant que je ne sçeusse le Louvre, et le Tibre avant la Seine. J'ay eu plus en teste les conditions et fortunes de Lucullus, Metellus et Scipion, que je n'ay d'aucuns hommes des nostres. Ils sont trespassez. Si est bien mon pere, aussi entierement qu'eux, et s'est esloigné de moy et de la vie autant en dixhuict ans que ceux-là ont faict en seize cens.[4] (*Essais,* 209)

Rome nourishes Montaigne, providing for his psychological and intellectual development, in juxtaposition to Paris. Rome's ruins,"the tomb of this city," though in theory lost in the past, have more effect on him than any monument in France. Once something becomes part of the past, "trespasses" the threshold between present and past, life and death, it becomes not further away in space or in consciousness, but eternal. The death of Montaigne's father eighteen years earlier does not seem closer than the death 1,600 years earlier of the literary Romans that nourished his youth. If they survive in the present, it is because of Montaigne, who feels a duty to honor the dead, who cannot help themselves (*Essais*, 209–10). Brulard also brings back the dead, though his motives seem less pure:

"Qui se souvient d'Alexandrine, morte en janvier 1815, il y a vingt ans? Qui se souvient de Métilde, morte en 1825? Ne sont-elles pas à moi, moi qui les aime mieux que tout le reste du monde?" (166) ("Who remembers Alexandrine, dead January 1815, twenty years ago? Who remembers Métilde, dead in 1825? Are they not mine, who loved them more than anyone else in the world?"). Montaigne holds "en teste" ("in his head") the time of the ancients and the present, Rome and Paris, the dead and the living.

The two writers collapse the space of two places and times into one textual moment, evoking the phantoms of the past. Montaigne, like Stendhal, does not describe Rome from the present, as he did in the *Journal de voyage en Italie,* but from his memory and from literary citation. Tom Conley, in "A Suckling of Cities: Montaigne in Paris and Rome," argues that in Montaigne, as well as Freud, the birth of the subject comes about through the city views of Rome.[5] Like Paris and Rome's simultaneity of place in the textual map, Montaigne's psychological past occupies the same space as his perception of the present. The textual trick of forcing two cities to be collapsed into one is the same as that used in *Brulard* to collapse the difference between subject and object, past and present. Conley extends his argument to Freud's analogy of Rome and the psyche in *Civilization and Its Discontents:* the ruins of the ancient city can be seen through an effort of imagination and can thus be contemporaneous with modern time, just as the psyche of the infant lives on in the unconscious of the adult (Conley, 170–71). The psyche destroys memories the same way that time destroys the city's structures, but the ruins of memories survive in the same way that ruins survive. The metaphor goes too far for Freud because it suggests a collective psychogenesis and therefore the metaphor leads to the paradox of a unique individual who is nevertheless identical to every other individual (Conley, 169). Freud concludes that it is impossible to occupy two different historical states or places in the same space at the same time (Conley, 169).

Henri Bergson elaborates this paradox (that one subject can occupy two times and spaces simultaneously) into a theory of consciousness and memory before Freud. The conscious is a mechanism to discard what is not useful to the perception of the immediate present; the unconscious would then be what is "impotent," what the conscious considers unnecessary. Just as objects that are not immediately perceived still really exist (the commonsense rebuttal to Berkeley's immaterialist *esse est percipi*—to be is to be perceived), "le souvenir-pur" ("pure memory") and the past coexist with the present. What is more unsettling is that "pure memory" is, according to Bergson, not stored in the brain, but exists independently, which suggests (though Bergson seems reluctant to extend his concept) that there may exist a universal memory shared by all.

Since space measures the proximity of a potential menace to the body in relation to time, what is essential to perception is a schema of the future; it seems preferable to open the space in front of the body (the future) and to close the time behind. The "real" seems to start with the present, but

> quand un souvenir reparaît à la conscience, il nous fait l'effet d'un revenant dont il faudrait expliquer par des causes spéciales l'apparition mystérieuse. En réalité, l'adhérence de ce souvenir à notre état présent est tout à fait comparable à celle des objets inaperçus aux objets que nous percevons, et l'*inconscient* joue dans les deux cas un rôle du même genre.[6] (Bergson, 161)

Bergson's version of the uncanny is simply the breakdown of the conscious's repression of the past. From here he assumes "notre *caractère* est bien la synthèse actuelle de tous nos états passés" (162) ("our *character* is really the present synthesis of all of our past states"). The bird's-eye view of Rome is a sublime experience that achieves the surpassing of space and time, the synthesis of our past selves. To reverse Bergson's syllogism, Stendhal (or Montaigne) must invoke all his past states in order to comprehend fully, or perceive in the present, his "character" (the expressed purpose of *Brulard* and the *Essais*). Stendhal's (or Montaigne's) conjuring up of his memory of Rome, an object not immediately present, also conjures up his ghosts, "les revenants" (in French "ghosts," or "that which comes back") of his past (hence the choice of Rome, "city of tombs"). This incantation temporarily unlocks the unconscious: "all of Titus-Livy's memories rushed back to me." The unconscious (and the memories it perceives) is always present, occupying the same space as the conscious. The contemporaneous presence of the past only resembles a paradox since the mind, in an economy of perception, represses memory as past. The bird's-eye view of Rome forces the two to coexist, or rather tricks the conscious into projecting the past onto the space in front of the body, what is usually occupied by the future. The return of the suppressed is thus superimposed onto the space of the future represented as map (Stendhal has his back to the West, against the usual progression of time).

Any attempt to analyze the mass of time revealed by this temporary unleashing of memory, that is, to use the conscious to select memories to bring forward to perception, would break the spell by reinstating the mechanism of repression; the unconscious becomes impotent. Indeed, this ideal moment brought on by the vision of Rome does not even last a few pages, since the narrator has trouble defining whom he was or is. The harmony ("j'étais heureux de vivre"—"I was happy to be alive") has disappeared and been replaced by confusion, as the narrator no longer knows which spatial and temporal reference points to choose, as seen by the narrative's wandering through space and time (Rome, Wagram, Paris, Ischia, Grenoble, 1793, 1832, 1835, 1880, 1935). Proust's insomniac suffers the same existential wandering upon waking. This "égarement" or "straying" leads, of course, to the Cartesian analysis that dominates the novel, an effort to cut through the different layers of time, the analysis and dismemberment of the subject.

There are very few other "panorama perspectives" like the one of Rome in the rest of the work that represent space as a function of time. However, those that exist take on special significance by their rarity and deliberate placement in the text. There are two "figures géométriques" or "cartes" ("maps") as he calls them, which could be described as representations from a panoramic perspective. Françoise Coulont-Henderson has categorized them as "des croquis à caractère allégoriques, sortes de cartes du Tendre" (149) ("sketches of an allegorical nature, a sort of map of the human heart"). More than just purely visual elements however, they serve to interrupt the text, revealing what the written text cannot. They are equally spaced in the novel: the first 130 pages after the beginning (*Oeuvres intimes,* 159), the second 130 pages after that (290); which is to say almost exactly one-third and two-thirds of the way into the text. Similar to the view of the first chapter (and thus different from the majority of the work), these are affective cartographies or itineraries where time is represented spatially and ideally. Because of their similarity and even spacing in the text, we can link together the first chapter, the last chapter, and these two sketches. These four textual moments serve to question, to undermine the authority of the autobiographical project, the truth in dividing up Henry Brulard's life into distinct (writeable and drawable) moments, suggesting that the subject cannot be contained by language or chronological narrative.

The first sketch schematizes the different "routes" one can take in life, seen from the point of view of the "moment de la naissance" ("moment of birth"). Facing the "moment of birth" (marked suggestively by a triangle and the letter "A") is an empty half circle. Extending from the half circle are four "routes" that continue open-ended: "Route de la folie" ("Route of madness"), "Route de l'art de se faire lire" ("Route of the art of getting oneself read"), "Route de la considération: Fx Faure se fait Paire de France" ("Route of esteem: Fx Faure makes himself a Peer of France"),

"Route de la fortune par le commerce ou les places" ("Route of fortune through commerce or appointments"). The map is personalized with the name of Stendhal's least impressive friend, Félix Faure, who, through luck and lack of personal ambition, rose to the elite of Restoration society. The sketch is included in a letter (now lost) to his friend Roland Colomb (cousin of Stendhal who discovered the world of letters late in life and who edited Stendhal's works after his death). He explains that once a person has chosen his path in life, he cannot suddenly choose another. He does not blame his friend, however, since if the narrator were to die and approach Montesquieu, he would not be surprised if the great writer were to tell him that he had no talent: "l'oeil ne se voit pas lui-même" (159) ("the eye does not see itself"). The modification of the phrase "Quel oeil peut se voir . . . ?" ("What eye can see itself . . . ?") to the affirmation "l'oeil ne se voit pas . . ." ("the eye does not see itself . . .") underscores the impossibility of this cartographic representation: for the map to work, the narrator would have to see himself, presumably by occupying the letter A, the moment of birth. This is exactly what *Brulard* attempts to do, reenter the moment of birth as text in order to see himself objectively.

The second sketch (figure 1.4) has a similar context to the first: the narrator ridicules successful politicians and financiers who decide to add to their megalomania by taking up literature (a vice rampant during the Restoration and July Monarchy, according to Stendhal). This second sketch is more elaborate than the first, since it now contains six routes instead of four. From left to right, they are "'F' la route de la folie" ("'F' the route of madness"), "'L' l'art de se faire lire: Le Tasse, Jean-Jacques Rousseau, Mozart" ("'L' the art of getting oneself read: Tasso, Jean-Jacques Rousseau, Mozart"), a route with no name, "la route de la considération publique" ("route of public esteem"), "'P' Route des bons préfets et conseillers d'Etat: MM. Daru, Roederer, Français, Beugnot" ("'P' Route of good Prefects and Councilors of State: Messrs Daru, Roederer, Français, Beugnot") and finally "'R' Route de l'argent: Rothschild" ("'R' Route of money: Rothschild") (290). Five routes have a small letter "B" assigned to them indicating that they are "Routes prises à 7 ans, souvent à notre insu. Il est souverainement absurde de vouloir à 50 ans laisser la route R ou la route P pour la route L. Frédéric II ne s'est guère fait lire et dès 20 ans songeait à la route L." ("Routes taken at seven years of age, often unconsciously. It is supremely absurd at 50 years of age to want to abandon Route R or Route P for Route L. Frederick II could hardly get himself read and already at 20 he thought about Route L."). It is "sovereignly [i.e., supremely] absurd," since only a sovereign like Frederick II would attempt it. It should be noted here that, although he expressed interest in

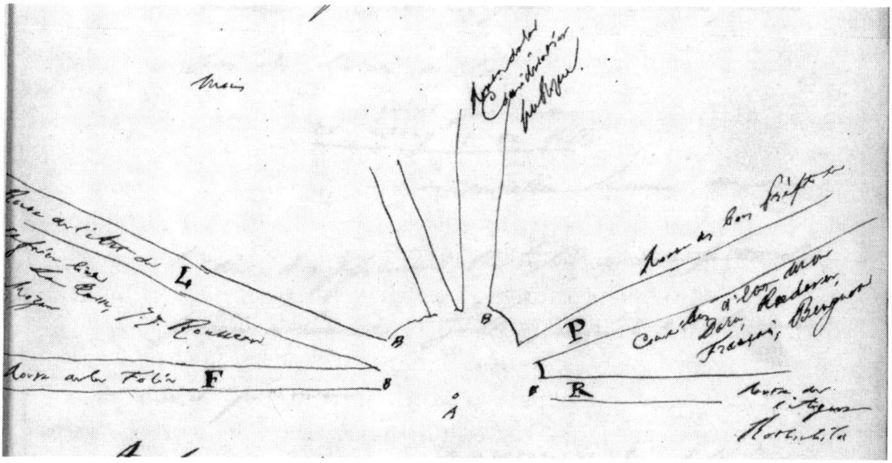

Figure 1.4. Routes taken at various stages of life. *Vie de Henry Brulard,* R299, vol. 2, no. 851, folio 424. Courtesy of Bibliothèque municipale de Grenoble.

writing plays "à la Molière" as he says early in life, Stendhal/Beyle did not publish until after his public career ("auditeur au Conseil d'Etat") ended with the fall of Napoleon I. Stendhal is himself the best example for why the proposition that one cannot change directions in life is invalid. The road is taken at the age of seven, "often unconsciously," the age of reason, and the age when Brulard lost his mother. The destiny of the text is determined by this event, but Beyle/Stendhal's destiny is that of someone who follows more than one path at the same time.

The significance of the letters is left playfully ambiguous, like the road without a name. Just as the analytic maps contain ambivalent letters (H, B, M) which could represent the narrator in the past or present, these letters ostensibly signify any individual, but more often refer indirectly to the narrator: is the moment of birth "A" because it is the first letter of the alphabet, and if so, why are five of the six paths labeled "B" (the second stage in development, or the paths attempted by Brulard?); is it "L" for "littérature" or "lire" (Sartre's distinction between life's two great divisions, writing or reading), "R" for "Rothschild" or for "riche," "P" for "public" or for "préfet"? As in the view of Rome, the first thing that is mentioned is the location of the subject (San Pietro in Montorio, or here "'A' the moment of birth"), then the periphery is described since the labels on the various roads are found at their end. Reading from left to right, the two roads on the left ("Folie" and "Littérature") move toward the subject at "A"; obviously Beyle/Brulard associated himself with literature, and in this text with madness, even if he states perhaps only rhetorically

"Rien n'empêche ma folie" ("Nothing prevents my madness") (428). The route with no name points directly to the word "mois" ("month") written in the preceding paragraph and perhaps referring to its homonym "moi" (Brulard could be considered to occupy the place between literature and public esteem, or taking a road with no name). The path of "public esteem" stands directly above "A" moving neither toward nor away, perhaps reflecting Stendhal's varying success as public official and diplomat. Finally, the roads of money and power are directed away from point "A," since Stendhal and his narrator had little of either.

These sketches would seem at first to describe a general theory of career advancement and the choices available to men of Stendhal's generation in the way that the *Rouge et le noir* was supposed to be a "chronicle of the nineteenth century." One could make an analogy to the view of Rome: anyone looking out from San Pietro would see more or less what the narrator describes. And yet, the "geometric figure," as well as the bird's-eye view, is encoded with very personal significance, containing the names and achievements of friends and acquaintances, letters with elliptical meanings, and especially hints concerning his life's itinerary. Unlike most of the drawings which represent a particular moment in time, these two outline past and future, transcending the present, but also, perhaps, the autobiographical discourse, since the itinerary they trace reinscribes the personal into the universal.

The semicircles found between the "moment of birth" and the various roads explain best the role of the two distinct cartographic systems in the text. If we consider, as the text itself claims, that Brulard/Beyle's career began when he went to Milan with Napoleon's army in 1800, then the empty space not gridded, the void contained in the semicircle, corresponds to the time period recounted by the *Vie de Henry Brulard* between the first "je vais naître" and the second. Similarly, in the first chapter with its view of Rome, there is no mention of his childhood in Grenoble, only the date of birth and the date 1800. This void indicates the difference in the text between what is recounted in *Brulard* and the life of Stendhal. The name Henri Beyle is inscribed throughout the text as guarantor of autobiography, as a sort of personal graffiti or a way to appropriate this textual "Life." The other, affective cartography has the opposite effect: to maintain the distance of the author from the text; to resist the universalizing tendency of language; in short, to prevent the destruction of the "dazling" [*sic*] of emotion and affection. The personal is erased from the surface of the text, but visible, as in a palimpsest, underneath the layers of time.

The "Dazling" of Memory

Representation, in all of its forms, is problematized throughout the *Vie de Henry Brulard,* to a degree which is much more evident than in Stendhal's "realist" novels.[7] Indeed, there prevails a constant fear, or hope, that the text will cross genre lines and "fall" into the novel: "Là, ce me semble, a été mon approche la plus voisine du *bonheur parfait.* Pour un tel moment il vaut la peine d'avoir vécu . . . Que dire d'un tel moment sans mentir, sans tomber dans le roman?" (407) ("There, it seems to me, was the closest I have gotten to *perfect happiness.* For such a moment it is worth having lived . . . What can be said of such a moment without lying, without falling into the novel?"). A "true" autobiographical narration that represents objective facts occupies figuratively a higher position than the novel, a genre that not only does not represent reality, but "lies" about it. For Stendhal's narrator, any description of facts tainted by subjective emotion is incapable of a truthful representation. At best such description is incomprehensible to the reader, since the content is too personal; at worst it creates an alternative narrative that would imitate the "flat" novels of Sir Walter Scott, a literary supplement to memory's lack. This hyperbolic distrust of descriptive representation is most acute during the narration of emotionally charged events. The narrator systematically despairs of any faithful rendering: "La sensation présente absorbait tout, absolument comme le souvenir de la première soirée où Giul[ia] m'a traité en amant. Mon souvenir n'est qu'un roman fabriqué à cette occasion" (420) ("The present sensation absorbed everything, absolutely like the memory of the first evening when Giul[ia] treated me like a lover. My memory is only a novel fabricated on this occasion"); "En me réduisant aux formes raisonnables je ferais trop d'injustice à ce que je veux raconter" (428) ("By reducing myself to reasonable forms I would commit too much injustice against what I want to say"). As the analyzing maps fail to grasp the totality of the subject and threaten to invent what they cannot represent, the "reasonable forms" of language become an unjust supplement.

The intensity of emotion exceeds not only the capacity of linguistic description, but also of memory itself. The narrator can only recall the sentiments surrounding the event, not the event itself: "Je n'ai aucune mémoire des époques ou des moments où j'ai senti trop vivement" (122) ("I have no memory at all of the periods or moments when I felt too vividly"). When description is not avoided altogether, a variety of rhetorical devices appears in the text that attempt a reconstruction of memory. Abstract and banal adjectives such as "bonheur" ("happiness"), "beau," and "parfait" ("perfect") are used to describe feelings and situations without providing any useful information. Foreign words and phrases express persons and ideas that are too evocative to be said in French: "my poor mother," "my life," "campo santo," "fiasco," "cette mort . . . me fit *pleasure*. Voilà le grand mot écrit" (177–78) ("This death . . . gave me *pleasure*. There, the great word is written"). Written and yet not written, "les grands mots" bypass the censorship regarding the sublime past; the sublime moment (good or bad) creates a sense of awe that surpasses understanding, rendering the event traumatic and thus unspeakable.

A recurring metaphor for the struggle with description reveals this mechanism of censorship:

> Je vois des images, je me souviens des effets sur mon coeur, mais pour les causes et la physionomie néant. C'est toujours les fresques du [ ] de Pise où l'on aperçoit fort bien un bras, et le morceau d'à côté qui représentait la tête est tombé. Je vois une suite d'images *fort nettes* mais sans physionomie autre que celle qu'elles eurent à mon égard. Bien plus, je ne vois cette physionomie que par le souvenir de l'effet qu'elle produisit sur moi.[8] (191)

In the manuscript a blank exists, perhaps indicating an intention of returning to the text, or at least suggesting a temporary lack of memory. The editor has supplied "Campo Santo" (which appears elsewhere in the text), Pisa's renowned monumental cemetery, where colorful medieval frescoes of heroic battle scenes are placed uncannily behind ancient Roman marble sepulchers. The image produced by the aging (or mutilation) of the frescoes evokes dismemberment and decapitation, thus indirectly referring to what language will not express, the fragmentation of the subject. Similar to the images of dismemberment in the view of Rome, Brulard's personal memory is linked to universal memory (the coexistence of medieval, classical, and modern reminders of death), hallucinating the ghosts of the past and the unweaving of the textual subject. The act of re-membering, of seeing the "physiognomy" of the past is too traumatic (or too revealing) and so can only come about through metaphor and wordplay, by studying the reaction of the subject, "the effect they had on me." The narrator vows not to describe events, but only the (sentimental and objective) effect the events had on him. The best description would be no description at all.

The final chapter of *Brulard* could be seen as the culmination of this threat of representation as the narrator, "un amoureux fou," progressively loses his capacity for language. The "life" narrative of Henry Brulard abruptly ends when he arrives in Milan, "le plus beau lieu de la terre"

(426) ("the most beautiful place on earth"). The first few pages describe in detail his arrival on horseback and his meeting with his relative Martial Daru. The text is accompanied by precise maps of Milan. But when he tries to outline the "bonheur céleste et complet" ("the celestial and complete happiness") of the succeeding days and months, and in particular his love for Angela Pietragrua, the narrator stops completely, apologizing for the excess of his emotions. The difficulty in representing Angela dates back to the *Journal,* since there is only one oblique mention of her in 1800. He decides three times to summarize, analyze, and catalogue the events and experiences, as he had done at the beginning of the text in the second chapter, without being able to write a single sentence. He then asks the reader to skip fifty pages to excuse his poor memory, but the novel ends a page later, leaving the reader in a void. The appeals for the patience of the reader, the questions as to how to describe perfect happiness without appearing insane, and the anguish at remembering a past too vivid, multiply and become more acute as each sentence becomes shorter. In the manuscript, the handwriting becomes progressively larger, each sentence forms its own paragraph, as if Stendhal were trying hopelessly to fill up the page with (empty) description. The work closes abruptly, undoing everything that precedes it with the final sentence: "On gâte des sentiments si tendres à les raconter en détail" (459) ("One spoils such tender feelings by recounting them in detail"). Has he suddenly discovered that all the "sentiments si tendres," what the narrator had previously claimed were the real object of the text, have been spoiled? That the text has ruined for the author everything that it has described?

The idea that narrating feelings in detail can in some way spoil or ruin them is a constant in Stendhal's autobiographical works. Already in the journal entry of 1805 (thirty years before the writing of *Brulard*), Stendhal writes, "Je n'écris plus les souvenirs charmants, je me suis aperçu que cela les gâtait" (*Oeuvres intimes,* 715) ("I no longer write charming memories, I have discovered that that spoils them"). One of the main stylistic traits of Stendhal, an almost stoic absence of detail, is theorized in one of his earliest writings. At least ten different formulations of the same sentence exist in the *Journal* and the *Souvenirs d'égotisme.* In the *Vie de Henry Brulard* this theme is developed and refined. The location of "one spoils . . ." as the last sentence marks its culmination as the last word in Stendhal's "autobiography," and the last time he expressed frustration at the harmful effects of writing.

The very act of converting an event into language, reducing it to metaphor, takes it out of the reach of memory. A precise objective rendering of memory necessarily kills the personal, the sentimental; as the *Journal* indicates, "Je trouve froid ce que j'ai écrit dans l'enthousiasme" (*Oeuvres intimes*, 1300) ("I find cold what I have written with enthusiasm"). *Brulard*'s narrator aims at the destruction of the "dazling" [*sic*] of an event, since an excess of sentiment distorts vision. The dominant form of cartography in the text, the "military" or "mathematical" analysis, exaggerates this distance from the event, reducing Brulard to an initial or a dot. By the text's own admission, the result of this analysis, of this classification, would be the erasure of memory, a substitution of the subjective by the objective. Thus the act of writing the self in text, of engraving one's memories with mathematical precision and distance not only spoils the "dazling" of events, the tenderness of feelings, but actually erases memory, erases being. As the view of Rome and the "figures géométriques" have shown, the narrative of Henry Brulard does not correlate with the schema of Beyle's life; Brulard is written text but unwritten or scratched-out memory. It is as if childhood memories must be erased, the link with Grenoble cut, in order for the individuation of the adult to take place.

Representations (writing, drawing, maps, engravings) enter into the mind and replace memory, threatening the self for the construction of the subject. All signs are conventions, whether linguistic, mathematical, or aesthetic, and therefore signifiers can never match that to which they refer. And yet the *Vie de Henry Brulard* is a text that fetishizes the ambiguity of language, that lives for and by the "danger" of the free play of meaning; any inscription of the subject, as the first chapter has shown, is reliant upon textuality.

Brulard as textual subject is both read by future readers and reads, inscribes himself within other texts (*Tristram Shandy, Zadig*). The reader constructs and deconstructs the text, just as the text frames and destabilizes the reading subject. The autobiographical simulacrum allows for a closed cycle of division and individuation of the subject. The "textuality" of the text as a game of multiplicity of meaning is guaranteed by the author's premature "death" (he can no longer honor the "autobio(thanato) graphical pact"), his ambiguous textual signature (the "five" letters in Brulard, the reader of the *Henriade* and the *Bélisaire,* the "point H"), and the fact that it is left "unfinished," the reader being encouraged to skip fifty pages ahead.

But the game is fixed, the cycle of meaning is already inscribed in the text. Beyle's memories, his personal experiences, that which cannot be confided to language, are erased from the text, protected from autobiography. Beyle/Brulard/Stendhal is reader and text, the meaning and the arbiter of meaning. Stendhal's narrator suspends the autobiography, in effect killing "Henry Brulard" to save Henri Beyle.

Stendhal's Privilege

The *Vie de Henry Brulard* produces the illusion of an objective distance between the author and the subject of his text (himself) by staging the birth of a new subject, simulating the "Life" of Brulard as text. The autobiographical is now displaced, its presence ensured by the game of textuality but nevertheless always questioned by it. Brulard is simultaneously an inscription of Beyle and also a citation of other ambiguous texts. The distance or perspective gained in this textualization or emblematization of the self is affirmed as well as destabilized by the eruption of image in the text. "Cartesian," analytic maps provide for an alternate play of meaning that multiplies the possibility for referentiality the more it tries to define and delimit the subject. The novel maps formed by other key "cartographic" moments in *Brulard,* however, seek to recuperate the self, the personal, remove it from the dangerous effects of textuality. The view of Rome unfolds the totality of time and space from memory. Beyle/Stendhal kills Brulard, simultaneously gaining control of the textual game while ensuring that the game will still be played.

The last stage of this autobiographical progression would be the "fall" of the text into the novel, the great fear and ultimate desire of *Brulard.* Chronologically, the entrance of Brulard/Beyle into Milan almost coincides with that of the French lieutenant in Stendhal's novel *La Chartreuse de Parme.* Almost, but not entirely, since the autobiographical referent is now lost. Similarly, the hero of that novel, Fabrice del Dongo, may be the son of the French lieutenant or even of Beyle, but there is nothing in the text to support the hypothesis except the coincidence of his conception and the lieutenant's passage. The novel, free of autobiography's paternal hold on meaning, unleashes the power of textuality almost to excess (the encoded signals exchanged through Fabrice's prison window are paragraphs long, "expressing" emotions and sighs). Truth, the obsession of Stendhal's autobiography, is detoured in favor of literary invention, of lies.

The impossibility of describing Italy in *Brulard* has been overcome through the relinquishing of the analysis of the self for the creation of myth. In 1840, Stendhal wrote a short list of "privileges," a sort of wish list of imaginary powers (invisibility rings, immunity from impotence, a steady income, etc.) that "God" would bestow on him:

> God me donne le brevet suivant: . . . Article 7. Quatre fois par an, il pourra se changer en l'homme qu'il voudra. . . . Ainsi, le privilégié pourra, quatre fois par an, et pour un temps illimité chaque fois occuper deux corps à la fois. (*Oeuvres intimes,* 1560)[9]

Stendhal's seventh privilege grants him the one power he already had in his novel maps, the power to occupy various identities at the same time. The literally countless pseudonyms, the literary characters whose lives curiously follow his own (Julien, Fabrice, Lucien), and Brulard, the textual subject between character and pseudonym, allow Beyle a second life in the text. Beyle turned Stendhal will forever be a novel self, immaterial and fleeting, bound to the destiny of the novel.

PART II
Nerval Beyond Narrative

> Comme Henri Beyle, mais sans aucune ironie, Gérard de Nerval semblait prendre plaisir à s'absenter de lui-même, disparaître de son oeuvre, à dérouter le lecteur. Que d'efforts il a faits pour rester inconnu!*
>
> —Théophile Gautier, cited in Chotard, *Nerval: Mémoire de la critique*, 55

Théophile Gautier was often an astute reader of his childhood friend Gérard Labrunie (known by his most common pseudonym, Gérard de Nerval). Gautier's characterization of Nerval as a version of Stendhal without the irony is more apt than Gautier himself could have imagined. Stendhal's *Vie de Henry Brulard* was not published in Gautier's or Nerval's lifetimes, and yet the similarities between the two men's works (at least concerning the stakes of first-person narrative) are remarkable. The first common trait would be what Gautier describes as the pleasure both writers take in sidetracking the reader through the play of the text. Both Stendhal and Nerval were obsessed by pseudonyms and the possibilities of inscribing the subject in a literary text while erasing the trace of an author (the subject of my analysis of *Voyage en Orient*). The second similarity between the two involves their understanding of the role of space in the creation of a textual self. Stendhal's maps propose two opposing systems of conceiving the subject in time which are explored in their own way by Nerval (seen in detail in chapter 4). The third parallel

*Like Henri Beyle, but without any irony, Gérard de Nerval seemed to take a pleasure in absenting himself, disappearing from his works, throwing the reader off. What effort he made to remain unknown!

between them, what Gautier considers the most salient, are the renewed attempts to "disappear" from their works, to write the self out of the text, and therefore to escape the dangers of textuality. The end of *Brulard* is strikingly similar to the *Voyage en Orient* and to *Sylvie,* where the narrative abruptly ends and the narrator replaces himself with another textual character. These literary substitutions allow the narrators to flee the death inherent in autobiographical narrative, as it is openly defined by both authors. Nerval, however, marks an advance in respect to Stendhal in his last work, *Aurélia,* where he directly confronts death by analyzing the process by which the narrated and narrating selves are fused.

Whereas Stendhal explored the boundaries of autobiography and fiction in one work, Nerval slowly modified the function of first-person narrative from the *Voyage en Orient* up until *Aurélia,* which was published immediately after his death. To write thematically about Nerval risks confounding the endless repetition of events, characters, and symbols with a real progression in style and narrative structure. The following two chapters analyze the structures of four of Nerval's key works (the *Voyage en Orient,* the "Généalogie fantastique," *Sylvie,* and *Aurélia*) in order to trace the development from a subjectivity where any one character can be substituted for the narrator in a text (as Stendhal had done with Tristram Shandy and Nerval does with exotic myths) to a subjectivity formed by a first-person subject who is able to incorporate multiple perspectives within a novel map (as Stendhal had done with his view of Rome and Nerval will do in *Aurélia*). The first chapter, "Orientations," studies how the *Voyage en Orient* introduces for the first time in Nerval's work a semi-autobiographical first-person narrator. The role of the narrator and the voyage is to write the subject in the text and to render the world of the imagination literal text (as the "Orient" is already a construction of the Western unconscious). The narrator becomes entangled in, and inseparable from, the references and citations in the text. He avoids the death inherent in narrative by substituting heroes of Arabic myths for himself at the close of the text. The second chapter, "Unfolding Nerval," follows the subject's attempts to untangle itself from the labyrinthine spaces of the text. In the "Généalogie fantastique" and in *Sylvie,* the spaces of memory and the spaces of the text envelop the subject; space isolates the subject from the harmful effects of textuality, time, and difference. In *Aurélia,* the "novel subject" itself is dissected into its two irreducible parts: the narrating (sane) "je" and the narrated (insane) "je." The two "je" inhabit the same textual space but radically different places and times. Together they invent a novel map, a dual perspective similar to that of Stendhal's bird's-eye view. The dual perspective of this novel map, or in Nerval's words, "double aspect," allows the subject to view itself as both same and other across time. It both replicates the divide between Nerval's sane and insane selves and produces a palliative image of a unified self in time and in discourse.

Chapter Three

Orientations: Writing the Self in Nerval's *Voyage en Orient*

Heading East

Gérard de Nerval's *Voyage en Orient* would appear to be the long first-person travel narrative of a Parisian erudite, who travels from Paris to Constantinople via Geneva, Constance, Vienna, Cerigo (Cythera), Cairo, and Beirut. Inscribed within the very popular genre of exotic travel literature, the text repeatedly claims to be the truthful account of its narrator's experience: "Ce que j'ai écrit, je l'ai vu, je l'ai senti. Ai-je eu tort de rapporter ainsi naïvement mille incidents minutieux, dédaignés d'ordinaire dans les voyages pittoresques ou scientifiques?" (*Oeuvres II,* 624) ("What I wrote, I saw, I felt it. Was I wrong to report in a naive way the thousand little incidents, ordinarily ignored in picturesque or scientific travel narratives?"). More truthful than mere picturesque voyages, such as the ones written by Chateaubriand and Lamartine that use the Orient as an object of style, more real than scientific accounts because it incorporates the subjective experiences of its narrator, the *Voyage en Orient* attempts to portray the perfect balance of ethnographic literature, anticipating Leiris and Lévi-Strauss by almost a century. This apparent balance, however, is only attained through the synthesis of two distinct trips taken by Nerval, the direct lifting of other travel logs and studies of the Orient, and the assimilation of various Western and Eastern mythologies. Neither entirely true, nor entirely fictitious, Nerval's work transcends categories and genres to create a unique work of literature based on paradox and the emergence of the subject as text.[1]

At the end of October 1839, Nerval traveled through central Europe, passing Lyons, Geneva, Berne, Zurich, Constance, Munich, Salzburg, and finally Vienna, where he stayed until March 1840. In a letter to his father, dated December 2, 1839 (*Oeuvres I,* 836), Nerval expressed the desire to continue on to Constantinople from Vienna on a mission from the French government, but his request was denied. This first excursion inspired a work published the following year, *Les Amours de Vienne,* which divides the narrator into two different characters, awkwardly distorting the facts of the journey. Before Nerval could realize his desire to travel to the Orient, he underwent his first documented mental breakdown and internment in an asylum in Paris at the beginning of 1841. In March of that year, Nerval's friend Jules Janin published a biting "biographie anticipée" (reprinted by Nerval at the beginning of *Lorely,* in *Oeuvres II*), the fallout of which threatened to destroy Nerval's personal reputation and literary career.[2]

It was not until more than a year later, on December 23, 1842, that Gérard de Nerval finally set out on a journey to Constantinople. In the numerous letters to his father and to Théophile Gautier, he continually justified his decision to leave, claiming that it would improve his physical and mental health and demonstrate his sanity to the reading public.[3] Thus before it had even begun, Nerval's journey had a literary end: to regain the respect of his peers, to re-create himself through the construction of a vastly complicated literary tour de force. Nerval's goal was to follow his imagination, his dreams, and his illusions of the Orient to their very limit, in order to accomplish his literary work and renew himself in literature. This creates a paradox, according to Ross Chambers, since he cannot travel both to escape his insanity and at the same time to intensify it (*Gérard de Nerval et la poétique du voyage,* 23). Travel intensifies perceptions, like an attenuated version of madness, promising to reveal other worlds, while remaining firmly entrenched in the real. Through travel, as he reiterates in his letters, Nerval will find a way to pursue his visions and collect material for his work by living his future text.

Nerval began negotiating the publication of his *Voyage* in the middle of the voyage itself. The first published account was an open letter to Gautier in the *Journal de Constantinople* on September 7, 1843 (*Oeuvres I,* 1436–37). Yet due to the vicissitudes of publishing houses and the Revolution of 1848, fragments appeared at uneven intervals; the crucial sections dealing with the initiation myths ("Les Pyramides," "Histoire du calife Hakem," and "Histoire de la Reine du matin") appeared only in 1850 (Bowman, *La conquête de soi par l'écriture,* 146–47). The two-volume *Voyage en Orient* blends the trip to Vienna and the one to Constantinople into one, often inventing itineraries not followed by Nerval (such as the journey across the Adriatic to Cerigo). It was finally published in 1851, some ten years after Nerval first planned his voyage to Constantinople, and only four years before his death.

The *Voyage* holds a privileged place in Nerval's corpus: it marks a regeneration of his literary career, it stands as his first major (first-person) narrative, and it introduces themes that will be central to all of his subsequent texts. A study of the construction of this text and a close analysis of the relation of the narrating subject to space will provide the key to understanding Nerval's final works (the subject of the next chapter). Tightly structured chapters present episodes and places that correspond, leading the narrator not so much in a circuitous journey as in a spiral, returning to the same place but not on the same plane.[4] Similarly, the narrator follows a double trajectory: as his experiences and knowledge of the Orient he perceives widen (destroying the illusions he had formed in Europe), the place reserved in the text for observation narrows until the recounting of myth dominates. The myths themselves repeat each other and increasingly reflect the experience of the narrator. Subject and subject matter, narrator and text, eventually become indistinguishable from each other, just as the "real" voyage was from the beginning both lived and literary, real and imagined. Nerval's subject becomes entangled in the fabric of the text; his final works *Sylvie* and *Aurélia* will attempt to free him.

Illusions, Lost and Found

The ninety-page introduction to the *Voyage en Orient,* entitled "Vers l'Orient," recounts the narrator's trip from Paris to the East (of Europe), south to the Greek islands, ending at his arrival in Alexandria. On a smaller scale, it reproduces the spiral structure of the whole, anticipates the themes, places, and myths of the remaining three chapters, renders the familiar neighboring Western countries as foreign as possible, while positing truth, as he imagines it, in the Orient. The continual disappointments faced by the narrator foreshadow his general disillusionment; his experience becomes progressively literary and textual as he approaches Alexandria. The narrator[5] addresses the text to a friend, describing himself as "un touriste parti de Paris en plein novembre" (*Oeuvres II,* 3) ("a tourist who left Paris in the middle of November"), without any particular itinerary or destination, depending on chance ("j'aime dépendre un peu du hasard" 12), and traveling on the tightest of budgets. Gérard's lack of entourage, absence of fixed plans, and minimal budget contrast with the extravagance of most European literary travelers (notably Chateaubriand) in the way they translate the instability of this textual and literary subject. Only when he arrives in Geneva does he "orient" his wanderings, and subtly suggests the purpose for the voyage/text: "Où vais-je? Où peut-on souhaiter aller en hiver? Je vais au-devant du printemps, je vais au-devant du soleil . . . Il flamboie à mes yeux dans les brumes colorées de l'Orient" (12) ("Where am I going? Where can you want to go in winter? I am going ahead of the spring, ahead of the sun . . . It flashes before my eyes in the colored fogs of the Orient.") Finding himself in the Alps in winter, surrounded by snow, Gérard is inspired by the metaphorical flames of sunset which transform into the colored haze of his imagined Orient. Already the perceptions of his sublime surroundings evoke their paradoxical opposites, transcending reality and reaching toward the heights of the imagination. This imaginary trip will render time spatial, as the narrator travels ahead of spring, ahead of the sun, to a country with an eternal summer, an unforgiving sun (his feelings of the Egyptian climate will become decidedly less optimistic: "Je ne veux pas dire, qu'un éternel été fasse une vie toujours joyeuse. Le soleil noir de la mélancolie" (132) ("I do not mean that an eternal sun always makes for a joyous life. The black sun of melancholy"). The narrator's motivation for traveling to the Orient is from the beginning expressed in terms of a renewed poetic imagery ("Le soleil noir de la mélancolie" will reappear in his much later poem "El Desdichado"), a surpassing of the subject's place in time.

The mechanism of the subject's inscription into text, the power of metaphor to bridge the distance between subject and object, along with the dangers involved in this process, are already apparent in the next paragraph: "Ce sont bien les hautes Alpes que l'on découvre de tous côtés à l'horizon. Mais où est le mont Blanc? . . . J'ai fini par l'admirer sous la forme d'un immense nuage blanc et rouge, qui réalisait le rêve de mon imagination" (12–13) ("Those are really the high Alps that one can see on all sides of the horizon. But where is Mont Blanc? . . . I ended up admiring it in the form of an immense white and red cloud, which fulfilled the dream of my imagination"). Searching for the ideal mountain, with all its symbolic majesty, in the "dream of his imagination," Gérard necessarily misses the real mountain. Nineteenth-century graphic representations of Geneva often exaggerated the view of Mont Blanc (the 1984 edition of Nerval's *Oeuvres complètes II,* 1406n), thus offering the narrator a misleading image. This "Mont Blanc," "Mount Blank," or phonetically "My Blank," is an illusion lacking a base, a blank in which the imagination can inscribe itself. The quest for the imaginary, as apparent here, progresses by a rewriting over the blank of perception. The "real" Mont Blanc can only cause him "little impression," as the imaginary one has already been imprinted. The real danger involved in this deceptive metaphor is humorously portrayed by the image of Gérard walking into the void to plant a flag on top of his cloud/mountain.

This scene is paralleled in the chapter "Druses et Maronites," when Gérard, led by a guide named Moussa ("Moses") (310), penetrates into the mountains of Lebanon. Just as the colorful sunset of Geneva called up images of the Orient, the whiteness of the Lebanese mountains evokes the Alps (330). He imagines all the possible etymologies of the word Lebanon ("Liban" in French), placing enormous symbolic value on the journey:

> En entendant ce mot *leben,* je me rappelais qu'il veut dire en allemand *la vie*. Le Liban tire aussi son nom de ce mot *leben,* et le doit à la blancheur des neiges qui couvrent ses montagnes, et que les Arabes, au travers des sables enflammés du désert, rêvent de loin comme le lait [*leben* in Arabic]—comme la vie![6] (318)

The blankness of the snow, the fantastic plurality of meanings of the word "leben," delude the Arab travelers as well as Gérard, just as the snows of Mont Blanc (l-[e]-banon) melt into the clouds. Instead of finding "life" near the summits, he happens upon the perpetual civil war between two religions, rendering literal the danger of Mont Blanc, the danger of confusing metaphors with objects.

Gérard's impressions of Constance develop even further his desire to transcend opposites, to pursue the illusions of the imagination, and divine the Orient from the Occident (17–18). Constance is a beautiful "name" (evoking permanence and calm), a beautiful "memory," the seal binding the contradictions of Europe together. It is also geographically and symbolically homologous to Constantinople (Constance/tinople), and is used by Nerval to tie together conflicting cultures as well as the chapters of his text. Constance, the "Stamboul d'Occident" (19) ("the Istanbul of the West"), however, does not live up to its imagined reputation: "En approchant, on trouvait ensuite la ville elle-même indigne de sa renommée et de sa situation merveilleuse . . . à la place de Constance, imaginons Pontoise, et nous voilà davantage dans le vrai" (19) ("Approaching the city, one then finds it unworthy of its reputation and marvelous setting . . . instead of Constance, imagine [the Parisian suburb of] Pointoise, you would be closer to the truth"). Time after time, Gérard describes the beauty of a city from afar, only to be disappointed at its vulgarity or unimpressive size seen from up close (as he will do most notably for the Pyramids and for Constantinople). The "true" Constance can never be one with itself, since it cannot embody the entirety of associations locked in its name:

either it is the unspectacular Pontoise, or it is the distant and faded reminder of Constantinople.

The narrating subject that passes through these cities must necessarily be elsewhere as well, existing in two different places (one imagined and one perceived), and often different times, simultaneously, as a reader engrossed in a novel or a spectator at the theater. The experience for the idealistic traveler is fatiguing, in so far as he becomes disenchanted with the world:

> C'est une impression douloureuse, à mesure qu'on va plus loin, de perdre, ville à ville et pays à pays, tout ce bel univers qu'on s'est créé jeune, par les lectures, par les tableaux et par les rêves. Le monde qui se compose ainsi dans la tête de l'enfant est si riche et si beau, qu'on ne sait s'il est le résultat exagéré d'idées apprises, ou si c'est un ressouvenir d'une existence antérieure et la géographie d'une planète inconnue.[7] (19)

The imaginary universe created by the child dreamer, and destroyed by the adult traveler, seems too beautiful, too full, not to be true. That this universe could be the memory of a past life and of another planet hardly seems like an extravagant idea to the narrator. Indeed, the text itself undertakes the mapping of the geography of the imagination and the exploration of the past, echoed in the three different initiation myths, all of which contain elaborate descriptions of an underground world open only to the privileged few who can unlock the past.

Instead of avoiding the possibly corrupting "readings," "paintings," and "dreams" that facilitated the creation of the imaginary universe, the text increasingly relies on their active presence to drive forward the voyage and the narrative. He compares Munich to a star in the fantastic voyages of a d'Assoucy or a Cyrano de Bergerac, where the only inhabitants are painters and where their creations have material existences. Every building in Munich seems to be the painted copy of a famous model; its museums overflow with precious canvases (24). His observations of Munich's other artistic treasures are tainted by the comparison, and thus he leaves the city the same day, before his theories can be disproved.

In order to describe his "impressions *sentimentales*" ("sentimental impressions") of Vienna, the "avant goût de l'Orient" ("the foretaste of the East"), Gérard calls upon the help of Sterne, Casanova, Captain Cook, Byron, and Molière (31–32). The plethora of citations across geographical and temporal boundaries creates a confusing web of references that threatens to prevent any authentic experience of Vienna for the narrator (and for the reader). Consequently, Gérard's first real impressions of the city are not favorable; he wanders the streets confused by the culture, ignorant of the language. Arriving in Vienna without understanding the local dialect, he sets out to find "quelque jolie personne de la ville qui veuille bien me mettre au courant du langage usuel" (31) ("some pretty person from the city who would like to catch me up to speed with everyday language"). In a theater he meets his perfect "interpreter": "Imagine que c'est une beauté de celles que nous avons tant de fois rêvées—la femme idéale des tableaux de l'école italienne, la Vénitienne de Gozzi, *bionda e grassota,* la voilà trouvée!" (33) ("Imagine that she is a beauty like those we have so often dreamed about—the ideal woman from the paintings of the Italian school, Gozzi's Venetian, *bionda e grassota,* has been found!"). His relations with the text's first love interest belie his obsession, not with romance, but with an artistic and linguistic ideal. The woman as walking canvas becomes an allegory for the city and the language: "J'ai expliqué à cette beauté qu'elle me plaisait, surtout—parce qu'elle était pour ainsi dire *Austro-Vénitienne,* et qu'elle réalisait en elle seule le Saint-Empire romain, ce qui paraît peu la toucher" (33) ("I explained to this beauty that I liked her especially because she was, so to speak, *Austro-Venetian,* and that she incarnated by herself the entire Holy Roman Empire, which seemed to touch her little"). She becomes, as Constance was the seal of Europe and Vienna the bridge between East and West, a symbol for the overcoming of opposites and a vehicle for the narrator's imagination, to her own genuine indifference. Needless to say, they fail to communicate effectively, and Gérard finds other loves, only leaving Vienna because of an eventual broken heart. Like Cairo, which it foreshadows, Vienna differs from the other cities in that it first appears vulgar, and only gradually discloses its splendor, like the lifting of a veil. It would seem to be a city that allows the narrator to create the story of his own adventures (56), adventures inspired by actual (sentimental) experience that enable him to let go of his previous images: "A Vienne, cet hiver, j'ai continuellement vécu dans un rêve. Est-ce déjà la douce atmosphère de l'Orient qui agit sur ma tête et sur mon coeur?" (60) ("In Vienna, that winter, I lived continuously in a dream. Was it the gentle atmosphere of the Orient that acted on my head and my heart?").

The Viennese dream ends on the Adriatic, and Gérard attempts in vain to realize an artistic ideal of the classical world on his journey past Greece. His first stop to this mythic land is Cerigo, the island of Cythera, inspiration for Watteau and home of a cult to Venus. The narrator bases his knowledge of the cult on the account by Francesco Colonna, itself related by a novella, *Franciscus Columna,* by Charles Nodier. Colonna, a Renaissance monk who wrote a bizarre treatise on erotic mysticism

(*Hypnerotomachia Poliphili*), becomes the archetype in the text for the mythic initiation of all artists (Schaeffer, 38–39). Colonna's description of Cythera is entirely imagined, his knowledge of true love as well. Gérard laments his own need for real experience and empirical evidence: "Et moi qui vais descendre dans cette île sacrée que Francesco a décrite sans l'avoir vue, ne suis-je pas toujours, hélas! le fils d'un siècle déshérité d'illusions, qui a besoin de toucher pour croire, et de rêver le passé . . . sur ses débris?" (67) ("And I who am going to stop on this sacred island that Francesco described without having seen it, am I not still, alas! the son of a century disinherited of illusions, which needs to touch in order to believe, and to dream of the past . . . on its ruins?"). Literary invention and imagination would be superior to empirical observation, and Gérard's need to experience the real, to wander ruins, reveals the inferiority of those who were born after the Revolution. However, Francesco's literary invention, and the citation of Nodier's interpretation of it, betrays Nerval's own literary fabrication. If Gérard is *el Desdichado,* the disinherited of illusions, Nerval himself certainly was not; like Colonna, he never traveled to Cerigo, basing his account solely on other texts and his own imagination.

The resurrection of imagination through writing is confirmed upon arrival in Alexandria, the city where Greece meets Egypt and the introduction comes to a close. Paradoxically, the narrator begins by writing, "Tu auras compris sans doute la pensée qui m'a fait brusquement quitter Vienne . . . je m'arrache à des souvenirs" (89) ("You will have understood probably the idea which suddenly made me leave Vienna . . . I am tearing myself away from memories"). Only after thirty pages of text that describe the ideal Greece of Gérard's memory and imagination does he "confess" to the reader that he is running away from his memories. More accurately it would seem that his memories are tearing him away from reality, or even away from life. The last paragraphs of the "Introduction: Vers l'Orient" not only elaborate the general aspects of Alexandria and Egypt, but also the psychological state of the narrator:

> L'Égypte est un vaste tombeau; c'est l'impression qu'elle m'a faite en abordant sur cette plage d'Alexandrie, qui, avec ses ruines et ses monticules, offre aux yeux des tombeaux épars sur une terre de cendres. Des ombres drapées de linceuls bleuâtres circulent parmi ces débris. . . . J'aurais mieux aimé les souvenirs de l'antiquité grecque; mais tout cela est détruit, rasé, méconnaissable.[8] (89)

Remarkably similar to Stendhal's Rome, another "city of tombs" that marks the death of the author and the birth of the textual subject, Alexandria is only a wasteland of ruins and ashes, the burial ground of the classical world. The ruins of Pompeii's Column and Cleopatra's Baths do not inspire Gérard's weakened imagination. The hills are too small to provoke the sublime emotion of the Alps, the 1,500 years of the "modern" Alexandria pales next to the mere memories of the ancient city. The narrator who attempts to "tear himself away from memories" admits to having "la pudeur de la souffrance, comme l'animal blessé qui se retire dans la solitude pour y souffrir longtemps ou pour y succomber sans plainte" (89) ("modesty with regards to suffering, like a wounded animal which cowers in solitude in order to suffer a long time or to die there without a whimper"). The suffering alluded to after Vienna, the mounting deceptions of Greece, and the desolation of Alexandria suggest not that Gérard is fleeing a romantic fiasco, but rather the lost world of his illusions, the death of himself as author or authority. The narrator's European imaginary, continually at odds with perceived reality, has been buried at the end of the introduction, allowing for the creation of a new, "Oriental," imaginary that will be written into the text in harmony with the narrator's experience and apprenticeship in Arab myth. The narrator will, from now on, be written with and into the text, until he will eventually become indistinguishable from it.

Assimilations and Translations

The remaining three chapters of Nerval's *Voyage*, "Les Femmes du Caire," "Druses et Maronites," and "Les Nuits du Ramazan," find Gérard attempting to assimilate Islamic culture and document his experience as a foreign "inside" observer. In contrast to the "Introduction: Vers l'Orient," where his imagination never coincided with perceived reality, the Orient itself will prove to be a continual mystery to be unraveled through the interpretation and rewriting of fragmentary information (personal observation, citation, and imagination). If Edward Said is correct, then the Orient is more a cultural construction of the Occident (which constructs itself in the process) than an actual geographical entity; the system of knowledge concerned with the Orient describes it less as a place "than [as] a *topos,* a set of references, a congeries of characteristics, that seems to have its origin in a quotation, or a fragment of a text, or a citation from someone's work on the Orient, or some bit of previous imagining, or an amalgam of all these" (*Orientalism,* 177).[9]

The Orient would, in short, be a text; one to be read, interpreted, condensed, or copied. In the distinctly literary pilgrimages undertaken by

Lamartine, Flaubert, and Nerval to the Orient, despite the sometimes overbearing presence of a "narrative consciousness" (in this case Gérard) that centers the text around the uniqueness of its experiences, there is the eventual realization on the part of this very narrative consciousness "that pilgrimage is after all a form of copying" (*Orientalism,* 177). Gérard, ever the polytheist, will make many pilgrimages to different temples, copying the various discourses that make up the "Orient" (and the Western subject), and reorienting them, layering them for the creation of a new textual subject. The *Voyage en Orient* is, then, not only the fictionalized work of Nerval's already literary voyage to Constantinople, but also Gérard's voyage through the text that is the Orient. In assimilating himself to the culture of the Orient, in becoming "Oriental," he becomes text. Indeed, this assimilation, this becoming text, happens through the learning of Arabic, the deciphering of cultural codes, the apprenticeship of religious and Masonic initiation rites: that is, through translation and writing.

The first of the "Oriental" chapters, "Les Femmes du Caire," relies on an extended allegorization of the city of Cairo as a veiled woman. The veil is a privileged figure of the allegorical mode, as it draws attention to the truth that allegory seeks to reveal and to hide (since allegory is to say one thing while meaning another).[10] The veil is, obviously, a screen that covers a woman's face, but it also is a screen onto which the gazing subject can project any image. As Gérard discovers, behind the screen of the veil is a woman gazing back, upsetting the power dynamic of the Western male subject objectifying the Oriental woman. If a veiled woman is an allegory of Cairo, then the narrator's experience of Cairo exposes his relationship to allegory and to language in general as the locus of repressed desire.

The first sentence states clearly, "Le Caire est la ville du Levant où les femmes sont encore le plus hermétiquement voilées" (90) ("Cairo is the city of the Levant where the women are still the most hermetically veiled"). Within this sentence, there is the anticipation that the veil will be lifted, the words "still" and "Levant" (in French "raising" or "lifting") suggesting that it is only a matter of time before Egyptian women conform to modernity. According to the narrator, the veils of Egypt discourage the "frivolous" European traveler, who usually only stays in Cairo a week. He sets himself apart by proclaiming that "la patience était la plus grande vertu des initiés antiques. Pourquoi passer si vite? Arrêtons-nous, et cherchons à soulever un coin du voile austère de la déesse de Saïs" (90) ("Patience was the greatest virtue of ancient initiates. Why pass through so quickly? Let us stop and try to lift up a corner of the austere veil of the goddess of Sais"). Gérard thus places himself in the position of an initiate into the ways of the Orient, though already conflating the ancient (the worship of a pharaonic goddess) with the modern (the veil as an element of Islam). His initiation will take place over time and will end with the lifting of the veil and the truth of the city: "La ville elle-même, comme ses habitantes, ne dévoile que peu à peu ses retraites les plus ombragées, ses intérieurs les plus charmants" (92) ("The city herself, like its inhabitants, only unveils little by little its darkest retreats, its most charming interiors"). As opposed to the cities of the North that offered all of their mysteries immediately (Gérard only spends one day in Geneva, Constance, and Munich), the space of Cairo, its mysteries, and the changes in Gérard's own consciousness unfold slowly over many months.

The initiation begins when the narrator decides to follow a wedding procession into the "labyrinth" of Cairo's streets. By following the wedding, by witnessing the husband's "journée de triomphe et d'illusion" (100) ("day of triumph and illusion") when he is finally able to lift his wife's veil, Gérard will simultaneously have a better understanding of "Les Femmes du Caire" and a map to the city streets. City space and the woman's veil are repeatedly confused. His dragoman, Abdullah, warns him of the danger of exploring the city at night, and so Gérard disguises himself to blend into the crowd. He witnesses the spectacle of dance and song that accompanies the celebration, comments on the variety and colors of the veils, and lists the various Arabic words that describe the event. Fearing that his identity will be revealed, he strives to imitate the gestures of the crowd; but he wishes to continue the procession indoors, as he is aware of the need for spoken language. His dragoman gives the first language lesson: "*Tayeb*! c'est une réponse à tout . . . Et d'ailleurs je suis là pour détourner la conversation" (97) ("*Tayeb!* is a response to everything . . . And anyways I am there to change the conversation"). Abdullah does in fact lead conversations, but not always where the narrator would like. *Tayeb* is the narrator's one-word pass into Egypt, a substitute word, like a blank, that allows him to be inserted into the Cairene populace:

> C'est un mot qui, selon l'intonation qu'on y apporte, signifie toute sorte de choses; on ne peut toutefois le comparer au *goddam* des Anglais, à moins que ce ne soit pour marquer la différence qu'il y a entre un peuple certainement fort poli et une nation tout au plus policée. Le mot *tayeb* veut dire tour à tour: *Très bien,* ou *voilà qui est bien,* ou *cela est parfait,* ou *à votre service,* le ton et surtout le geste y ajoutant des nuances infinies.[11] (97)

Unlike Figaro's "goddam," which marks the speaker's relation to the world as one of revolt and negation in the face of a policing society, the narrator's *tayeb* underscores his general philosophy of affirmation and his willingness to place himself on the same level as his interlocutor. Those who use this word are very "polie" ("polite" or "polished"), permitting a smooth transition across space and language. This verbal passport of affirmation gains him access to any location in the city, and stands in place of any detailed knowledge of the language.

Gérard's observations of marriage rites become more personal when he is told by his neighborhood sheik that in order to rent a house in the non-European area and conform to local custom, he must live with a woman. Ensue long negotiations with the sheik, various consultations with friends and the French Embassy as to his options, and descriptions of the Coptic, European, Islamic, African, and Asian candidates. This gives the narrator the opportunity not only to attempt to delineate the class and racial categories of Cairene women (which proves impossible), but also to underscore the tight social fabric of Islamic society. Gérard, the solitary wanderer who travels on hardly any budget, inadvertently finds himself at the head of an important household, employing seemingly dozens of people in order to integrate into a society that is not his own.

Still obliged to find a woman in order to become a "citizen of Cairo," but unwilling to marry a woman who is not his ideal, he settles upon the idea of buying a slave who can also cook. His good European conscience promises to set her free at the end of the journey and to treat her with respect. Reversing his European prejudices, the expectations of his slave reveal the complexities of Islamic society, where according to Nerval the women wield more real power than women in Europe and where the masters have more responsibilities than the slaves. Gérard's greatest difficulties in appropriating his slave are linguistic. She is from the Indian Ocean, perhaps Javanese, and so doubly foreign to the narrator. When he is in negotiations to purchase her, he asks for her name, in order to make the process appear less commercial:

> Je demandai son nom . . . j'achetais le nom aussi, naturellement; *–Z'n'b !* dit Abd-el-Kérim. *–Z'n'b,* répéta Abdallah avec un grand effort de contraction nasale. Je ne pouvais pas comprendre que l'éternuement de trois consonnes représentat un nom. Il me fallut quelque temps pour deviner que cela pouvait se prononcer Zeynab.[12] (173)

Unable even to buy her name, he can never truly possess her, and must make do with approximations and condescension.

His second Arabic lesson after *tayeb* occurs when he tries to communicate with her to discourage her from looking out the window at some young men (183–84). He remembers the word *Lah,* the relatively polite way of saying "no," but is taught by Zeynab a harsher word as she refuses the food he offers. Only later does he discover that the word, *Mafisch,* "comprend toutes les négations possibles" (190) ("includes all possible negations"). *Tayeb* and *mafisch* represent the affirmative and the negative, creation and destruction, inscription and erasure, acceptance and refusal, providing the two poles on the axis of language that allow Gérard to navigate the Orient. Armed with his slave and these two words out of which his intelligence will supply the rest of the language (189), Gérard can now dismiss his dragoman, and attempt to live without an interpreter. He no longer requires the mediation of the "Oriental," since he now imagines that he has immediate access to the Other.

Through his relationship with his slave, Gérard begins to understand the allegory of Cairo, to see what is underneath the veil. The veil has been lifted, his ideal glimpsed, but his desire is not fulfilled. At the end of his stay in Cairo, Gérard, on top of the Great Pyramid, is told by a traveler from Berlin the first of the three myths that structure the *Voyage.* According to various authorities, the ancient Egyptians held initiation rites under the pyramids; the neophyte had to find his way across many obstacles through labyrinths over a period of forty days. He then would witness the veil of the goddess Isis fall, and his ideal woman would appear for a brief instant. His last test would be similar to the story of Adam and Eve: placed in an idyllic garden with the incarnation of this ideal woman, would he take the forbidden fruit? If the neophyte imitates Adam, "sa punition devait être alors d'errer dans le monde, et de répandre chez les nations étrangères les instructions qu'il avait reçues des prêtres" (226) ("his punishment was then to wander the world, spreading to foreign nations the teachings he had received from the priests"). Gérard's first initiation is similarly unsuccessful. The "secrets" of Cairo prove to be pleasant, but hopelessly domestic and full of responsibility, like the day after a honeymoon. Having lifted the allegorical veil, his desire for the fruit of knowledge is frustrated and he is destined to wander.

A Deadly Dénouement

The following chapter, "Druses et Maronites," presents Gérard's travel in Lebanon through his discovery of two of its religious sects, the Druse and the Maronites. Once again he will proceed literally to initiate himself into the Orient through symbol and marriage, but in an even more explicit way than in Egypt. Though still accompanied by and devoted to Zeynab, the narrator decides to marry a young woman from this "sol sacré qui est notre première patrie à tous, que je me retrempe à ces sources vivifiantes de l'humanité" (338) ("sacred soil which is everyone's first homeland, where I bathe myself again in the invigorating springs of humanity"). Marriage to a woman from Lebanon would be marrying into the sacred culture of humanity that would complete the narrator's assimilation into the Orient and guarantee a rebirth in the text.

The cliché of the Orient as the rejuvenating source of civilization and the renewal of the self through marriage is here taken at face value, despite the anticipation of the reader's mockery (338). The ironic tone of the next passage suggests that there is now a critical distance between the text and the narrator, one that will soon close up as the author/narrator's "life" becomes a novel:

> J'aime à conduire ma vie comme un roman, et je me place volontiers dans la situation d'un de ces héros actifs et résolus qui veulent à tout prix créer autour d'eux le drame, le noeud, l'intérêt, l'action en un mot. Le hasard, si puissant qu'il soit, n'a jamais réuni les éléments d'un sujet passable, et tout au plus en a-t-il disposé la mise en scène; aussi, laissons-le faire, et tout avorte malgré les plus belles dispositions. Puisqu'il est convenu qu'il n'y a que deux sortes de dénouements, le mariage ou la mort, visons du moins à l'un des deux . . . car jusqu'ici mes aventures se sont presque toujours arrêtées à l'exposition.[13] (338–39)

Here, near the center of the work (page 338 out of 624), the theories of the novel, of the *Voyage,* and of marriage are fused together in a complicated syllogism. The novel, according to the narrator (and the placement of this citation in the text), centers all the apparently divergent discourses of fiction through drama, the narrative knot, "interest," and action on the "active and resolute hero," in this case, the often inactive and irresolute Gérard. Conducting his life like a novel, or more precisely writing himself into a roman-ticized travel narrative, the narrator becomes his own author (and thus does away with the implied author). The master of his own textual destiny, he can write himself into the text of the Orient.

"Le hasard," chance or perhaps simply reality, has never been able to unite the various elements that make up a "passable subject": both in the sense of the subject of theater (the truth is stranger than fiction, and so does not make for good drama) and in the sense of the subject as individual who must create an origin and a narrative in order to tie together the random events that make up lived experience. If left to chance, everything fails. The only solution, according to this passage, would be to embrace the conventions of theater, of literature. By confusing life and text, everything is given meaning in the teleological economy of narrative, where there are no remainders and every event leads to the dénouement. Now in the middle of the text, Gérard has already placed himself in a narrative, but must invent an ending that will make sense of his wandering. The conventions of theater only allow two types of dénouement, marriage or death, and Gérard chooses the least grim. Though it may seem comic that both marriage and death have the same effect, the narrator takes this literally. The end of the text would also mean the end of the textual subject, an eventuality to be avoided at all costs. The remainder of the *Voyage* will see the narrator successively approach and then move away from any sort of dénouement.

Gérard's chosen object of affection is a young blond Arab woman, Zeynab's friend at the French School in Beirut. What piques his interest is not only the paradoxical fact, for Gérard at least, that she is blond and Arab, thus reuniting supposed opposites, but that her father is the imprisoned rebel Sheik Eschérazy, member of the mysterious Druse religion. The narrator's goal is to use his connections and his stature as a European to arrange for the release of the father with the hope of obtaining the hand of the daughter, Salèma. Through multiple ruses, Gérard coaxes the sheik to explain the details of his secret religion, one that blends elements of Christianity, Judaism, Islam, and a belief in the transmigration of souls (354). Predictably, this "universal" religion, whose believers worship indiscriminately in mosques or in churches, represents for the narrator (like Salèma's blond hair) the key to bridging East and West, and by extension text (in the form of the Orient) and subject.

The sheik's story corresponds to the second myth of the text, the forty-page "Histoire du caliphe Hakem." Nerval's Hakem (Al-Hakim) is more or less in conformity with the more fantastical versions of history: as the ruler of Egypt around 1000 A.D., he married his sister and set fire to Cairo in a bout of insane rage reminiscent of Nero. According to Nerval's account, the caliph had a *ferouer,* a double, who reigned in his place, while the real Hakem was imprisoned. The story of this divine madman intersects with Nerval's own preoccupations, hints of his previous mental health problems, and foreshadows *Aurélia.* Within the text itself, the caliph's projected marriage with his sister, the incarnation of the ideal woman, repeats the theme of the first myth heard on the Great Pyramid, and the narrator's own obsession with the daughter of the storyteller. This second myth reflects not only the beliefs of the Druse, but invokes other places and passages within the text (the story is told in Lebanon, but refers back to Cairo), and events in the life of the author, Nerval. The distinction between the life of a reincarnated god and the life of the narrator and author, the tensions between first-person travel narrative and fictional novel, have been so blurred that they coexist on the same level in the text.

After listening to the sheik's story and negotiating his release from prison, Gérard asks for Salèma's hand in marriage. The sheik refuses since the narrator is not a Druse, and the Druse accept no converts: "*la plume est brisée, l'encre est sèche, le livre est fermé*" (426) ("*the pen is broken, the ink is dried, the book is closed*"). No one, it is implied, can enter the Druse communion whose ancestor was not also Druse; the book of members is shut; it is impossible for Gérard to write himself into the Oriental text, since it has already been written. Desperate, he remembers vague similarities between the beliefs of the Druse and Freemasonry, convincing himself and the sheik that the Knights Templar (spiritual ancestors of the Masons) adopted the ways of the Druse during the Crusades (an affirmation not unique to Nerval's work). For further proof, Gérard presents his Masonic diplomas, full of cabalistic signs, to the sheik, who finally agrees to the union (429). Through a ruse bordering on forgery, the narrator is able to pass himself off as "Oriental," to insert himself into the closed book of the Druse.

However, just as the marriage becomes a possibility, Gérard suddenly comes down with a suspicious fever whose only remedy is to leave the country (432). Gérard claims that "l'homme s'agite et Dieu le mène" (432) ("man moves about and God leads him"), inferring that the "man of action" who wrote his own destiny is now at the mercy of a higher power. Moreover, the subchapter following the sheik's tale is entitled "Correspondance (Fragments)," the "chain" of time is broken (421), the succession of logical events is fragmented. Renouncing his hopes (or fears) of marriage, he places Zeynab in the care of the sheik and his daughter, and travels on to Constantinople. The narrator continues to flee any deadly dénouement, and abandons any agency to God or, perhaps, to the text.

The concluding chapter of the *Voyage,* "Les Nuits du Ramazan" ("Ramadan Nights"), brings the narrator to Constantinople, and metaphorically back to the beginning of the text as this city recalls Constance. As Constance was the "seal" that held Europe together, Constantinople is "le sceau mystérieux et sublime qui unit l'Europe à l'Asie" (622) ("the mysterious and sublime seal which unites Europe and Asia"). The city serves as a real and metaphorical bridge across the Bosporus, literally translating ("moving across") the languages and cultures of the East and West. The narrator is constantly surprised, and often bewildered, at how European the city is, culturally, religiously, linguistically, and politically. The vastly different ethnic and religious groups all cohabit in relative peace, providing a model for Gérard's ideal society of "universal tolerance" (624). Having traveled from the closed spaces of the mountains of Europe and Lebanon, the islands of Greece, the stifling deserts and marshes of Egypt, Gérard has finally arrived at the liminal space of the Ottoman capital. The stage is set for other translations and transitions. Constantinople is even personified as a translator of nature, as it transforms the sublime swamps of the Egyptian delta into the harmonious northern landscape (609).

This final chapter finds Gérard no longer at the center of the action. His interest in marriage has waned, and, perhaps as a result, death poses no immediate threat. While avoiding the two possible dénouements, he has still found a way to narrate his life in literature, though indirectly, through translation. He is now the unassuming observer of his surroundings, relating to his French readers his insights on this paradoxical society (while in Constantinople, Nerval had Gautier publish his letters, and Gérard claims to write for journals as well). Whereas his goal in Cairo and Beirut was to become "Oriental" through initiation and marriage, his purpose in Constantinople is simply to give "l'idée d'une promenade à travers ses rues et ses places à l'époque des principales fêtes" (622) ("the idea of a walk through its streets and squares during the principal holidays"). This statement of apparent banality hides a more complex experience that the text elaborates: in order to participate in the religious holidays, in order even to enter Stamboul, the narrator must pass for Muslim.

He performs the same role as the city itself, continually moving from the "franc" sector, Pera, to the Islamic sector, Stamboul, and interacting with Armenians, Greeks, and Muslims indiscriminately. In order to penetrate the city and stay at an inn during the nights of Ramadan when non-Muslim visitors are prohibited, Gérard dresses like a Persian and must abstain from speaking any European languages (470). During the day when the revelers of Ramadan are sleeping, he travels back to Pera, in order to "reprendre langue avec les Européens" (472) ("take up language again with Europeans"). His relation to the two parts of the city is thus linguistic, spatial, and symbolic: Stamboul is the city of night and Oriental mystery, Pera its mirror opposite. Gérard becomes a mediator for the two cultures, successively occupying the position of outsider and insider, Oriental and Occidental.

Yet this role of mediator is brought about not through interpretation, which would imply that Gérard was in both places simultaneously and communicated the information orally, but rather through translation, that is, through reflection and the mediation of a text across space. Now that he claims authority as an authentic Oriental, or at least as someone who can pass for one, he is free to provide his own translations, with his own particular distortions. This leads him to inscribe himself to an even greater degree in the text. Though effacing his place in the narrative, since he no longer heads toward any goal, his presence in the translated stories is ubiquitous. No other chapter in the *Voyage* is as anecdotal: for every observation the narrator offers for a local custom, an elaborate and witty story or theatrical play (opera, vaudeville, or marionette show) provides an illustration and proof.

The most revealing of these translated stories is the "Histoire de la Reine du matin et de Soliman prince des génies" ("Story of the Queen of the Morning and Solomon Prince of Genies"), which dominates the chapter, spreading over one hundred pages (it was published twice separate from the *Voyage*). Sitting in a café during Ramadan, surrounded by various sorts of artisans (who will be the indirect heroes of the tale), the narrator listens over a period of several days to a professional storyteller. Gérard admits that he only knows the most "indispensable" words of Eastern languages (504), but with the help of his friends and his imagination, he is able to understand the subject. The very complexity of the story betrays his own additions to the translation.[14] The role of the storytellers themselves is to come up with a different way of recounting familiar tales (504). Gérard will follow this tradition by composing his own version of the story of Soliman (Solomon) and Saba (Queen of Sheba), borrowing from the Bible, Oriental dictionaries, Masonic legend, and his own imagination (Richer, *Nerval et les doctrines ésotériques,* chapter 8, "La Reine de Saba").

The "Histoire de la Reine du matin" performs the same function as the other two myths of the *Voyage:* it heightens the experience of the narrator by its correspondences within the text that tie religious myth to the life of Nerval. It is the rewritten tale of King Soliman, his gifted architect Adoniram (Hiram), and the Queen Saba, who has come to Jerusalem to marry Soliman, but then prefers Adoniram. Like the founding myth of the Druse, the two men are described as mirror opposites, struggling for power and for the love of an ideal woman. Soliman, a mediocre poet and planner of Cartesian cities, attempts to trick death and decay through logic and science, conjuring spells to stave off the animals that prey on dead bodies. This vain attempt to "accomplir l'INFINI" ("accomplish the INFINITE") (605) fails, and he decomposes in his gem-filled mines. Adoniram, by contrast, discovers that he belongs to the race of Geniuses and is a descendant of Cain (as the narrator of *Aurélia* will also claim);

destined to creativity and rebellion, he reveals the power of workers. He secretly weds Saba, but is killed by three fellow artisans under the order of Soliman (one of the Masonic rites is to pursue the murderers). He lives on through Saba's child and the cries of rebellion against kings (perhaps a reference to the Masonic role in the French Revolution) (602).

This "double" dénouement, the marriage and death of Adoniram, centers the narrative on the architect, who fittingly deprives Soliman of either kind of dénouement. In order for the text to follow the narrative laws that Gérard draws up in the middle of the *Voyage,* a marriage or death must occur. The narrator refuses to perform either of these and so, like Scheherazade, tells more and more tales to postpone his textual execution. He replaces his own death and marriage with those of other characters. This substitution is made possible by Gérard's disguise as an "Oriental" and his liberal translations that graft elements from the rest of the *Voyage* to ensure a smooth transition. This last-minute exchange provides for the textual subject's material safety, as it is only the rewritten incarnation of an older text, destined itself to be rewritten in Nerval's own future texts. Just as an autobiographical simulacrum made Henri Beyle's metamorphosis to Henry Brulard and then to Tristram Shandy almost imperceptible, Gérard escapes death through the virtual metempsychosis of intertextuality.

CHAPTER FOUR

Unfolding Nerval

The *Voyage en Orient* reveals that the presence of the subject is constantly shifting, avoiding any definitive reading, escaping the fatalism of narrative. If the subject can be compared to any character and substituted in any text, if there are no limits either to metaphor or to the metamorphosis of language, then the subject loses all coherence and becomes a floating signifier. The power of this universal subject is that it is adaptable to any context, and it can write and erase its own context. Gérard literally writes himself as Oriental during the Druse wedding, and just as soon writes himself out of the text, when he exchanges his role with Soliman and Adoniram. The price of universality is the dissolution of the self. The ruse of literature is to combine the powers of the universal with the essence of the particular, to become *causa sui*. Nerval's mystical and poetic dilemmas converge and, as a result, force the writing both to explore the nature of the subject and to usurp the mystery of the divine. Nerval's final works offer compelling, if not always complementary, techniques to fix the subject in space, to draw a map around the textual subject, and at the same time they attempt to alter the boundaries of language and identity.

The aim of this chapter is to trace the development of subjectivity through three texts by Nerval (the "Généalogie fantastique," *Sylvie,* and *Aurélia*). Gérard de Nerval attempted to redefine the boundaries of his own subjectivity through a remapping and enveloping of both internal and external space. Through a crossed reading of Nerval's little known "Généalogie" and one of his most illustrious works, *Sylvie,* the liberating possibilities as well as the eventual dangers (at least to the sanity of the author) of a spatial conceptualization of the subject are revealed. The juxtaposition of the "Généalogie" and *Sylvie* uncovers the centrality of the fold to Nerval's spatial and textual imagination. In these two texts, he abandons the logical, modernist Cartesian grid in favor of the ambiguous curved fold, as the distinction between inside and outside disappears in the pleats of his convoluted narrative. Nerval's folds manipulate space itself to envelop the subject in the world.

The fold, according to Gilles Deleuze in *Le Pli,* is the philosophical and aesthetic figure that structures the work of Leibniz and the baroque. Deleuze's reading of the baroque proposes that "le propre du Baroque est non pas de tomber dans l'illusion ni d'en sortir, c'est de *réaliser* quelque chose dans l'illusion même, ou de lui communiquer une *présence* spirituelle qui redonne à ses pièces et morceaux une unité collective" (170) ("what is unique to the Baroque is not falling into the illusion nor leaving it, but rather to *achieve* something within the illusion itself, or to give to it a spiritual *presence* which would return a collective unity to its pieces and bits").

In this sense, we could call the folds of Nerval's texts baroque; the "Généalogie" and *Sylvie* realize through folds in the text the illusion of the unity of the subject, a unity based on the inextricability of folds in matter to the folds of the perceiving or hallucinating subject. Inside and outside, memory and reality are confused and hallucinated in the fold, which is the site of a perpetually shifting subject. Nerval's quixotic quest is to unify his visions, create his illusions at will, to make the world conform to his desire. Space folded in on itself pulls the subject out of time, thereby sparing the subject from change. The folded narrative subject replicates the world in its own image. *Aurélia,* by contrast to *Sylvie,* narrates the struggle to overcome the solipsistic structuring of the fold. Space is opened outward, and as a result, the subject embraces time and alterity.

The Fantastic Genealogy

The document commonly referred to as Nerval's "Généalogie fantastique"[1] condenses a wide variety of spatial and thematic concerns onto one manuscript page (figure 2.1). Probably composed at the end of March 1841 during his first internment in the clinic of Dr. Esprit Blanche (Richer, *Nerval: Expérience vécue & Création ésotérique,* 47), the "Généalogie" predates the voyage to the Orient and previews the obsessions of *Les Filles du feu* (1854) and *Aurélia* (1855). According to Richer, the first version of *Aurélia* (also from 1841) presents remarkable similarities to the "Généalogie," which suggests that 1841 may indeed be the defining moment in Nerval's imagination (Richer, 51). Richer and Richard (*Microlectures*) have done considerable work to situate the "Généalogie" within Nerval's opus and to interpret the development of the inner logic of the

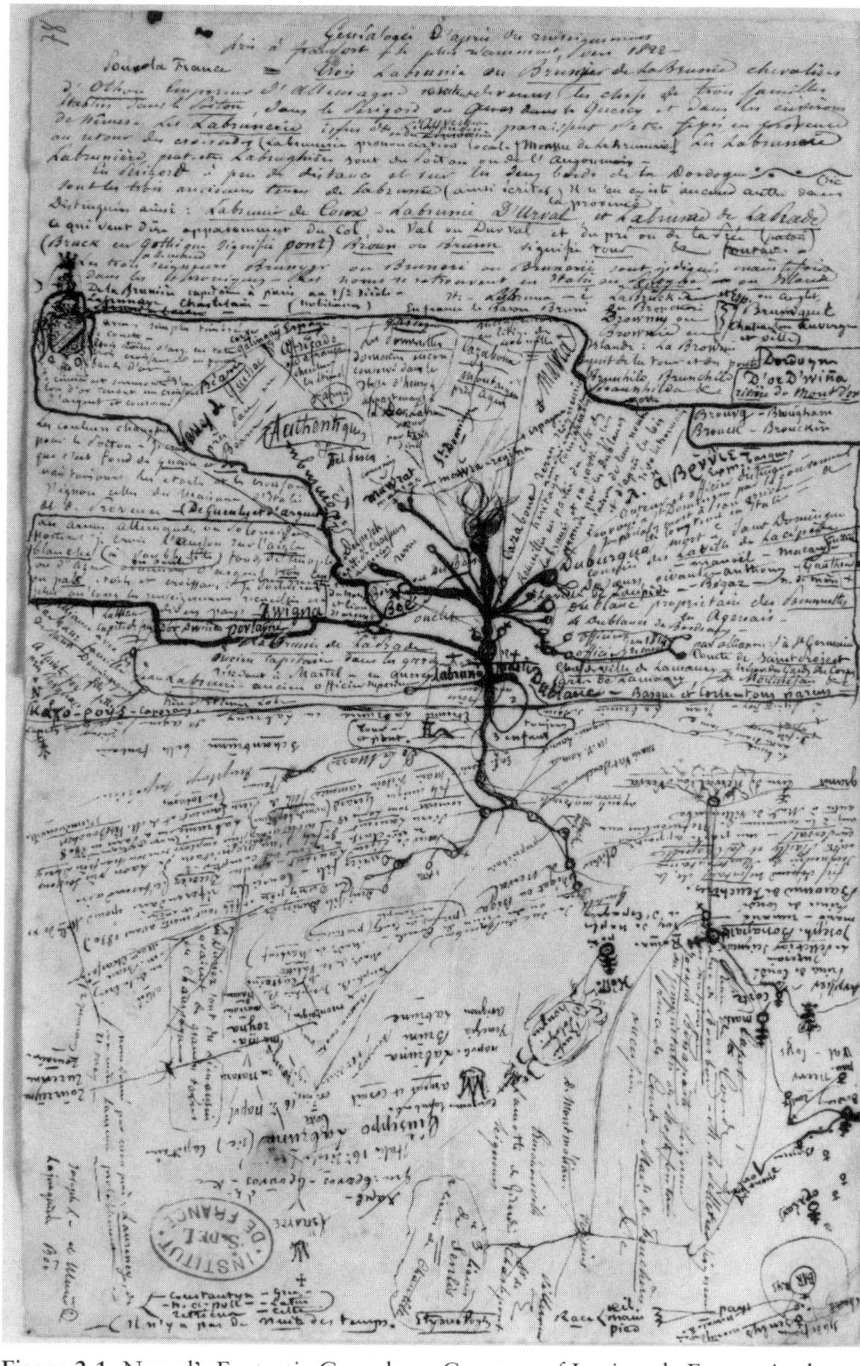

Figure 2.1. Nerval's Fantastic Genealogy. Courtesy of Institut de France, in the Collection Spoelberch de Lovenjoul, D 741, folio 78.

manuscript. However, the form of the "Généalogie," its quality as image, has literally been overlooked, as the function of the visible is key to the interpretation of this labyrinthine text.

The manuscript page is divided into three uneven regions of Nerval's self: his father's family (Labrunie), his mother's family (Laurent), and his literary pseudonym (Nerval). As many critics have remarked, Nerval is the anagram of his mother's maiden name (LAVREN), a partial anagram of his father's name (LAbRVNiE), and the name of his uncle's property, the *clos de Nerval.* Nerval claims that the property near Senlis was an ancient Roman camp and he traces the name back to the twelfth Roman emperor, Nerva. The literary and textual name Nerval links the two families and situates them in space and epic time. The "Généalogie" sets out to create the matrix from which Gérard Labrunie de Nerval emerges. The goal of the drawing and the lineage is to make sense (both as meaning and as direction) of the disparate origins of the self.

The "Généalogie" is divided exactly in half, as if folded in the center. The top half begins, with Nerval's characteristically precise and orderly writing, with a description of his paternal origins. The bottom half, devoted mainly to the maternal side, marks a distinct change, since the writing is the reverse of the top half, the page rotated 180°. Connecting the two halves is a peculiar mass of lines vaguely resembling a tree trunk. The "trunk" of a traditional family tree is here inverted with its roots pointed upward, which suggests that it is not a tree at all. This plant is composed only of roots that branch out from what appears at first to be a center. A closer examination reveals lines in every direction, which stem from multiple centers. Deleuze and Guattari's concept of the "rhizome" is a particularly tempting explanation for the "Généalogie fantastique," as they define a rhizome as an "anti-genealogy" (*Mille plateaux,* 32). They affirm the possibilities of "rhizomatic systems" (decentered, without origin, spreading out horizontally like grass) over "arborescent systems" (vertical, hierarchical, centered on meaning and truth). Connections are made, in the "Généalogie," to apparently unrelated names and places that bridge great spatial and temporal distances and create new meaning. The "Généalogie" is not, however, a purely rhizomatic system; the borders of the page mark an outer limit and the main root, or trunk, draws the corners toward the center, the location of Gérard Labrunie. The "Généalogie" could be described as a hybrid between the arborescent and the rhizomatic.[2]

These two systems, each with their own functions, find their expression in the "Généalogie," not only through the ambiguous plant, but also in an inscription and rebus at the center of the text, drawn over the plant:

"Tour—et pont [a drawing of a tower and a bridge] toujours 3 enfants" ("Tower—and bridge always 3 children"). The meaning of the inscription is explained in the top (paternal) half, of the text, where Nerval claims that three Labrunie brothers, knights of the emperor Othon, founded three families in Poitou, Périgord, and Quercy. Nerval's branch would be from Périgord, where there are three "anciennes tours de Labrunie" ("ancient towers of Labrunie") (in his poem "El Desdichado," he is "le Prince d'Acquitaine à la Tour abolie"). He then gives an etymology which links his name to the tower and to the bridge: "(Bruck en gothique-allemand signifie pont) Brown ou Brunn signifie tour . . . La Brownie, esprit de la tour et des ponts" ("(Bruck in Gothic German signifies bridge) Brown or Brunn signifies tower . . . La Brownie, spirit of the tower and bridges"). The geographical and etymological musings of the name Labrunie unite two very different symbols, the tower and the bridge. Towers connote elevation, hierarchy, surveillance, and stability, having the same symbolic function as trees. Bridges are already double, connecting two or more places; they, by definition, imply movement and change (and therefore could be considered "rhizomatic"). In the *Voyage en Orient* we have seen the fascination with the dangerous heights of Mont Blanc and with the liminal space of the Hellespont, in Constantinople. Michel de Certeau proposes that narrative delimits the borders of places as a practice of space. He conceives of frontiers and bridges as the two contradictory mechanisms of narrative: "Les récits sont animés par une contradiction qu'y figure le rapport entre la frontière et le pont, c'est-à-dire entre un espace (légitime) et son extériorité (étrangère)" (*L'invention du quotidian 1: Arts de faire,* 185) ("Narratives are animated by a contradiction which the relationship between border and bridge figures, namely between a (legitimate) space and its (foreign) exteriority"). Nerval's genealogy similarly transgresses the frontiers it draws and invokes the other that lies in the self. A reading of the "Généalogie" through the lens of the metaphors of the Tower/tree and Bridge/rhizome will frame the tensions of control and metamorphosis.

The most salient aspect of the "rhizomatic" is the etymological frenzy of the text. On the bottom of the maternal half of the manuscript, the word "étymologies" is boxed and set apart, as if an invocation of the transformative powers of language. As any reader of Proust knows, etymology and toponymy are very imaginative "sciences," which seek to find the origins of a lexical unit, and connections are invented when needed. A combination of fanciful etymology and creative genealogy subverts "arborescent" linguistic structures and paternalistic lineages. Instead of finding one origin, the text's etymologies spread out over all humanity, encompassing families from France, Italy, Germany, Spain, Russia, Poland, Hungary, Africa, America, ancient Rome, and elsewhere. Two branches from his father's side, Labrunie (brown or burnt) and Dublanc can encompass the entire page, uniting the white space of the blank page with the dark blots of ink. The most bewildering etymologies are Nerval's Greek inventions. Besides transforming Orléans (a virtual homonym with his mother's Laurent) into the "Greek" `Ορλέανς, he suggests another Greek root for Labrunie: Λαμβ-βρωνος-βρούνος (Lamb-Bronos-Brounos). Richer gives the translation as "qui saisit le tonnerre" ("he who seizes the thunder"), linking Labrunie to the heroic race of Prometheus (Richer, 49), and by extension, the heroes of the Oriental myths of the *Voyage* and *Aurélia*.

Nerval's etymologies steal the fire from the "Name of the father," displace origins, and produce subversive connections. In the bottom half, the words "Bourgogne 16e—Origine Dordogne—Joseph B[onaparte]—Joséphine B[onaparte]" form two triangles around the word/name Montaigne. The rebus that results is a visible figure and a readable allusion to Montaigne. Nerval seems to link himself to Montaigne, the original introspective writer of the Renaissance who was also famous for his tower in Aquitaine. If the connection between Mountain/Montaigne/Tower were not obvious enough, Nerval draws a line from the "a" of Montaigne to the edge of the page where he writes "Toūrrēyne, Turenne, Touraine." Once again, Nerval combines different symbols (here tower and queen) to produce the name of a famous "ancestor" and a place of origin (Richard, 16). The metamorphosis of "Tour" undermines the semiotic stability of the mountain. He plays with his (literary and spiritual) fathers' names, creating chance relationships, substituting an official lineage with a spiritual affiliation. Writing and drawing take the place of the father's name and question the authority of order. On the maternal side of the text, there is less of a need for etymology, as any association will suffice to tie a name and person to Nerval. Near the toponym "Senlys" (Senlis), the town where his mother was born, Nerval places the word "voisins" ("neighbors") out from which stem the names of all the lords who owned property in the region. The names and the myths that nourished Nerval's childhood are just as influential in his vision of identity as any genetic link.

Folded space provides a surrogate order for the domination of the father, as it performs the same control over lineage and identity as language. The two folds of the page channel the excess of etymology and link the bridges. The borders of the manuscript page prevent a run-off of the text; an incredible amount of information is condensed, like in a dream, into a small paginal area. Consequently, no space is left blank; everything has its place. Dividing branches of the family into distinct segments are very thick lines, especially on the paternal half, that find their way back to the main "trunk."

The metaphorical "tours" have corresponding visual markers that anchor the names to places: a Count's coat of arms, the points of a Lombard crown, a map of the Dordogne river valley and its three towers, and numerous crosses indicate geographical locations. Next to the toponym "Terre de Nerval ou Nerva" is the word "granit," which provides a solid foundation. Under the "Terre de Nerval" is a thick horizontal line out of which grow vertical lines that lead to the city Roma. These lines literalize the etymology of granite ("grain") and sprout another genealogical plant that links Nerval (or the emperor Nerva) to Rome.

The map in the lower right-hand corner offers a totalizing view that grafts genealogy onto geography. The top of the map is labeled "Isle de France" under which is a small circle—Barrys (Paris)—inside a larger circle, Senlys (home of the Valois dynasty and Nerval's maternal family). The circles render Paris an island, separating Nerval's native city from the rest of the world. South of Barrys/Paris are `Ορλέανς, Mont d'Or, Bordeaux, Toulouse, Marseille, Roma, and Corte. The cities are connected by a line to emphasize the absolute relationship between them: Nerval's ascendance. The correspondence between family, body, and place is revealed by a diagram placed next to the map of the "Isle de France":[3]

oeil
Race < main >—pays
pied

The physical self is caught between the determining factors of race (used by Nerval as synonymous with family or clan) and country, genealogy, and space. The body itself is divided into three symbolic parts and functions: the eye, the hand, and the foot. In the "Généalogie" the diagram brackets the subject between two hierarchical concepts (race and country) and, by extension, the city space of Paris (Race–Pays: Parys/Paris). The subject of the "Généalogie" is contained within and disciplined by the lines of space and race that it drew for its own expansion.

The necessary focal point of the "Généalogie" reveals and obscures the controlling mechanisms of the text: the fusion of the two halves into Gérard Labrunie de Nerval. On the maternal half of the main trunk stems a branch linked to Étienne Labrunie (Nerval's father) where, in relatively small letters, is written "fils unique Gérard (nom de baptême) Labrunie (nom patronymique) né à Paris en 1808" ("only son Gérard (Christian name) Labrunie (family name) born in Paris 1808"). If one were not aware of the author of the "Généalogie," the inscription of Gérard's name would not be readily apparent. And yet, it appears at exactly halfway between the two ends of the genealogical plant, providing the keystone that supports the entire structure of the text. The extraordinary wanderings across time and space are supplanted by the simple facts of place and date of birth. All other events in the genealogy are subsumed under the relatively modest assertion of Nerval's official identity. However fantastic the rest of the genealogy might be, Gérard's own place in the text is absolutely serious; he avoids his pseudonym and clearly affirms the fact that he is his father's son. Underneath Gérard Labrunie's "birth" is written "Et[ienne] L[abrunie] marié à Marie Victoire Laurence fille de Pierre Laurent et de M. Vict[oire] Boucher d'Ermenonville" ("Et[ienne] L[abrunie] married to Marie Victoire Laurence daughter of Pierre Laurent and of M. Vict[oire] Boucher of Ermenonville"). Nerval's mother appears only in this line (the father's name is written numerous times), but erroneously; her actual name was Marie Antoinette Laurent, and was often called Laurence. The text repeats the grandmother's name twice (Marie Victoire), and feminizes the grandfather's name, in order to inscribe a sort of matriarchy into the genealogy. Moreover, the mother's actual name is absent, escaping the direct representation of language (which is reminiscent of Stendhal's inability to describe his mother). Curiously, this is the only line of the "Généalogie" that Richer does not transcribe, as if he were obeying the text's own erasure of the mother.

Time itself is arrested by the inscription of Gérard Labrunie. His birth date, 1808, is one of only three exact dates (one being the date of the genealogical "research" mentioned in the text's heading). Throughout the "Généalogie" time is spatialized by placing a very vague chronological order to the spatial lists of family members; yet everywhere unexpected juxtapositions of names emerge from vastly different places and epochs. Indeed, the fantastic etymologies work to question the idea of chronological progression, temporal cause and effect. The manuscript's towers watch over time, seeing into the past and fusing it with the present. "Tour," in the masculine, is also "turn" or "return," as in the expression "tour à tour"; the eternal return of genealogy, etymology, and space guarantee the continuation of the subject. At the bottom of the page, near the word "étymologies" and the diagram linking "race" to "pays," is the phrase "Il n'y a pas de Nuits des temps" ("There are no mists of time," the French expression is literally the "nights" of "times"). This ambiguous affirmation may suggest that nothing is lost in time, that through the proper lens (memory, etymology, or geography) the past can be observed and spatialized. The inscription of time onto the page, the end of time's progression, represents the ultimate control over the subject's identity. All possible links with the past and future coexist with the subject in the text; the subject is all being and no becoming.

The "Généalogie fantastique" is the totalizing representation of Gérard de Nerval's identity. The carnivalesque overturning of the traditional genealogical family tree upsets paternal hierarchy; and yet, other structures of perception and control are left in place to inscribe and delimit the subject. Instead of sketching a purely arborescent structure that constructs truth based on value and order, Nerval draws a rhizomatic plant that stretches across time and space to subsume everything under the momentous birth of Gérard Labrunie.

The space of the manuscript page reinforces both the control of the subject and the control over the subject. The borders of the page limit the expanse of writing, the extent of metaphor. The two folds of the text (the horizontal fold separating the paternal from the maternal, and the vertical fold formed by the genealogical "plant") divide space and time into quadrants (Nerval's "quartiers de noblesse"). The page is in effect folded in on itself, pulling the disparate elements together into the location of Gérard's birth. The etymological derivations serve as an incantation that invokes all of Nerval's virtual selves in order to trap them in the folds of the "Généalogie." The world is re-created in Nerval's image, the subject is mesmerized by its own reflection.

The Dénouement Escapes You

Nerval's 1853 novella, *Sylvie, souvenirs du Valois* (later included in the collection *Les Filles du feu*), expresses and extends the tensions of the "Généalogie fantastique" in narrative form. The textual subject, which in the "Généalogie" was able to anchor all possibility, is no longer able to be its own foundation, nor that of the objective world. A persistent fear of solipsism in *Sylvie* drives the narrator to search for a foundational referent. The fold, as had been the case for the "Généalogie," structures the text, channels and focuses all experience on the subject. The subject in *Sylvie* depends both thematically on the isolation of the Valois region (the subtitle is *souvenirs du Valois*) and structurally on the mirroring of the chapters.

Caught in a hallucinatory world of his own creation, the Nervalian subject struggles to regain control of his illusions. As he becomes progressively lost in a (post)modern labyrinth, devoid of inside and outside, he must, as Nerval says in his introduction to *Les Filles du feu,* "saisi[r] le fil d'Ariane, et dès lors toutes mes visions sont devenues célestes" (*Oeuvres*

I, 158) ("seize Ariadne's thread, and from then on all my visions will become heavenly") The seamstress Sylvie plays the role of Ariadne for Nerval's Theseus; by way of her narrative thread, she leads the narrator out of his psychic labyrinth and exchanges the preeminence of space and simulacrum for that of time and difference.

Sylvie is the story of salvation through narrative, yet the exact genre of the text is indeterminable. In a letter to Maurice Sand asking him to illustrate the work (November 6, 1853), Nerval describes the text as "un petit roman qui n'est pas tout à fait un conte" ("a little novel which is not quite a fairy tale") in which he tried to set down on paper his memories of the Valois region (Kofman, 11). *Sylvie* is thus somewhere between a first-person novel, an autobiography, and a fairy tale. The places and events reflect vaguely the life of the author, but the form and style evoke the mystical setting and timeless nature of a fairy tale. The play of genre will have repercussions on the formation of the subject, as the narrator exploits the tensions between the repetition and illusion of the tale and the progress and realism of linear narrative.

In *Sylvie* the power of the subject to surpass its temporal and spatial limitations (offered by intertexuality in the *Voyage* and by etymology in the "Généalogie") is everywhere put into question. The confusion of perception and memory, of author and narrator, instead of allowing the textual subject to rewrite the world in its image, undermines the faith in the subject's ability to organize and control its relationship with the outside. Christopher Prendergast has argued that mimesis in *Sylvie* is internalized, and that each part of the story, linked to other parts of the story, prevents any representation of a world outside the text (*The Order of Mimesis*). Consequently, there prevails an absence of a stable referent to fix the subject and object: "The psychological and affective drama of *Sylvie* is also an epistemological drama; it operates what we might call an 'epistemological suspension,' whereby both the knowing subject and the object of knowledge remain irreducibly uncertain entities" (Prendergast, 150). The textual subject, which in the "Généalogie" was able to anchor all possibility, is no longer able to be its own foundation, nor that of the objective world.

A persistent fear of solipsism in *Sylvie* drives the narrator to search for a foundational referent. Space, as had been the case for the "Généalogie," structures the text, mapping and focusing experience on the subject. The ordering of space substitutes for the dissolution of the subject and the uncertainty of perception, simulating unity and stability and abating the changes wrought by time. The subject in *Sylvie* depends both thematically on the isolation of the Valois region (the subtitle is *souvenirs du Valois*) and structurally on the mirroring of the chapters.

Most critics and readers have taken the novel for a nostalgic and enchanting tale of the French countryside. This interpretation is encouraged in Nerval's letter to Maurice Sand: "C'est une sorte d'idylle . . . J'ai voulu illustrer aussi mon Valois" (cited in Kofman, 11) ("It's a sort of idyll . . . I wanted to illustrate as well my Valois"). The use of the Valois is not, however, as innocent as it appears. The evocative and memorable Valois landscape provides the propulsion that drives the narrative and defines the narrator. The first half of the text tells the tale of a cultivated Parisian who begins to fall in love after a long obsession with an actress named Aurélie. While musing about the actress, he reads in a newspaper that he has become rich again in the stock market, perhaps allowing him to obtain his love. In his words "je touchais du doigt mon idéal. N'était-ce pas une illusion encore, une faute d'impression railleuse?" (*Oeuvres I*, 244) ("I had my ideal in my grasp. Was it not still an illusion, a mocking typographical error?"). It soon becomes clear that her material reality does not interest him. In the same newspaper, he notices an announcement for a village fete in the Valois region, which recalls tender childhood memories. Half dreaming, his entire youth unfolds before him. He remembers his love for a mysterious noble girl named Adrienne who became a nun, and the jealousy of his other love, Sylvie. The love for the actress Aurélie is suddenly explained by her uncanny resemblance to the nun Adrienne, but this is deeply troubling for the narrator: "Aimer une religieuse sous la forme d'une actrice! et si c'était la même!—Il y a de quoi devenir fou!" (*Oeuvres I*, 247) ("To love a nun in the form of an actress! And if it were the same woman!—It's enough to become crazy!"). He decides to go to the village fete in the hope that Sylvie can save him from the "dangerous passion" (dangerous, presumably, since it could lead to madness), and in the hope that he can take a foothold in reality ("Reprenons pied sur le réel," 247). In the carriage ride to the countryside in the middle of the night, he "recomposes the memories" from the time he used to frequent the Valois. Other memories ensue, leading the narrator further into a dream-state.

The purpose of the voyage is to find the solution to an unsettling enigma: whether Aurélie is the same woman as Adrienne. The answer is to be found within the narrator's memory, triggered by his presence in the Valois and his discussions with Sylvie. Space does not offer more objective evidence for the identity of the two women, but instead plunges the narrator deeper into his own self-centered memories.[4] The exclusively subjective character of the Valois is made possible by its unique geographical location: as Nerval writes in other texts such as *Promenades et souvenirs* and *Les Nuits d'octobre,* the Valois is relatively close to Paris, and yet there is no easy transportation to the region (to this day, the modern traveler has to take a bus from Chantilly). Cut off from the modern world, Nerval and his narrator imagine that the Valois is hermeneutically sealed off from time. In *Sylvie,* the voyage to Senlis at night from Paris allows for the narrator to write, "to recompose," the text through memory, creating a virtual Valois and the illusion of a stable subject.

The spatial isolation of the subject is reproduced by the structure of the text. The chapters do not follow a strictly chronological order, but, rather, correspond transversally with each other. The fourteen chapters of *Sylvie* reflect upon each other like a mirror, with a complex double symmetry. Chapters from the beginning and the end echo each other in concentric circles and share parallel themes. An episode of representation, reenactment, or remembering occurs in each chapter of the first half, which effectively brings to life a memory or an ancient tradition (similar to the revival of the narrator's desire). The second half of the text marks the narrator's disillusion as he chases after the ideals sprung from the memories or dreams of the first half, each one proving to be a "chimera." The narrator will literally try to reinscribe himself into the past in order to recreate and restage the visions of his memory (as evoked in the first half) into text. If he can prove that Aurélie and Adrienne are the same person, and if he can win Sylvie's love, time will be stopped, the "I" of the past will be identical to the "I" of the present. Léon Cellier has meticulously catalogued the correspondences (episodes, themes, and recurring objects) of the chapters in order to propose a diagram of the overall structure (Cellier, 28):

i ii iii / iv v vi vii / xii xiii xiv
/viii ix x xi /
a B a

According to Cellier, the first three chapters are repeated in the last three, but inversely ("123 . . . 321"), indicating a closed structure, as opposed to the open structure of *Aurélia* (35). The central eight chapters also replicate each other, creating a separate configuration. These eight chapters, in fact, are where the memories of the Valois are most concentrated. Like the two axes of the "Généalogie fantastique" formed by the horizontal fold in the page and the vertical fold of the genealogical plant, the arrangement of the chapters creates a space in which the enveloped Valois is coextensive with the narrating subject.

The pivotal moment of the novella lies in the seventh chapter (the final chapter of the first half), "Châalis," which reproduces in miniature the mechanisms of the fold found in the rest of the work. Within the narrative, it marks the transition between the memories and dreams of the Valois, and the harsh present reality experienced in the second half. At the center of the text, the chapter folds space inward, such that the narrator/subject is imprisoned within the Valois. The first sentence of the chapter literalizes the enveloping of the narrator as he approaches the region: "Il est quatre heures du matin; la route plonge dans un pli de terrain; elle remonte. . . . Nous nous arrêtions à la maison du garde, à l'ancienne abbaye de Châalis.—Châalis, encore un souvenir!" (256) ("It is four o'clock in the morning; the road dips in a fold in the terrain; it climbs back up. . . . We stop at the guardhouse, at the former Abbey of Châalis.—Châalis, another memory!"). The fold in the terrain announces the complete enfolding of space, in which the Valois and the narrator are enclosed. The transition from the present to memory or dream is revealed in the repetition of the Abbey of Châalis, the first instance being the real, the second the memory/dream. There is a further repetition within the word itself, the very unusual double "a" that smoothes over differences. The fold creases space into two seemingly identical halves. Châalis evokes the English word "chalice" and the French "calice," simultaneously reinforcing the function of containment (the chalice as cup) and the sacred space of the Valois (the "chalice abbey").

The space of Châalis produces the most dense and hallucinatory experience of *Sylvie,* as the narrator's desires are confirmed by his memory or dream. The narrator, along with Sylvie's brother (another double), observes a private party that happened some point in the past. The uncanny quality of the event is induced by the mix of the abbey's architectural styles (Byzantine, Gothic, Italian Renaissance) and the sense that the two (modern) observers are intruders (257). An allegorical play is performed by the young girls of the neighboring convent. Adrienne, the narrator's first love whom he suspects later to be the actress Aurélie, plays the role of a holy spirit who incites angels to admire Christ. The scene, as the narrator remembers it, realizes his desire to fuse the spiritual nun with the heartless actress. The vision is so perfect that the narrator wants to doubt that it ever happened: "En me retraçant ces détails, j'en suis à me demander s'ils sont réels, ou bien si je les ai rêvés" (257) ("Retracing these details, I wonder if they are real or indeed if I have dreamed them"); "Mais l'apparition d'Adrienne est-elle aussi vraie que ces détails et que l'existence incontestable de l'abbaye de Châalis?" (257–58) ("But was Adrienne's apparition as true as these details and as the incontestable existence of the Abbey of Châalis?"). The realism and vividness of memory's details correspond to the accuracy of perception, either substantiating the memory/dream or questioning the sanity of the narrator.

In the last sentence, another fold in the terrain brings him out of his illusions into reality: "Ce souvenir est une obsession peut-être!—Heureusement voici la voiture qui s'arrête sur la route du Plessis; j'échappe au monde des rêveries, et je n'ai plus qu'un quart d'heure de marche pour gagner Loisy par des routes bien peu frayées" (258) ("This memory is an obsession perhaps!—Luckily here the carriage came to a stop on the Plessis road; I escaped the world of dreams, and I only have a quarter of an hour to get to Loisy by rather untrodden paths"). Plessis is a common toponym in France that has its origins in the Latin stem *plecto* (to fold or to plait) and comes from *ples*, a terrain enclosed with hedges that have branches folded over each other. The fold at the beginning of the chapter is mirrored at the end, setting the chapter apart from the rest of the work (as the text is detached from the outside, and the Valois cut off from modernity). The folds form a spatial envelope outside of time, where everything corresponds and repeats and where distinctions are broken down.

The hallucination ends when the narrator leaves the fold. Daylight comes to the Valois, and the narrator/Nerval slowly comes to realize that the region no longer reflects his nocturnal reverie. The second half of the text marks the narrator's disillusion as he chases after the ideals sprung from the memories or dreams of the first half. The narrator tries to reinscribe himself into the past in order to restage the visions of his memory (as evoked in the first half) into text. If he can prove that Aurélie and Adrienne are the same person, and if he can win back Sylvie's love, the "I" of the past (or of his hallucination) will be identical to the "I" of the present. The narrator proceeds by coaxing both Sylvie and Aurélie into revisiting the Châalis Abbey and reenacting the hallucinated scene of chapter 7, with the hope that the young women will confirm the identity of Adrienne. Sylvie refuses to reveal all that she knows. At the end of the penultimate chapter, Aurélie, however, becomes enraged that the narrator loves her only because of an empty resemblance to another woman, declaring, "Vous ne m'aimez pas! Vous attendez que je vous dise: 'La comédienne est la même que la religieuse'; vous cherchez un drame, voilà tout, et le dénouement vous échappe" (271) ("You do not love me! You expect me to say to you: 'The actress is the same as the nun'; you are looking for a play, that's all, and the dénouement escapes you").

The dénouement does not, in fact, come about through the efforts of the narrator, but rather through a last-minute disclosure from Sylvie. Following Aurélie's rebuttal, the final chapter of the novel jumps forward to the present, a number of years after the main events of the rest of the text (indicated by the use of the present tense instead of the simple past). The overwhelming desire in the first thirteen chapters to repeat the past, to celebrate ancient traditions and songs, to find harmony in nature, and to root identity in space is resolutely denied in this last chapter. Space is no longer the container of memory, of the self; as the narrator declares, "Châalis—que l'on restaure—vous n'avez rien gardé de tout ce passé!" (272) ("Châalis, which is being restored, you have not kept anything of this past!") He recounts that he often travels to visit Sylvie, who is now married with children.

In the final lines of the text, he confesses that he forgot to include an important detail; he had taken Sylvie to see Aurélie's theater troupe and had asked her if there was any resemblance between the actress and the nun Adrienne. Sylvie laughs at the idea, and then, more seriously, pronounces the last words of the text, "elle est morte au couvent de Saint-S . . ., vers 1832" (273) ("she died at the Saint-S convent . . . around 1832"). Sylvie's revelation turns the repetitive tale into a linear novel. She has fulfilled her role as the actual narrator of the novel; her profession as lace-maker or seamstress implies that it is she who ties and unties the narrative knot. This dénouement evokes the first date in the text, thus rupturing the timelessness of the tale, and connecting narrative to death. At the same time, however, Adrienne has become a real person through her death; the narrator no longer doubts whether she ever existed (and thus can be sure of his own sanity), because of Sylvie's confirmation. A narrative thread offers a way out of solipsism, away from the endlessly obsessive repetition of the past, and toward an acceptance of time and of the difference it engenders.

Gérard de Nerval's experiments with textual space, the "Généalogie" and *Sylvie,* revolt against the Cartesian mapping of space that produces rational, homogenized subjects. Instead, external and internal, social and psychic space are folded into each other, are literally complicated and multiplied, with the result that the subject occupies the ever-changing line of the fold. As the "Généalogie" so graphically illustrates, enfolded spaces proliferate connections and possibilities, upset borders, and deliver to the subject an almost limitless power to redefine itself in time and language. However liberating this new spatial model may seem, it creates a labyrinthine world in which the subject can no longer distinguish inside from outside, past from present, self from other. The rhizomatic roots of the "Généalogie" structure and control space even more effectively and insidiously than the Cartesian grid, since they pull and manipulate everything in space toward the subject.

Sylvie exposes the dangers of and offers a tentative solution to Nerval's textual folds. The narrator of the novel confuses memory and identity with the space of the Valois as he searches for a foundation upon which to base his sense of self. The text is structured not according to chronological narrative, but rather according to spatial contiguity. The narrator only regains his sanity after he abandons control over the outside and accepts the inherent difference of others revealed by time, and not space. Subjects change over time, in a sense they are because of what they become. A text based solely on the association of place would tend to confuse time periods, negating the temporal progression of narrative, and therefore any progression of the self. The distinction of subject and object, inside and outside, self and other can only occur through the introduction of time, not necessarily of chronological time or of a "grand narrative," but rather through the true time that makes possible becoming and difference. The real narrator of the novel would be Sylvie herself; she is the only character who changes substantially over the course of the text, from peasant seamstress to a modern industrial worker, from a young innocent girl to a proud mother. It is she who introduces time, through the date of Adrienne's death, and thereby imposes her difference on the narrator. As long as the dénouement escapes him, as long as he is unable to grasp the narrative thread, the narrator is destined to wander the labyrinth of his own illusion.

Aurélia's Double

Nerval's final work, *Aurélia ou le rêve et la vie,* breaks from his previous first-person narratives in its dissection of the novel subject. The *Voyage en Orient* sought to inscribe the subject in the text and spaces of the "Orient" through the ruse of intertextuality, exploiting the ambiguities between a fictional and a real Gérard de Nerval. *Sylvie* rooted the subject within the uncanny spaces of the Valois and depended on an "outside"/ heterodiegetic *narratrice* to sew together the ends of the text, allowing Gérard to remain within the concentric circles of solipsism. Whereas these texts relentlessly repeat the same motif of the subject defined by space and text, continually fleeing the menace of alterity and temporality, *Aurélia* directly counters the textual mechanisms that had anchored the subject and seeks a new definition for subjectivity based on time and communication with the other.

Instead of assimilating the narrated "je" and the narrating "je," instead of erasing the difference between the past/written Gérard and the present/writing Gérard, *Aurélia* unravels the autobiographical simulacrum (as defined in relation to Stendhal). The text explores with astounding clarity the division of the subject by its inscription in text. As the analyses of the previous texts have shown, the narration of the self can only lead to death. Nerval's final text draws the implications of textual subjectivity to their extreme consequences through an investigation of "death" itself (which Nerval, following an ancient tradition, associates with dream and insanity) and the possibilities of writing about it.

Within its first few sentences, *Aurélia* announces the inscription of the narrating subject and the exploration of life beyond death:

> Le Rêve est une seconde vie. Je n'ai pu percer sans frémir ces portes d'ivoire ou de corne qui nous séparent du monde invisible. Les premiers instants du sommeil sont l'image de la mort; un engourdissement nébuleux saisit notre pensée, et nous ne pouvons déterminer l'instant précis où le *moi,* sous une autre forme, continue l'oeuvre de l'existence. C'est un souterrain vague qui s'éclaire peu à peu, et où se dégagent de l'ombre et de la nuit les pâles figures gravement immobiles qui habitent le séjour des limbes. Puis le tableau se forme, une clarté nouvelle illumine et fait jouer ces apparitions bizarres;—le monde des Esprits s'ouvre pour nous.
>
> Swedenborg appelait ces visions *Memorabilia;* il les devait à la rêverie plus souvent qu'au sommeil; *L'Âne d'or* d'Apulée, *La Divine Comédie* du Dante, sont les modèles poétiques de ces études de l'âme humaine. Je vais essayer, à leur exemple, de transcrire les impressions d'une longue maladie qui s'est passée tout entière dans les mystères de mon esprit; et je ne sais pourquoi je me sers de ce terme de maladie, car jamais, quant à ce qui est de moi-même, je ne me suis senti mieux portant. Parfois, je croyais ma force et mon activité doublées; il me semblait tout savoir, tout comprendre; l'imagination m'apportait des délices infinies. En recouvrant ce que les hommes appellent la raison, faudra-t-il regretter de les avoir perdues? . . . Cette *Vita nuova* a eu pour moi deux phases. Voici les notes qui se rapportent à la première.[5] (*Oeuvres I,* 359)

This extraordinary passage proceeds by a series of complex substitutions, metaphors, and citations that propose an understanding of death by means of transcribing experiences in which the mind loses consciousness of the body. Dream, as we saw in relation to the *Voyage en Orient,* is taken by Nerval as a higher plane of existence, a second life. The text valorizes the Dream as a second life, with the ambiguous connotation of a double life or an afterlife. The second sentence evokes the narrator's emotion or fright while entering "the invisible world" of sleep, referring to Homer's *Odyssey* (book 19): there are two gates of Sleep, one of horn and one of ivory. The horn gate opens onto the real shadows of the underworld; the ivory gate, however, reveals only illusory phantoms.[6] The text elides the difference between the two gates, collapsing dream, illusion (madness), and the underworld into the same "invisible" world of the unconscious. The first moments of sleep are the "image" of death, disturbing the thought process, and separating the "moi" or ego from the new, otherworldly, existence of the self. The new subject has shed the materiality of the "moi" just as the subject of autobiography must be reborn as text; the voyage through dark subterranean landscapes into the clear light of the spiritual world literalizes the rebirth.

What the narrator describes here is reminiscent of Stendhal's rebirth through the textual cogito ("after so many general remarks, I am going to be born") and Descartes's cogito, where the anonymous "je" feigns to ignore everything but pure consciousness and the revelation of God through the clarity of thought. Nerval, of course, reverses Descartes's ontological proof based on reason to propose another based on Dream (or hallucination). This new proof requires not the single perspective of a universal Cartesian subject (a subject that only realizes the truth through the negation of its own uniqueness), but rather the dual perspective of the dreamer (who is grounded in the place and time of the dreaming body, and yet also present in the Dream, outside of time and space). The presence of a narrating subject (necessarily in the material world) excludes the assimilation of a subject in the "other" world; the narrator of *Aurélia* claims to separate the two, thus allowing for a dual perspective. Proust will also begin "Combray" with the metaphysically troubling experience of a dreamer who awakens without being able to "reenter" the body.

The text then proceeds to inscribe the narrator's endeavor into the well-worn path of previous writers (Swedenborg, Dante, Apuleius), who by citation guarantee the validity and sanity of the project. Their example justifies the transcription of the apparently irrational delusions of the narrator, who admits to his mental illness, while he simultaneously undercuts the diagnosis of his doctors. The questioning of the "illness" itself reinforces the foundation of Nerval's new ontology: disdaining vulgar "reason," the narrator valorizes the knowledge he has gained, the "doubled" strength (of the dual perspective) and activity of his mind.

The goal of *Aurélia* is thus to transcribe the world of dream/death/madness into the language of reason (or more generally the "other" world, or the world of alterity, into the understanding of the self). Shoshana Felman, in *La Folie et la chose littéraire,* has studied the relationship of *Aurélia* to the discourse of madness in the wake of Jacques Derrida's critique of Michel Foucault. As Derrida argues in *L'Écriture et la différence,* any defense of madness amounts to a "praise of reason," since there is no "outside" of reason's discourse; if the insane have been silenced, as Foucault claims, for Derrida writing as silent speech would be a mad form of reason. Nerval breaks the silence about his own madness through his writing even as writing itself is "mad." Felman links the split of the narrating subject into (insane) hero and (sane) narrator to the problem of reading and writing signs. Nerval's illness can only be cured by the process of becoming a writer: "Si l'hallucination était une lecture de signes, un déchiffrement du *réel,* l'écriture, en revanche, s'efforcera d'être un déchiffrement du *rêve.* L'écrivain deviendra, de la sorte, l'interprète, le lecteur de sa propre folie" (77) ("If hallucination were a reading of signs, a deciphering of the *real,* writing, on the other hand, would try to be a deciphering of the *dream.* The writer would become, consequently, the interpreter, the reader of his own madness").

Similarly Ross Chambers, in *Mélancolie et opposition,* argues that Nerval uses contemporary medical discourse about madness to overturn it from within, creating a textual madness to heal the narrator's madness: "La guérison narrative ne va donc point sans une certaine forme de 'folie' textuelle, et c'est dans cette folie d'un texte radicalement décentré que nous pouvons reconnaître le signe le plus sûr de son modernisme" (127) ("Textual healing does not proceed without a certain form of textual 'madness,' and it is in this madness of a radically decentered text that we can recognize the surest sign of its modernism"). Whereas most critics have focused, with good reason, on the discourse of madness within *Aurélia* as it is related to Nerval's own mental illness, I base my reading of the text on the constant movement between the metaphors of dream, madness, and death, which are inseparable from their "other," which is reason.

As Théophile Gautier said of his friend: "On dit d'*Aurélia* que c'était le poème de la Folie se racontant elle-même. Il eût été plus juste encore de l'appeler la Raison écrivant les mémoires de la Folie sous sa dictée" (cited in Chotard, 147) ("*Aurélia* has been said to be the poem of Madness told to itself. It would have been more apt still to call it Reason writing the memoirs dictated by Madness"). Gautier's description of Nerval's writing process as dictation is perhaps more apt than Nerval's own characterization of his project as transcription, since dictation implies the simultaneous physical presence of the other.

Aurélia is the story of this dictation and transcription of the two opposing halves of the self (according to the narrator, each man is double and "Il y a en tout homme un spectateur et un acteur"—"there is in each man a spectator and an actor" (380). The "spectator"/narrator/sleeper listens as the "actor"/dreamer dictates. They necessarily occupy the same space in the text, and yet are in two different places and times. In a rewriting of the first paragraph near the end of the text, the narrator declares:

> Le sommeil occupe le tiers de notre vie. . . . Après un engourdissement de quelques minutes une vie nouvelle commence, affranchie des conditions du temps et de l'espace, et pareille sans doute à celle qui nous attend après la mort. Qui sait s'il n'existe pas un lien entre ces deux existences et s'il n'est pas possible à l'âme de le nouer dès à présent?[7] (412)

Sleep once again describes a separation with the body linked with the experience of death, while also freeing the subject from the conditions of time and space. The goal of the text is to allow consciousness ("the soul" or perhaps the subject) to combine the existence of everyday life (confined by a particular time and place) with the perspective of the "other" life that overcomes space and time. This synthesis can only be accomplished by palimpsest, where the experience of the dreamer is written over that of the sleeper.

The first psychotic episode of the text (a recounting of Nerval's own first documented illness shortly before his trip to the Orient) introduces the coexistence of "real" place with oneiric space. The narrator describes being led through the streets of Paris by his friends. Suddenly he sees a giant star in the sky indicating his destiny. Deciding to follow the star, the city streets transform before him: "Je croyais voir le lieu où nous étions s'élever, et perdre de ses formes urbaines; sur une colline, entourée de vastes solitudes, cette scène devenait le combat de deux Esprits et comme une tentation biblique" (363) ("I thought I saw the place where we were rise up, and lose its urban forms; on the hill, surrounded by vast solitudes, this scene became the combat between two Spirits, like some biblical temptation"). The actual place and time of the incident (Paris, 1840) are given by the narrator and can also be inferred from the presence of Gérard's friends who try to convince him to return home. At the same time, the city streets are transformed into a psychic space (a theatrical "scene") somewhere between dream and text (it is a scene of "biblical temptation," and Gérard voices his intention to go "Vers l'Orient"—"Towards the Orient," which refers to the introductory chapter to the *Voyage*). The reader is aware of the reality and validity of the two very different spaces occupied by the narrator and is not forced to decide which of the two is more "real" than the other.

The key to Nerval's textual vision is revealed in the narrator's analysis of the scene in the next chapter, where he describes a dual perspective:

> Ici a commencé pour moi ce que j'appellerai l'épanchement du songe dans la vie réelle. A dater de ce moment, tout prenait parfois un aspect

> double, et cela, sans que le raisonnement manquât jamais de logique, sans que la mémoire perdît les plus légers détails de ce qui m'arrivait.[8] (363)

The overflowing of dream into real life proceeds with complete lucidity; it follows its own logic (one familiar to any reader of Nerval's other works) and yet is able to coexist with the observations of the real world, creating a "double aspect."

The logical consequence of this dual perspective would be to allow the narrator to see himself as other. Indeed, the presence of the "double" or *Ferouër* (which Nerval uses in the *Voyage*) is first thematized and then eventually literalized in the text as a threat. At the end of chapter 3, the narrator elaborates upon the effects of the dream state and the ensuing double perspective after he is taken in by a group of soldiers:

> Couché sur un lit de camp, j'entendais que les soldats s'entretenaient d'un inconnu arrêté comme moi et dont la voix avait retenti dans la même salle. Par un singulier effet de vibration, il me semblait que cette voix résonnait dans ma poitrine et que mon âme se dédoublait pour ainsi dire, distinctement partagée entre la vision et la réalité. Un instant, j'eus l'idée de me retourner avec effort vers celui dont il était question, puis je frémis en me rappelant une tradition bien connue en Allemagne, qui dit que chaque homme a un *double,* et que, lorsqu'il le voit, la mort est proche.[9] (364–65)

This scene reverses the habitual "dictation" in the text where the rational narrator in the real world observes the dreamer; instead, the dreamer/madman describes the physical sensation of the separation of "vision and reality." Here the narrator is able to render the familiar "real world" mad, while at the same time describing the alienation of an out-of-body experience. Though he feels the physical presence of the double in his chest, it becomes other to him, announcing impending death (just as the autobiographical form had already done).

Nerval's palimpsest of dreamed experience reproduces the liberation of time and space he associates with death. The writing self thus has the ability to be at once grounded in material reality and to occupy a position of universality beyond the constraints of time. The "double aspect" of dream's pouring into real life functions the same way as Stendhal's bird's-eye view of Rome, where the narrator, situated at the edge of the city, is able to see all of time projected onto the space in front of him. Stendhal's spiritual state, provoked by the heights of the Gianicolo Hill, allows him to tap in to his own memory and to that of the entire city. His state conjures up the ghosts of the past, and an idea of his whole life (death included). Bergson's metaphor, that seeing the past in present space has the same effect as seeing a ghost (Bergson, 161), seems as appropriate to Nerval as to Stendhal. In the majority of dreams in Nerval's text, the narrator is visited by the ghosts of his family, or of all humanity, coming to him to tell the story of the human race.

The observation of the progress of time and metamorphosis, as opposed to the halting of time and the obsession with stability in *Sylvie,* forces the narrator to take account of his actual place in time. Nowhere is the role of time better expressed than in a dream in the fourth chapter that prefigures Proust's famous "bal de têtes" at the end of *Le Temps retrouvé:*

> J'entrai dans une vaste salle où beaucoup de personnes étaient réunies. Partout je retrouvais des figures connues. Les traits des parents morts que j'avais pleurés se trouvaient reproduits dans d'autres qui, vêtus de costumes plus anciens, me faisaient le même accueil paternel. Ils paraissaient s'être assemblés pour un banquet de famille.[10] (367)

Time itself is seen in the changing faces of his relatives, recognizable as the "same" person, and yet the faces occupy different times. The narrator's uncle reveals to him that "notre passé et notre avenir sont solidaires. Nous vivons dans notre race, et notre race vit en nous" (368) ("Our past and our future are in solidarity. We live in our race, and our race lives in us"). Instead of identity being rooted in one place and one instant in time (as the narrator of *Sylvie* feared), identity is the actualization of an essence that exists across time.

The concentric circles and enclosed spaces of *Sylvie* that sought to freeze time and banish difference have given way to the eccentric spaces of *Aurélia.* Dreams and visions are filled with forms that constantly change nature, growing enormous or shrinking, metamorphosizing into apparently different objects or persons, though recognizable by their essence. The folds in the "Généalogie" and in *Sylvie* that defined the subject, locking it in one place and time, are now in *Aurélia* opened outward, unfolding a world of endless possibilities from the unconscious of a text written from two perspectives.

Part III
Sand's Utopian Subjects

> Homme, mon ami, tu plaisantes volontiers les oeuvres, fatalement autobiographiques, de la femme. Sur qui comptais-tu donc pour te la peindre, te rebattre d'elle les oreilles, la desservir auprès de toi, te lasser d'elle à la fin? Sur toi-même?*
>
> —Colette, *La Naissance du jour,* 81–82

Of all the writers I study in this book, George Sand was the most successful, not only in terms of earning a living from her pen, but especially in her international celebrity during her lifetime. As Naomi Schor in *George Sand and Idealism* and others have shown, Sand's innumerable novels and plays awarded her what seemed like an unquestionable place in the French literary canon in the nineteenth century. The most famous woman writer of her time, Sand could not escape a visibility brought on by her exceptionality as artist and woman. This double exceptionality meant that she was already inscribed in a public discourse, caught in the impossible position between authorial subject and the inferior status of feminine subject accorded to her by law and social convention. Unlike Stendhal or Nerval, who wrote unpublished texts meant to explore the limits of their own subjectivities, Sand avoided a candid, personal examination of her own life. Her apparently exhaustive multivolume memoir *Histoire de ma vie,* for all its inclusion of minute detail, leaves out the most well-known episodes of her infamous love affairs. Sand's fictional texts, instead, propose new models of subjectivity that refuse simple rep-

*Man, my friend, you willingly make fun of women's inevitably autobiographical works. On whom did you count on then to paint them until you were sick of hearing about it, to turn you against her, to make you tired of her in the end? On yourself?

resentations of gendered subjects and create new spaces where women and men interact with each other and in society. In the next two chapters, I examine Sand's first signed novel, *Indiana,* and one of her last novels, *Nanon,* each of which use textual space to reinvent social ties and to rectify historical injustice.[1]

George Sand's unique place in history might seem to suggest that her works are not representative of a woman's subject position, that she somehow freed herself from the constraints placed on other women of her time. Many of her male contemporaries, such as Balzac, certainly felt that she was different, masculine, or more like themselves (Naginski, *George Sand: Writing for Her Life,* 1). Yet her texts work through and reconfigure women's subjectivity, independently of her own extraordinary life. Reading Sand's texts biographically, an approach which often yields insights about the emergence of her ideas, nevertheless obscures the richness of Sand's thinking about subjectivity.

Contemporary feminist scholarship confirms what Sand's writing teaches us: the stakes of writing the subject are fundamentally different for women. As Margaret Cohen and others have argued, the choice of literary genre in the first half of the nineteenth century and beyond was largely gender-determined. The hybrid texts of Stendhal, Nerval, Proust, and others combined the genres of realist novel and autobiography. Cohen claims that the dominant literary genres chosen by women were sentimental or idealist novels and that realism was later constructed as a genre on the basis of realist texts written by male authors.[2] Some scholars claim that men more easily overcame the taboo against the exhibitionism inherent to autobiography since Rousseau.[3]

Women's writing was therefore caught, until very recently, in a critical double bind, where women's fiction was read as autobiographical, and any truth in women's autobiography was considered compromised because of the gender of the author.[4] Women writers were seen as women first and writers second, a critical perspective that casts the inevitable glare of autobiography onto the most fictive of their productions. As Domna Stanton remarks, "[autobiography] had been used . . . to affirm that women could not transcend, but only record, the concerns of the private self; thus it had effectively served to devalue their writing" (4).

While the female author's novel was read as autobiography (and her autobiography read as novel), the discourse of autobiography itself reproduced the notion of a universal, and implicitly male, subject.[5] The suspension of the distinction between autobiography and fiction within a single text, as practiced by Stendhal, Nerval, and others, did not provide a satisfactory option for women writers since the very denial of their authorial position relied on a supposed blurring of autobiography and fiction. Instead of unraveling the authorial subject, which constitutes a positive goal for the male writers I study in this book, in women's writing the affirmation of separate genres, the inscription of a female subjectivity through an autobiographical signature (an "autogynograph"), and an assertion of the right to create truly fictive novels proves to be, ultimately, more liberating.[6] In my readings of Sand's works, I make an effort to avoid interpreting her novels as veiled autobiographies, preferring rather to analyze how her texts invent new subjects.

Just as the nineteenth-century literary field attempted to marginalize women's writings, and thereby determined their textual strategies, women did not enjoy the same freedom of movement, the same ability to explore physical space, as their male counterparts. Political oppression goes hand in hand with restrictions on travel. Gérard de Nerval's wanderings across Europe showed not only his personal conflation of psychological and physical space, but they also revealed the resistance of the bourgeois order to the perceived dangers of vagrancy, all the more exaggerated in the case of women. The sexist ideal of women's domesticity in the nineteenth century was rendered concrete in their exclusion from the political sphere and objectification by the male gaze in public spaces. The *flâneur* as a dispassionate, objective observer of city streets served to solidify the neutral, male, subject position, and his very powers of observation rendered it impossible for the *flâneuse* to walk the streets unnoticed. As Catherine Nesci shows in her book *Le flâneur et les flâneuses,* women writers such as George Sand, Delphine de Girardin, and Flora Tristan employed inventive means of taking back the streets, ranging from cross-dressing to assuming masculine pseudonyms. Their texts, she argues, deployed "countermyths" of the modern city, constituting urban utopias where women and men could interact as equals (41–42).

Sand's novels, I argue, figure the double bind of women's textual subjectivity—the impossibility of writing either pure fiction or pure autobiography—as a function of textual space. The utopias of Sand's literary imagination are ideological structures that use space to redefine language and society. In *Indiana,* texts and urban spaces are represented as dangers to the heroine's body and sanity. The symbolically rich natural utopia of the Île Bourbon (today the French overseas department La Réunion in the Indian Ocean) renews identity and language for both Indiana and Ralph. *Nanon,* by contrast, portrays a female narrator whose mastery of writing proceeds in tandem with her mastery of maps, and who eventually builds her own agrarian utopia. These two novels which bookend Sand's long literary career from the aftermath of July 1830 to the tragedy of 1871 suggest that fictional women subjects for Sand overcome the limits imposed on women by their specific historical situations and propose transcendent forms of subjectivity in imaginary spaces of their own creation.

Chapter Five

Drowning in the Text: Space and *Indiana*

When *Indiana* was first published under the pseudonym G. Sand in 1832, the first reviewers proclaimed the new male writer a profound analyst of contemporary society, but at the same time one whose novel undoubtedly benefited from revisions by a woman's pen; according to Sand's *Histoire de ma vie:* "Les journaux parlèrent tous de M. *G. Sand* avec éloge, insinuant que la main d'une femme avait dû se glissait çà et là pour révéler à l'auteur certaines délicatesses du coeur et de l'esprit, mais déclarant que le style et les appréciations avaient trop de virilité pour n'être pas d'un homme" (*Histoire de ma vie II,* 380).[1] If some readers were led to believe that the author was a man, others more in the know at first thought that *Indiana* was another collaboration between George Sand and Jules Sandeau under the name Jules Sand, after their previous novel *Rose et Blanche* from 1831. The blatant misogyny of the male narrator (who at one point exclaims "la femme est imbécile par nature"—"woman is an imbecile by nature"; *Indiana,* 251) and the mastery of realist codes clearly indicated to the supposedly savvy reader that this novel could only have been composed by a man, albeit a sensitive one capable of understanding the plight of women caught in the chains of marriage. If Sand's cross-dressing were enough to befuddle men about her gender despite her tiny stature, writing as a man came even easier—all that was necessary was a change in grammatical gender and a suitably paternalistic tone.

Soon enough, however, in the small world of Parisian letters Sand's authorship was quickly recognized and *Indiana* suddenly became unmistakably the work of a woman. As Béatrice Didier writes, once the gender of the author was discovered, any perceived fault in the novel became attributable to Sand the woman and any quality such as the flaunting of social convention became scandalous (Didier, preface to Sand's *Indiana,* 11). In his very favorable review in the *Journal des Débats* of July 21, 1832, C (whom Didier identifies in a note as Victor Charlier, *Indiana,* 375) proclaims astonishment that such a brilliant work of fiction has as its creator a young woman: "Après l'avoir lu et relu, on demeure confondu d'étonnement, quand on songe qu'une femme en est l'auteur, qu'une femme délicate et frêle possède cet admirable don d'écrire" ("After having read and reread it, we remain confused and astonished, when we think that a woman is the author, that a delicate and frail woman possess such an admirable gift for writing"), concluding that the reader is compelled to reread about the awful character of Raymon described in these "pages idéales et vraies, tout à la fois, qu'une femme seule pouvait écrire" ("at once ideal and true pages which only a woman could write.") The critic, while applauding the novel's realistic social portraiture and critique, seeks desperately to place Sand's gendered body back into the text to the point of suggesting that the vivid description of Indiana's tortured and torturing love interest has to be a representation by a woman, presumably drawn from her own personal experience.

The weak yet passionate *créole* Indiana can hardly be mistaken for the cross-dressing, liberated woman George Sand and so what a critic insinuates to be inspired by personal experience in a woman's text, he might call keen observation in a Balzac or a Stendhal. In *Histoire de ma vie,* Sand attempts to escape the double bind of literature written by women by proclaiming that her personal life is not the subject of her novels:

> On n'a pas manqué de dire qu'*Indiana* était ma personne et mon histoire. Il n'en est rien. J'ai présenté beaucoup de types de femmes, et je crois que quand on aura lu cet exposé des impressions et des réflexions de ma vie, on verra bien que je ne me suis jamais mise en scène sous des traits féminins. Je suis trop romanesque pour avoir vu une héroïne de roman dans mon miroir.[2] (*Histoire de ma vie II,* 364–65).

Her truthful autobiography, she claims, will finally prove that her novels are entirely fiction. Moreover, actual women do not fit fictional types, and even less so a woman as extraordinary as Sand. Yet a novel's shifting context determines the various and contradictory ways it can be read, and its author's gender above all else orients the reader's expectations. The misogyny of the narrator in *Indiana* convinces the unsuspecting reader of the masculine gender of the author and predisposes him to the validity of the novel's argument for greater social freedom. At the same time, this gap between narrator and narrative demonstrates how social prejudice is constructed along gender lines. As Sandy Petrey argues, *Indiana* is Sand's only truly realist novel, a pure product of the destabilizing July Revolution of 1830; the duality of *Indiana*'s misogynistic narrator and feminist narrative convincingly performs a brutal sexism, all the better to expose its workings (*In the Court of the Pear King*, 92).

That gender, politics, and history influence the "truth" of a text, that a text itself can multiply meanings and disintegrate the unity of the self is the structuring principle of *Indiana.* The different prefaces and the novel itself warn again and again of the dangers of writing and of interpretation, notably for women. Whether a love letter by a manipulative chauvinist or a disingenuous review in a literary journal, the written word distorts the truth and misleads a naive reader. Women who themselves try to write in order to convince men inevitably fail in the novel, as their gender already determines how men read their texts. This powerlessness to control meaning manifests itself in the novel through the wandering, hallucinations, madness, and the suicidal impulse of the female characters, Noun and Indiana. Haunted by yet drawn to the dissolution of body and self that accompanies her forays into both textual and physical space, Indiana repeatedly holds herself back, literally and figuratively, from taking the plunge.

Manipulations

The two "Préfaces" (an original from 1832 and one from 1842) and one "Notice" (1852) that introduce the novel denounce repeatedly any manipulation of the truth by texts, without apparent irony even as they maintain the fiction of the masculinity of the author. The role of the novel and of writing in general would not be to interpret facts to fit an argument but only to reflect reality; in a decidedly Stendhalian turn of phrase, Sand remarks, "L'écrivain n'est qu'un miroir" ("The writer is only a mirror") (Préface de 1832, *Indiana,* 37). The writer and his/her novel cannot be held accountable for representing the truth, since only society is to blame for its own corruption. Sand's novel claims to influence public opinion while respecting the sacred institutions it implicitly critiques (39).

In her second preface ten years later, Sand admits that an unmediated representation of society in the hopes of persuading the public cannot have an impact without reforming laws and institutions. She writes that it had been her intention not to undermine or even critique society when she wrote *Indiana:* "Longtemps après avoir écrit la préface d'*Indiana* sous l'empire d'un reste de respect pour la société constituée, je cherchais encore à résoudre cet insoluble problème: *le moyen de concilier le bonheur et la dignité des individus opprimés par cette même société, sans modifier la société elle-même*" (44).[3] Sand, or her masculinized author, seems to anticipate Lampedusa's aristocrat Tancredi in *Il gattopardo,* who exclaims, "Se vogliamo che tutto rimanga com'è bisogna che tutto cambi" (50) ("If we want everything to stay the same, everything must change"); yet in the topsy-turvy world after the July Revolution, everything must stay the same in order for everything to change. Words must keep their meaning, referents must remain stable, if representations of the social order are to be accurate and politically effective. Moreover, as a female author usurping a masculine writing position, it was a clever maneuver to recall how the system is supposed to work in order to accuse the hypocrisy of those who unjustly benefit from it.

Along with this desire for transparent writing and truthful representation, the novel's prefaces try to guard against and then eventually attack readers, journalists, and politicians who put words in the mouth of the author, bending the meaning of a "simple" novel to fit an ideological agenda. In the original preface, the author warns against all the possible misinterpretations of "his" work, a novel "sans importance" ("without importance") (37), rehearsing a familiar trope in nineteenth-century prefaces which often display a false modesty. Indeed, the author expects his readers not to agree with him: "le narrateur s'attend à des reproches" ("the narrateur expects criticism") (40); "l'auteur s'abandonne tout entier à la critique" ("the author gives himself entirely over to the critics") (41). Yet here Sand seems to be anticipating more than an average succès de scandale; as we have seen, the first reviews were rather positive and not terribly concerned with any immorality displayed in the novel.

The real scandal, the trap set by Sand, is of course the not-so-secret gender of the author. In her preface from 1842, Sand reveals how journalists overinterpreted her novel, which is to say read it as a woman's novel with a specific agenda: "Certains journalistes qui s'érigent de nos jours en représentants et en gardiens de la morale publique . . . se prononcèrent avec rigueur contre les tendances de mon pauvre conte, et lui donnèrent, en le présentant comme un plaidoyer contre l'ordre social, une importance et une sorte de retentissement auxquels il ne serait point arrivé sans cela" (43).[4] Her "Notice" from 1852 is even more blunt when it reiterates that *Indiana* was Sand's first novel, that it was written without any theory or ambition, and so those critics who refuse to read "naively" what was written "naively," who denounce works as immoral, betray their own talent and betray the writing profession (35). It is the critic's own intelligence that does him in: "La critique a beaucoup trop d'esprit, c'est ce qui la fera mourir" (35) ("Critics have too much wit, it will be the death of them").

The novel's plot mirrors the textual strategies of its "Prefaces" and "Notice." The unflattering portrait of the critic in Sand's "Notice" corresponds exactly to that of *Indiana*'s roguish aristocrat Raymon de Ramière, who not coincidentally earns his reputation in society as a brilliant essayist. Raymon's wit, like that of the critic, does ultimately lead to his demise, but a symbolic one in the form of a castration and silencing by his new wife, the former Mlle de Nangy, who is the only woman in the novel not to fall for his eloquent lies (298). As a young, handsome, and well-spoken member of the Restoration's ruling class, Raymon possesses all the qualities needed to secure a bright future as well as to seduce women. He differs from the stereotype of the suave seducer in one very important respect according to the narrator in another observation reminiscent of Stendhal: "Un homme qui parle d'amour avec esprit est médiocrement amoureux. Raymon était une exception; il exprimait la passion avec art, et il la ressentait avec chaleur. Seulement, ce n'était pas la passion qui le rendait éloquent, c'était l'éloquence qui le rendait passionné" (83).[5] In romance and also in politics, Raymon falls in love with his own eloquence. For the sake of a beautiful phrase or a well-wrought argument, he abandons the truth and deceives himself. His narcissism is such that when he gazes at a woman he only sees the image projected by his own romantic discourse. As soon as the love affair loses his interest or becomes inconvenient, he writes a new woman into his life.

The reader is first introduced to Raymon when M. Delmare, Indiana's husband, takes him for a burglar and shoots at him on his property (63). The novel's first of many cases of mistaken identity is resolved when Raymon's elegant hunting outfit proves his social rank. Unlike the female characters, his gender and class repeatedly protect him from harm. Raymon is caught trespassing on Delmare's estate because of a rendezvous with his first love interest in the novel, Noun—Indiana's Creole maid and childhood friend. Noun's natural beauty attracts Raymon, but he cannot or will not overlook the enormous gap in their social positions and so rejects as ludicrous Noun's desire to be his wife. Once Raymon sees Noun's mistress Indiana, he falls in love with her more graceful beauty, even though the narrator insists that Noun is the more stunning of the two. Noun, increasingly desperate after she discovers she is pregnant, attempts in vain to borrow Indiana's class markers (she writes on Indiana's stationery, she uses her bedroom, and she wears her clothes), though Raymon only sees the unbridgeable distance between Indiana's refined elegance and Noun's vulgar beauty. After Noun commits suicide, Raymon pursues Indiana, hoping to have an affair, but counts on Indiana's sense of decency, as well as her husband's vigilance, to guarantee that he will not be burdened by a serious, and potentially socially disastrous, relationship.

Raymon misguidedly depends upon Indiana to act according to Parisian social conventions by staying with her husband and accepting to be Raymon's mistress; at the same time, he seems to trust Indiana to understand that his lover's discourse is rhetoric for its own sake, meant to incite passion and not inspire everlasting devotion. Noun and Indiana both foolishly take Raymon's statements and promises at face value, and not as part of an elaborate game of seduction. For them, Raymon should be bound by his words, and the narrator agrees: "L'amour est un contrat aussi bien que le mariage" (76) ("Love is a contract just as much as marriage is"). In the end, he woos Indiana back from the far-off Île Bourbon in another deceitfully passionate letter and then promptly forgets about her when he marries Mlle de Nangy. His new wife proves that the marriage contract can, when properly exploited, be empowering for women when she uses Indiana's pathetic return as the pretext to subordinate her husband, delighting in "la position d'infériorité et de dépendance où cet incident venait de placer son mari vis-à-vis d'elle" (298) ("the position of inferiority and dependence which this incident placed her husband toward her").

Raymon's wife can turn the tables on her husband because his fame as a loyal and vocal supporter of the old regime puts him in danger after Louis-Philippe comes to power. Before 1830, Raymon seduced public opinion in favor of the conservative government with the same skill he used to seduce women: "[Il] est un des hommes qui ont eu sur vos pensées le plus d'empire ou d'influence, quelle que soit aujourd'hui votre opinion. Vous avez dévoré ses brochures politiques, et souvent vous avez été entraîné, en lisant les journaux du temps, par le charme irrésistible de son style, et les grâces de sa logique courtoise et mondaine" (128).[6] The narrator introduces a rare second person, "vous," which equates the (male) reader of the novel and of Raymon's newspaper articles with the apparently equally gullible women readers of Raymon's love letters. The language of nineteenth-century political punditry resembles that of romantic lovemaking: "empire," "entraîné," "charme irrésistible," "grâces."

Raymon and his conservative colleagues wrote in defense of the "Charte," Louis XVIII's quickly outdated constitution, fooling themselves into believing they were communicating to the public the letter of the law and not their own self-interested ideological interpretations: "ce [la Charte] n'était plus qu'un texte sur lequel chacun s'exerçait à l'éloquence, sans qu'un discours tirât plus à conséquence qu'un sermon" (128) ("it [la Charte] was nothing but a text on which everyone would practice his eloquence, without reasoning having any more consequence than a sermon").

Just as Raymon falls in love with his own eloquence, he manages to indoctrinate himself through his own political rhetoric. His ability to distort reality is recognized and rewarded by the Restoration government:

"Cette rare faculté qu'il possédait, de réfuter par le talent la vérité positive, en avait fait un homme précieux au ministère" (130) ("this rare ability that he possessed, of refuting positive truth through talent, made him a precious man for the ministry"). But when the political winds begin to shift in 1829 and the government takes a radical move to the right, Raymon finds himself caught between his loyalty to the king and his own better judgment. Worse for a narcissist like Raymon, the new political turn reveals that all of his previous tracts were ridiculous (261). When revolution finally happens and the bourgeois king Louis-Philippe takes the throne, Raymon finds himself without political allies, and thus without a future. His calculated marriage to the wealthy aristocrat Mlle de Nangy guarantees him a comfortable, if forever dull, future.

Raymon and the literary critics mocked in the novel's prefaces share the same talent for molding reality through language in order to fit their worldview and the same fatal flaw of believing their own falsifications. As long as facts remain hidden, such as the tendency of monarchies to turn absolutist or the inconvenient difference between narrative voice and authorial gender, manipulators of language can take advantage of textual ambiguity to promote their interests. For women, structurally disempowered in such a system, the best tactic is to force a confrontation between word and referent, between the letter of the law and social reality. Sand's "masculine" narrative possesses all the stylistic virtues of a text written by a man, but the gender of the author renders the novel scandalous; if virtue as well as masculinity are performative, then they are societal constructions and not naturally determined. Similarly, Mlle de Nangy obliges Raymon to confess his marriage to her in front of Indiana; she thus humiliates him both by taking command of the situation and by showing Indiana that Raymon's passionate letters were nothing but an illusion. The lesson for Raymon and for Sand's literary critics is that writers of shifty texts may eventually be targets themselves.

Lost in Space

Indiana's main women characters, Noun and Indiana, do not have Sand's mastery of writing or Mlle de Nangy's dispassionate, calculating mind. They take Raymon at his word, and when they do try to influence others through writing or in their actions, they tend to mistake signs for reality. Trapped in what they imagine to be a transparent world, they lose their bearings whenever their surroundings change. Near the beginning of the novel, the narrator presents the reader with a tableau of domestic boredom and stability, a fantasy of harmony endangered by the slightest movement: "On eût dit, à voir l'immobilité des deux personnages en relief devant le foyer, qu'ils craignaient de déranger l'immobilité de la scène; fixes et pétrifiés comme les héros d'un conte de fées, on eût dit que la moindre parole, le plus léger mouvement allait faire écrouler sur eux les murs d'une cité fantastique" (53).[7] For Indiana's husband, the moral is even clearer, since, as the narrator writes, the only social contract he recognizes is the dictum "*Chacun chez soi*" with the ambiguous meaning of "to each his own" or "everyone is master in their own home" (132). Bourgeois order depends not only upon the fiction of stable linguistic meaning, but also upon the immobility of people and things, who must respect each other's borders.

Indiana is a novel about the dangers of and desires for exposing oneself to polyvalent texts and open spaces, especially for women. When Indiana leaves the comfort of her home, her own identity and sense of self is undone in the confusing jumble of images confronting her. Whether the countryside of the Brie, the streets of Paris, or the sublime volcanic landscape of the Île Bourbon, the novel's spaces contain a richness of signs and possible meanings that always invite the characters to superimpose the image of their own desires onto what they see: Raymon projects an image of Indiana onto the body of Noun; Indiana sees Noun's form on the quays of the Seine; the narrator imagines all of art history emerging from the rock formations on the island. These rare moments of truth, instead of being seen as epiphanies, are described, in Indiana's case especially, as hallucinations or madness. Unable to seize a chance at real freedom, Indiana repeatedly surrenders control of meaning and of her own narrative.

Marked by her presumed race and class as Indiana's ill-fated mirror image, Noun serves as the novel's paradigm of a woman's inability to command her own fate, to write her own text. Noun's indeterminate identity is reflected in how literary critics have described her; Pratima Prasad shows how scholars have tended to see only Noun's class difference with Indiana or, conversely, have classified her as a woman of color ("Espace colonial et vérité historique dans *Indiana*"). As Adlai Murdoch convincingly argues, the novel itself labels both Noun and Indiana "créoles," playing on the ambiguity of the word meaning person born in the colonies of European stock, person of mixed race, or person of African blood, and so paradoxically, either colonizer or colonized (Murdoch, 3). Nevertheless Noun's traits suggest, without ever affirming, mixed-raced ancestry (black eyes, curly hair, orientalized name) and Indiana's those of a woman of Spanish descent from the colonies (passionate, noble, pallid) (Murdoch, 18). Noun's fluid identity in the text allows her to attract Raymon with her "exotic" beauty and yet still attempt to impersonate Indiana, passing for a different class or a different race. Her eventual suicide serves as a narrative end point toward or away from which Indiana will move throughout the novel.

Much critical attention has been focused on one passage in particular, when Noun tries to win back Raymon by dressing as Indiana and inviting him to sleep in her mistress's bedroom. Noun leads a mystified Raymon into a brightly lit room where she has placed exotic flowers and which is decorated with furniture from far-off lands as well as engravings of Paul and Virginie and the Île Bourbon. Raymon begins to imagine that the "fantôme d'une femme" ("phantom of a woman") who led him to Indiana's room was Indiana herself, but then he unflatteringly contrasts Noun with Indiana (101). When he temporarily comes to his senses, he is bewildered to be in such an intimate place belonging to the woman he really loves, exclaiming to Noun: "Sortons de cette chambre, nous ne sommes pas à notre place" (102) ("Let us leave this room, we are not in our place"). Ultimately, he succumbs to Noun's "volupté tout orientale" ("very oriental voluptuousness") (104), but only to see, entranced, the image of Indiana in the reflections of Noun between two mirrors: "Les deux panneaux de glace qui se renvoyaient l'un à l'autre l'image de Noun jusqu'à l'infini semblaient se peupler de mille fantômes. Il épiait dans la profondeur de cette double réverbération une forme plus déliée, et il lui semblait saisir, dans la dernière ombre vaporeuse et confuse que Noun y reflétait, la taille fine et souple de madame Delmare" (104).[8] Twice in this passage Raymon's vision of Indiana is that of a phantom, one who presumably haunts the space of the bedroom and takes over Noun's body. After their night of lust, Raymon wakes up to find Noun once again a maid and Indiana's room unremarkable, with its air of "decency" (105). But after Noun slowly realizes that Raymon has used her body to make love to another woman, she quietly wanders off and drowns herself in the river, where Indiana eventually faints upon finding her. Noun trades places with Indiana, becoming herself a phantom to haunt Indiana and the text.

As Béatrice Didier has argued, the novel's many references to Ophelia (even Indiana's dog, who also drowns, is named Ophélia), to drowning and the theme of water, underline the repressed desire on the part of the novel's heroines for absolute passivity (Didier, *Sade,* 154), a passivity, I would argue, that extends to the vicissitudes of textual meaning. Noun dies less than a third of the way into the novel, but her presence is felt throughout since the characters are drawn back to where she drowned and Indiana and Ralph, her unlikely final love interest, repeatedly contemplate suicide. By giving herself over to the constant motion of the river, Noun ensures the dissolution of her self (in the text), but also decides the flow of the narrative—"Noun" becomes a subject. If Indiana is drawn again and again to water, if she sees the ghost of Noun every time she manages to break free from the influence of a man, it may, of course, be because she wants to lose herself completely, as she had tried to do in her relations with men. And yet by imagining that she can abandon her identity and her body to chance by wandering through space, as an author does over her writing, Indiana may be trying to envision the dangers and the joys of composing an alternative narrative of her life.

The first time Indiana considers suicide, she had just been forced to leave Raymon's Parisian *hôtel* by his mother and wanders the foggy streets of the city in a daze. Because she tried to leave her husband for Raymon, Indiana believes herself to be a damned woman, "une femme perdue dans l'opinion publique" ("a fallen woman according to public opinion") (218). Picturing her husband's hand shoving her into the stream of the gutter, she keeps walking, eventually becoming emboldened by the din of the streets. Indiana is unconsciously attracted to the water:

> Elle descendit le quai depuis l'Institut jusqu'au Corps Législatif; mais elle oublia de traverser le pont, et continua à longer la rivière, absorbée dans une rêverie stupide, dans une méditation sans idées, et poursuivant l'action sans but de marcher devant elle.
>
> Insensiblement elle se trouva au bord de l'eau, qui charriait des glaçons à ses pieds et les brisait avec un bruit sec et froid sur les pierres de la rive. Cette eau verdâtre exerçait une force attractive sur les sens d'Indiana. On s'accoutume aux idées terribles; à force de les admettre, on s'y plaît. Il y avait si longtemps que l'exemple du suicide de Noun apaisait les heures de son désespoir, qu'elle s'était fait du suicide une sorte de volupté tentatrice. . . . Quand elle sentit le froid cuisant de l'eau qui baignait déjà sa chaussure, elle s'éveilla comme d'un état de somnambulisme, et, cherchant des yeux où elle était, elle vit Paris derrière elle, et la Seine qui fuyait sous ses pieds, emportant dans sa masse huileuse le reflet blanc des maisons et le bleu grisâtre du ciel. Ce mouvement continu de l'eau et l'immobilité du sol se confondirent dans ses perceptions troublées, et il lui sembla que l'eau dormait et que la terre fuyait. Dans ce moment de vertige, elle s'appuya contre un mur, et se pencha, fascinée, vers ce qu'elle prenait pour une masse solide . . .[9] (226–27)

This passage confounds the reader as much as Indiana; objects trade places with their reflections, and screens with their projections. Indiana herself is portrayed as being void of any ideas or motivation, save for the drive to continue walking straight ahead. Yet she is entirely free for the first time in the novel, having earlier escaped out the window from her husband's reach and then being left by her lover. Moreover, her dreamlike stupor leads to a superimposition of images onto the spaces of Paris and a free association of place and memory quite the contrary of a "meditation without ideas."

For the reader, the text indicates Indiana's trajectory very precisely, from the Institut on the Quai Malaquais heading west toward the Corps Législatif on the Quai d'Orsay by way of the Quai Voltaire; from there she neglects to cross the bridge (the Pont Louis XVI) to return home, instead following the river until she has left the city. The many references to water, to the morning gloom, and of course to Noun's suicide suggest that in her trance Indiana imagines she is back on her property in the Brie, near the river where Noun drowns. Strangely though, after the passage describes her waking up from the sensation of cold water leaking into her shoe and she leaves behind her "state of somnambulism," she becomes more, not less, susceptible to hallucination. She seems able to recognize the stone buildings and blue-gray sky of Paris behind her, but only as they are reflected in the quickly moving flow of the Seine. The contrast of the steady river current and the unmoving ground of the quay provoke a sense of vertigo; Indiana mistakes the river for a reflection of land and leans over to step on it. Earlier, the passage depicted the extreme cold of the river water as hardening into ice, but at the same time Indiana's shoes are bathed in the water rolling over the riverbank. Water and land have exchanged places, like Elstir's marine landscapes in Proust's *A l'ombre des jeunes filles en fleurs,* confounding Indiana's already fatigued senses and once again juxtaposing immobility and movement.

Indiana's cousin Sir Ralph, led by her dog Ophélia, prevents her from jumping at the last minute and slowly shakes her out of her reverie. Still out of her mind, she asks him if he met Noun on the "chemin" ("path"), pointing at the river, then asks him to "cherchez mes pieds" ("go fetch my feet"), which she claims to have left on the rocks (228). Later, as she recovers and tries to remember what happened, Ralph insists to her that she tried to commit suicide and makes her promise to him, not that she will never try to kill herself again, but that she will discuss it with him beforehand! At first Indiana denies she ever thought about suicide: "Pourquoi me parlez-vous de suicide? . . . Je n'ai jamais voulu attenter à ma vie" (229) ("Why do you talk to me about suicide? . . . I never wanted to take my own life"). Eventually she gives in to Ralph's interpretation and then returns to her husband; but a close reading of the passage shows that Indiana, while attracted by the "sensual pleasure" of Noun's suicide, made an effort to regain what she took for solid ground and so did not consciously try to kill herself. Ralph did in fact rescue her, but in the process ensured that she was bound to him and to her husband.

Indiana experiences a similar vision when she returns to her native Île Bourbon with her husband Delmare and Sir Ralph. Left to herself most of the time, she wanders the mountains outside her home in the evenings, gazing out at the sunset, but averting her eyes from the "magnetic" sight of the ocean in the far distance—presumably the pull of the water is too much for her. Beyond the waves, in the strange cloud forms above the horizon, her mind wanders off to distant lands:

> Quelquefois les nuages de la côte prirent pour elle des formes singulières: tantôt elle vit une lame blanche s'élever sur les flots et décrire une ligne gigantesque qu'elle prit pour la façade du Louvre; tantôt ce furent deux voiles carrées qui, sortant tout à coup de la brume, offraient le souvenir des tours Notre-Dame de Paris, quand la Seine exhale un brouillard compact qui embrasse leur base et les fait paraître comme suspendues dans le ciel; d'autres fois c'étaient des flocons de nuées roses qui, dans leur formes changeantes, présentaient tous les caprices d'architecture d'une ville immense. L'esprit de cette femme s'endormait dans les illusions du passé, et elle se prenait à palpiter de joie à la vue de ce Paris imaginaire dont les réalités avaient signalé le temps le plus malheureux de sa vie. Un étrange vertige s'emparait alors de sa tête. Suspendue à une grande élévation au-dessus du sol de la côte, et voyant fuir sous ses yeux les gorges qui la séparaient de l'Océan, il lui semblait être lancée dans cet espace par un mouvement rapide, et cheminer dans l'air vers la ville prestigieuse de son imagination. Dans ce rêve, elle se cramponnait au rocher qui lui servait d'appui; et pour qui eût observé alors ses yeux avides, son sein haletant d'impatience et l'effrayante expression de joie répandue sur ses traits, elle eût offert tous les symptômes de la folie. C'étaient pourtant là ses heures de plaisir et les seuls moments de bien-être vers lesquels se dirigeaient les espérances de sa journée. Si le caprice de son mari eût supprimé ces promenades solitaires, je ne sais de quelle pensée elle eût vécu; car, chez elle, tout se rapportait à une certaine faculté d'illusions, à une ardente aspiration vers un point qui n'était ni le souvenir, ni l'attente, ni l'espoir, ni le regret, mais le désir dans toute son intensité dévorante.[10] (253–54)

Like Stendhal looking out at Rome from on top of the Janiculum, Indiana sees her past projected onto a landscape below. The passage shares many points in common with Indiana's "suicide" attempt in Paris: atmospheric detail which provokes a dream state; one place melting into the space of another; a "vertigo" caused by the difference between her stable position and a moving one; finally, a dissonance between Indiana's experience and Ralph's. Whereas the episode in Paris is a singular and unpleasant event in her life, the imperfect tense indicates that Indiana sought out this "vertigo" and "madness" over and over as if compelled to relive the experience, not because it was traumatic but because she finds in it an unexplainable joy. For her, "tout se rapportait à une certaine faculté d'illusions" ("everything was related to a certain power of illusions"), toward a single intense "desire," but whereas in Paris that desire revolved around Noun, here she imagines the monuments of Paris, the Louvre and Notre Dame. The narrator supposes that Paris is the site of Indiana's worst traumas, where Raymon had seduced her and left her. Yet nowhere else does the novel make explicit reference either to the Louvre or to Notre Dame. However, during her delirious walk along the river, these two monuments would have been visible through the fog across the water on the opposite bank and perhaps were reflected in the current. Moreover, their very monumentality signifies places of memory, history, and artistic and religious beauty absent elsewhere in Indiana's life and in the novel.

According to the text, her "joy," her "pleasure," and her "desire" in these "illusions" comes from the view of her imaginary Paris and also from the sensation of "rapid movement" as she crosses the ocean and moves through the city. As if to highlight her delusional *flânerie,* the almost sexual pleasure she takes in her virtual walk through Paris, she lives for this "pensée" ("idea"), which would disappear if her husband ever suspended her solitary walks. The narrator implicitly suggests that Delmare has every reason to prevent Indiana from wandering when he insists upon her madness and her lack of ideas. But on the following page, Ralph's hikes through the gorges of the Île Bourbon and subsequent meditations on his past merit respect as the reflections of a stoic philosopher. Indiana's daydreams project images of her desire onto changing, mobile, natural forms. Far from just an obsession over Raymon, her evening strolls show that she delights in the creations of her imagination, temporarily freed from her subservience to Delmare, Raymon, and Ralph.

The twists and turns of *Indiana*'s plot in the novel's fourth part find the heroine lost and wretched twice as she enters urban spaces, exposing the distance between her dreams of mobility and the dangers, especially for a woman, of unaccompanied travel. Indiana makes one final effort at escaping her abusive husband to return to France and Raymon. She bribes a ship's captain to allow her passage to France (necessary because any traveler was required by law to announce his or her departure in the local newspaper), and arrives in Bordeaux during the July Revolution. Disoriented by the strange new political reality, symbolized by the revolution's tricolor flag flying on Bordeaux's city hall, Indiana leaves the ship without her money or her identity papers and is stopped as a suspect by the National Guard. With the news of the monarchy's demise, she loses consciousness and wakes up days later in a hospital, where she is registered simply as "inconnue" ("unknown") (293). After two months she is able to leave the hospital, but remains in a feverish daze. She wanders the streets until she ends up once again by the port, eventually sleeping in an abandoned house and begging for food until the ship's captain recognizes her and sends her to Paris.

After her final rejection by Raymon and dismissal by Mlle de Nangy, she is taken in a carriage, again unconscious, and not knowing anyone, dumped in a hotel. The narrator's description of Indiana's hotel room corresponds to what Marc Augé calls a "non-lieu," a transitory place of anonymity that is the polar opposite of places of memory like the Louvre or Notre Dame; according to the novel, "ce local où nul n'a laissé de trace de son passage qu'un nom inconnu, . . . ce cachot de l'esprit et du coeur, voyez Paris, ce beau Paris, que vous aviez rêvé si merveilleux!" (299) ("this place where no one has left a trace of his passing except an unknown name, . . . this dungeon of the mind and of the heart, see Paris, this beautiful Paris, which you have dreamt as being so marvelous!"). This miserable hotel room, where she is even more immobilized than in the Île Bourbon, shatters her dream of the limitless city. Alone, unknown, her imaginary Paris vanished, Indiana wastes away in her room until Ralph once again miraculously arrives to rescue her.

Whether in the wilderness of her volcanic island in the Indian Ocean or in the political wilderness of France during the July Revolution, Indiana finds herself liberated from her ties to society and from her dependence on men, and eventually from her sense of identity. The spaces she traverses present to her a layered landscape where visions of the city compete with projections of her own desires. Indiana's experiences reveal a creative mind that invents metaphors of freedom and movement in order to imagine a world beyond the confinement of society's laws—which become all the more poignant when she is confronted with the harsh reality of institutional misogyny. Ralph's constant surveillance of Indiana, Raymon's cynical manipulation of her desires for recognition and adventure, and Delmare's domineering orders for her subordination all amount to different iterations of the same tactic used by the novel's sexist narrator:

to reinscribe Indiana's search for meaning as a product of madness and to reassert her subservience to men.

The Narrator's Story

Indiana's unexpected dénouement presents more than a few narrative, stylistic, and ideological problems that have puzzled critics. The novel's fourth part ends with Ralph and Indiana deciding to leap to their deaths into a gorge on the Île Bourbon; in the conclusion, the narrator discovers Indiana and Ralph living happily in the island's interior apparently cured of their suicidal urges. What is perhaps more disquieting for a novel that portrays the suffering of a woman at the hands of patriarchy, Indiana becomes almost voiceless in the conclusion as the narrator and Ralph engage in long emotional conversations and she retires to her quarters. After Indiana's many unsuccessful struggles to write her own fate, the scene of two men chummily discussing the past seems hardly like a satisfying ending. I would argue, however, that the conclusion marks a fundamental shift in the narrator's discourse as he embraces the creative possibilities of fantasy and Indiana and Ralph's dream of building a utopia beyond the tyranny of public opinion.

The narrator reveals himself to be a young man traveling to the Île Bourbon for no concrete purpose except to daydream. While exploring the island's interior and describing its geological peculiarities, he experiences an imaginative leap almost identical to Indiana's vision of Paris in the clouds. Within the confused disorder of volcanic rocks strewn across the "arena" of the volcano's crater, the narrator imagines he sees increasingly complex "architectural" forms; first a wall, then the delicate arabesque design of a Moorish building, followed by an obelisk, a Gothic fortress, and a pagoda (331). These natural ruins evocative of the history of civilization serve as inspiration and a challenge to the artist: "il semble que les génies de tous les siècles et de toutes les nations soient venus puiser leurs inspirations dans cette grande oeuvre du hasard et de la destruction" (332) ("it seems that geniuses of every century and of every nation have come to draw their inspiration from this great work of chance and destruction"). Volcanic forms, like artistic inspiration, are the work of chance, but also the work of destruction as they make way for new creations.

Predisposed to interpretational flights of fancy by the playful rock formations, the narrator stares at what he takes to be an inscription carved in a gigantic crystallized monument seemingly written by an ageless hand, but in reality formed by chance in the volcano's cauldron:

> De ces rencontres fortuites sont résultés des jeux bizarres, des impressions hiéroglyphiques, des caractères mystérieux, qui semblent jetés là comme le seing d'un être surnaturel, écrit en lettres cabalistiques.
>
> Je restai longtemps dominé par la puérile prétention de chercher un sens à ces chiffres inconnus. Ces inutiles recherches me firent tomber dans une méditation profonde pendant laquelle j'oubliai le temps qui fuyait.[11] (333)

The narrator loses himself deciphering a text he knows to be imaginary. Though he qualifies his activity as childish and perhaps meaningless, he nonetheless connects the interpretation of these natural "signs" to the mystic art of divination, to ancient civilization, to the earlier rock formations which inspired the history of architecture, and so by extension to his own creative textual practice. As Jacques Rancière has shown in works such as *La Parole muette* or *Politique de la littérature,* one of the characteristics of literature which emerged during what he calls the "aesthetic regime of art" at the beginning of the nineteenth century was a "petrification" of literature, a proliferation of inanimate objects in literary texts which were made to speak: "une parole qui n'est proférée par personne, qui ne répond à aucune volonté de signification mais exprime la vérité des choses à la manière dont les fossiles ou les stries de la pierre portent leur histoire écrite" (Rancière, *Politique de la littérature,* 23) ("a speech which is proffered by no one, which responds to no particular will for meaning but expresses the truth of things just like fossils or striations in stone are marked by a written history"). By giving the meaning of his text over to the "silent speech" of stones, the narrator both abandons his "will to meaning" and taps into the truth of things rather than the vanities of society.[12]

Just as Indiana's joyful vision of Paris led to reverie and "madness," the narrator is caught in a daze. He loses track of time as clouds form, and when a torrential rain begins to fall, he takes refuge in a cave and wanders the island's interior, lost for two days. The downpour overflows the riverbeds, flooding the mountainsides and forming one "immense cascade" (333). The rest of the conclusion abounds in references to water, from the Bernica Falls into which Indiana and Ralph attempt to jump, to the "furious" cataract and overflowing lake below the couple's cabin. In the increasingly unrealistic ending, as the narrator resembles more and more Indiana herself, his strict control over the novel is lost and meaning overflows its narrative gates. In her Indian Ocean utopia, no longer held back by her fear of society's laws, Indiana finally dove into the water.

George Sand's first novel established her reputation by guarding against the various ways women's writing was misread. She exposes the bias of masculine narrators and realist tropes by parodying it perfectly and undermining it from within. She realistically portrays, in the character Indiana, the struggles of women in dangerous texts and hostile spaces. The narrative's hero, Ralph, vows he will not be the "brute haïssable" ("detestable brute") (340) he had been. Judging by the vocabulary used in the conclusion, where Indiana is only referred to as either Mme Delmare or as Ralph's "compagne" ("companion"), the couple have successfully managed to avoid embracing the oppressive institution of marriage on their island paradise. The utopian conclusion to this, Sand's most realist novel, confirms that for society to change not only must the causes of inequality be laid out, but there must also be a leap of imagination toward a better world.

Chapter Six

Carte Blanche: Charting Utopia in Sand's *Nanon*

George Sand's last major novel, *Nanon* from 1872, narrates the appropriation of a tool of elite power, the Cassini "Carte générale de la France," by a humble peasant girl, who uses these maps to internalize and negotiate the space of revolutionary France. The novel presents the history of the French Revolution from a displaced perspective: it is told as a memoir by Nanon, an old woman, who remembers her experiences as a young girl in the countryside. Nanon's story is thus very far from the center of the Revolution in terms of time (the story is told sixty years after the events), space (the novel takes place in an isolated region days from Paris), and gender. *Nanon*'s new perspective on the French Revolution reiterates republican values but also invents new textual spaces for thinking about ideological conundrums—both those posed by the original Revolution of 1789 and also by the Paris Commune of 1871.

The violence of 1871 required a different novelistic response from that of the hypocrisy of July 1830. As I have argued, Sand's first novel, *Indiana,* portrayed the political necessity for women in the wake of the Revolution of 1830 to expose the widening gap between discourse and deed, between language and its referents. If the realist mode, with its tendency toward ironic distance and objective detail, proved the most effective way to depict society's cynical opinion of itself, realism in fiction has difficulty breaking away from mimetic representation in order to invent new social structures. The unrealistic, utopian ending to *Indiana* signals the need within the novel to create new, virtual spaces in which women and men can exist equally. As Naomi Schor argues in *George Sand and Idealism,* "idealism for Sand is finally the only alternative representational mode available to those who do not enjoy the privileges of subjecthood in the real" (73). Sand's position as a woman writer marginalized by the social order led her to see in idealism a mode of writing capable of affirming equality as a precondition of social harmony.

Whereas the utopian spaces imagined by Indiana are islands of idealism within a realist novel, *Nanon* portrays in realistic detail an alternative experience of the Revolution of 1789 and so affirms that revolutionary ideals do not have to lead to violence and destruction. At the fragile beginnings of the Third Republic, born out of the chaos of Napoleon III's defeat by the Prussians and immediately challenged by the Paris Commune, the legacy of the French Revolution and the viability of republicanism were very much in question. The head of state of the provisional government, Adolphe Thiers, was the same man who played the decisive role in 1830 by thwarting any attempt at a republic in favor of a new monarchy. Sand, along with many other intellectuals, reluctantly backed Thiers in the hopes of founding a stable republic incrementally, instead of a more radical government, which might easily collapse (as had the First and Second Republics). As she wrote in a letter to Edmond Plauchut on March 27, 1871, "Mr Thiers n'est pas l'idéal, il ne fallait pas lui demander de l'être. Il fallait l'accepter comme un pont jeté entre Paris et la France, entre la République et la réaction, car la France, *hors des barrières de Paris, c'est la réaction*" (Sand, *Correspondance XXII—avril 1870–mars 1872*, 352–53) ("Mr. Thiers is not the ideal, we shouldn't ask him to be it. We have to accept him as a bridge between Paris and France, between the Republic and reactionaries, since France, *outside of Paris, is the reaction*"). From her home in Nohant far from Paris, Sand had limited first-hand knowledge of the events unfolding in Paris; the often exaggerated tales of savage violence on the part of the Communards horrified her, and politically she felt that their actions would undermine the possibility of an eventual republic as Thiers laid siege to the city. For these reasons, the Commune tested Sand's faith in equality and the wisdom of the common people.[1] At the same time, the Commune produced an astonishing number of political innovations in a brief amount of time (73 days): the first government ruled by the working class; the separation of church and state; a push for free, compulsory education; the unprecedented participation of women in government as well as significant advances in gender equality. The Commune, despite Sand's pragmatic objections, resonated with her sympathy for the people and her ideological agenda.

In *Nanon,* Sand displaces her concerns about violence, women's rights, and education that come out of the events of the Paris Commune of 1871 and works through them by returning to the original French Revolution of 1789. Sand's novel manages to remain faithful to the actual events of the French Revolution as well as to its spirit, while at the same time it proposes new ways of thinking about community. *Nanon*'s many communal spaces are at once identifiable on the Cassini map of France and imaginary utopias produced by a fictional text. This doubled space, both real and ideal, both historical novel about 1789 and treatise on 1871, allows Sand to replicate the Commune as site of social innovation and to deny the Commune the quality of event or singular intensity, which would spread violent revolution around the world.[2]

As Nicole Mozet argues in her preface to the novel, while the narrative taken as a whole may be improbable, even utopian, each element of the story is realistic (Sand, *Nanon* 7). Nancy E. Rogers has written that though the history of the French Revolution in Sand's novel is exact, "the disjunction between historical accuracy and the effect of these key events on the peasants of *Nanon,* who are lost in ignorance and without access to accurate news from the capital, creates a distancing, or an ironic stance, on the part of the reader" (Rogers, "Nanon: Novel of Revolution," 138). The peasants of the novel's fictional village are alienated from the events in Paris, but I argue that this very distance from the Revolution, and from what the reader knows about it, allows for a rethinking of the essence of revolution and the possibilities for collective action in the future. Consequently, interpreting the events in the novel requires particular attention not only to the historical context, but especially to the counterfactual, the break with history opened up by the fictional text.

From Shepherdess to Marquise

Nanon combines the realism of detailed descriptions of everyday peasant life with the idealism of what the French Revolution could have been outside of Paris, starting with a shift in narrative perspective. According to Janet Beizer in her article "History's Life Story: *Nanon* as *Histoire de ma vie,*" *Nanon* is one of only a few novels by Sand, out of dozens, to have a first-person woman narrator (4). Sand's novel about revolution also narrates the revolution that allows a peasant girl to become a historical agent and a writing subject. Nanon recalls her own story beginning at the age of twelve, as an orphan who lives with her uncle and two cousins in extreme poverty. The novel is set in a fictional village named Valcreux in the Creuse region near the geographical center of France. Valcreux is dependent on the local monastery, "le moutier," whose ignorant monks serve as incompetent if relatively harmless landlords. Nanon's fortunes change when her uncle decides to buy a sheep, Rosette, and give it to her to raise. Having a purpose in life, another being to care for, inspires

Nanon with a sense of self, hygiene, economy, and eventually public and private space as she follows Rosette around town looking for new pastures. Rosette quickly leads her to the green pastures of the *moutier*'s vast property where Nanon meets a young nobleman, destined to a life of sacrifice as a monk by his family's archaic devotion to primogeniture. The young novice, Émilien de Franqueville, teaches Nanon to read, to use maps, and to challenge received ideas.

News of the events of the Revolution of 1789 eventually filter down to Valcreux, and the peasants learn with joy and incredulity that they are no longer serfs. What began as an eighteenth-century pastoral novel becomes an adventure story as the Revolution speeds up the pace of the novel and complicates the lives of the characters. The monastery is sold off by the state to a bourgeois lawyer from Limoges, Costejoux, but entrusted to the last remaining monk, Père Fructueux, and to Nanon and Émilien. A short idyllic interlude ensues before Émilien's noble ancestry leads to his arrest and condemnation during the Terror. Nanon along with Émilien's former servant Dumont break Émilien out of prison and flee to a remote part of Sand's cherished Berry, in a mystical place named "l'île aux Fades" ("isle of fairies") near the town of Crevant. Another brief few months of isolated bliss follow before Émilien goes off to join the Republican Army, and Nanon returns to Valcreux to make enough money to marry Émilien. She believes that only money can compensate for her lowly social status, given his aristocratic birth. Through a little hard work and especially a very large inheritance after the death of Père Fructueux (who thereby lives up to his name), Nanon amasses a fortune and buys the *moutier* outright from Costejoux. Émilien returns from the war, proud at losing his right forearm and thus merits the right to be a French citizen, Costejoux marries Émilien's snobbish aristocratic sister Louise, and Émilien and Nanon finally marry, have numerous children and live happily ever after as the marquis and marquise de Franqueville. Nanon writes the story in 1850, and an anonymous narrator appends a concluding paragraph to inform the reader that the marquise died in 1864 at the symbolic age of 89, after carrying for the sick.

The novel's narrative arc, as told by Nanon, follows the systematic unraveling of the old order, the *ancien régime* and its replacement by a community of equals led by Nanon. Starting with the fall of the Bastille, which Nanon believes at first was the name of a person who was put in prison, the peasants are liberated from serfdom. The monks themselves are forced to be independent and eventually disband when the *moutier* is sold by the state. The aristocracy, in the form of Émilien's family, discredits itself by emigrating and then actively works to destroy the republic.

When Nanon's uncle dies and Émilien's family flees the country, there is no stable family structure to dictate the actions of the two main protagonists, who, still more or less adolescents, take charge of their community.

Nanon, the poorest girl in town, and Émilien, the youngest in the *moutier*, have no qualifications to lead, no experience, and no authoritative position from which to speak. But during the days of mass hysteria at the start of the Revolution known as *la grande peur*, when peasants all over France feared roving bands of armed vagrants (who never appeared), Nanon and Émilien confront the illusion in order to calm the rest of the town, in the absence of leadership from the monks or the town's mayor. Similar events abound in the novel where Nanon protects the community from an external danger, either real or imagined, because no one else proves able to do so. The spontaneous and courageous Nanon struggling in the face of repeated violence from the outside evokes the image of the popular leaders of the Paris Commune. After Parisian revolts following the capitulation of the provisional government to the Prussian armies, the Commune began unexpectedly on March 18, 1871, when Adolphe Thiers ordered troops to confiscate 400 cannons controlled by the Parisian National Guard on Montmartre. The troops resisted firing on their fellow citizens (many of those defending the cannons were women), and the two commanding generals were shot.[3] Having broken relations with the provisional French government, the Central Committee of the National Guard found itself suddenly the highest authority in Paris. The Central Committee decided to hold elections and, instead of parliamentary representatives, simple delegates were chosen by arrondissement. These delegates, mostly workers with no political experience, could be revoked at any time by their constituents. The Commune was therefore run by those considered by the political class to be "incompetent" and without authority.[4]

The novel appropriates some of the structural specificities of the Commune, such as a greater role for women and rule by the inexperienced, but rejects the singularity of the urban event in favor of a multiplicity of idealized communities situated in no particular place. The greatest danger faced by the Commune was from the "Ruraux" ("Rurals"), the army made up largely of provincials that the provisional government assembled in Versailles to attack Paris. Danger in *Nanon,* however, comes from Paris and from other cities and workers, in the form of ideology.[5] In her travels Nanon is always sure to avoid larger towns. Her short stay in Limoges is marked by the impression that cities are ugly, dirty, and dangerous. In the novel, there is no solidarity among the poor, since city workers cannot speak in the name of peasants; Nanon chides bourgeois revolutionaries like Costejoux who, because they live in the city, only listen to the violent workers:

> Je sais, pour l'avoir entendu assez déplorer chez nous, que c'est le peuple de Paris et des grandes villes qui vous pousse et vous mène, parce que vous demeurez dans les villes, vous autres gens d'esprit et de savoir. Vous croyez connaître le paysan quand vous connaissez l'ouvrier des faubourgs et des banlieues, et, dans le nombre de ces ouvriers moitié paysans, moitié artisans, vous ne faites attention qu'à ceux qui crient et remuent.[6] (231–32)

Nanon can form her community in Valcreux only because of its distance from Paris and other cities, from the bourgeoisie, and from outside political influence. The initial moment of the Revolution proves to be the most liberating for the peasants, when the chains of the old order are broken. Jacobinism, centralization, and the Terror all become linked in the novel to the unfortunate radicalism associated with cities, which threatens the tranquil revolution of the countryside.

The Revolution brings to Valcreux a radical new equality among the peasants, one that is made all the more apparent because the poor village has neither bourgeois nor aristocrats. Its isolation from urban centers, and thus from dangerous political influence, forces the peasants to rely on each other; moreover, the sweeping away of the old order can allow for a young woman like Nanon to exercise power for the first time and to organize a new community along rational lines. Nanon's success is due in large part to her ability to find isolated, abandoned places, the blank spaces on a map, and transform them into viable habitations. The novel's rejection of cities as well as radical politics suggests that utopias neutralize politics in nondescript places far from the historical events of the capital. The novel's utopian, neutral or blank, spaces, while the result of Nanon's tireless efforts, nonetheless reflect the profound changes in the conception of French space during the Revolution.

Mapping a New France

French national space went through drastic and unprecedented transformations at the end of the eighteenth century. The Revolution reapportioned public space by seizing and then selling church property and émigré estates; as *Nanon*'s portrayal of the auction of the "moutier" suggests, the bourgeoisie (embodied in the novel by Costejoux) profited the most, while for the peasants, the absence of church and aristocratic domination desacralized space, subjecting it to the apparently more democratic movement of capital.

Political boundaries, too, were redrawn during the Revolution as large ancient regions were divided into *départements* along natural, geographic borders. Regionalism, it was hoped, would disappear along with political regions, to be replaced by new ties to an abstract and idealized nation. As Nanon herself says, "j'étais devenue moins paysanne, c'est-à-dire, plus Française" (234) ("I had become less of a peasant, which is to say, more French"). A precise image of the whole of France became possible for the first time as the completion of a decades-old cartographic endeavor, the "Carte de l'Académie" or Carte de Cassini, coincided with the founding of the First Republic, thereby greatly facilitating the restructuring of French political space.[7] The Carte de Cassini was the first attempt to map an entire country using very accurate geodesic triangulation. Surveys of France were taken from 1756 to 1789, and the 180 individual maps were published by subscription, successively from 1756 to 1815. By the simple fact of its mathematical cartographic method, the Carte de Cassini relied on a survey of the natural, supposedly immobile, landscape and not on the changeable man-made landscapes of political borders and cities and towns. France could be imagined as a country whose unity was not subject to human history because its natural boundaries were self-evident.

In his *Reflections on the Revolution in France,* Edmund Burke famously argued that human nature is far too complex to be understood by any single rational intellect, and so the French Revolution's blind destruction of tradition in favor of abstract notions could only lead to disaster: "I cannot conceive how any man can have brought himself to that pitch of presumption, to consider his country as nothing but *carte blanche,* upon which he may scribble whatever he pleases."[8] Taking Burke's pronouncement both literally and figuratively, the French Revolution's organization of society and space was at once the unauthorized assumption of divine power by the new government, a new beginning or blank slate that ignored history and tradition, but also a blank map upon which anyone could draw up new connections and new boundaries between places and citizens. Opposed to the conservative and skeptical Burke, Sand's *Nanon* demonstrates that the new blank map born of the Revolution allowed not just the abstract "scribbles" of Parisian elites, but also and especially the more intuitive rewriting of space by peasants, those who have for centuries worked on the land but who could only take possession of it with the Revolution.

Burke's carte blanche critique suggests, however, that sweeping away religion and history in favor of "nature"—whether in the form of natural borders or natural laws—relies on a more or less hidden Enlightenment ideology even as it seeks to eliminate ideology in the abstract. A new map of France cannot help but reveal the paradigms governing its reconfiguration of space. Similarly, as I have tried to show, Sand's novelistic cartography of the French countryside during the Revolution, while plausible, still betrays the ideological signature of its author, who was simultaneously inspired and traumatized by the Paris Commune. *Nanon*'s innocent story of community building and business success proposes an ideological alternative to violent revolution.

Louis Marin's *Utopiques: Jeux d'espaces,* written in 1973 as a reflection on the neutral places of the French university after May '68, offers a conceptual framework for describing utopian texts. Marin asserts that utopia is an ideological critique of ideology, one which consists of the textual creation of a neutral space for the fictional resolution or play of contradictions: "L'utopie est une critique de l'idéologie dominante dans la mesure où elle est une reconstruction de la société présente (contemporaine) par un déplacement et une projection de ses structures dans un discours de fiction" (249) ("Utopia is a critique of the dominant ideology in so far as it is a reconstruction of present or contemporary society by a displacement and projection of its structures in a fictional discourse"). Marin connects utopian discourse as it developed from the sixteenth through the eighteenth centuries to the emergence of modernity, and in particular to the foretelling of a capitalist transformation of the world. Utopia is above all a spatial and textual construction, for Marin: "L'utopie est organisation de l'espace comme texte et discours construit comme espace" (25) ("Utopia is the organization of space as text and discourse constructed as space"). Space is organized around opposing concepts and thus is readable and writable, while the utopian text itself becomes a space that can be navigated. Spatialized, opposing concepts can only coexist side by side; the utopian text produces multiple places (concepts) in a unified project and set in a neutral space of play (10). The nonplace suggested by utopia's etymology is also a neutral or neutralized place, whose referent is a placeholder, real but absent.[9]

Nanon's utopias, like Burke's carte blanche and Marin's utopian neuter, construct places according to Sand's socialist ideology in the blank spaces of the Carte de Cassini. On the textual level, the novel's fictional places can be easily situated on the map, often in places where the map gives no toponym. The novel's places, just like its retelling of historical events, are at once fictional and entirely possible. Within the narrative itself, Nanon repeatedly insists that the understanding of her environment only occurs in tandem with her slow acquisition of reading and writing, as the places around her become translated into text. After she learns to read texts and then maps, she understands how to master space, not only in order to navigate safely the routes of France, but also so that she can work the land for profit. In the *mise en abîme* of the character and the novel, the writing of *Nanon* requires imagining what could have occurred in the blank spaces of a map and the blank spaces of history, whereas Nanon's very survival depends upon finding isolated places where she can forge new ways of being.

The novel's utopias have their origin in Nanon's education and her subsequent exploration of the countryside, which turn space into text (as she learns to describe her world in writing) and text into space (as she memorizes maps in order to walk long distances in unfamiliar territory). On the very first page Nanon humbly observes that she may have difficulty accurately narrating the story of her life and that of her husband because she lacks a formal education:

> Je ne sais pas si je pourrai raconter par écrit, moi qui, à douze ans, ne savais pas encore lire. Je ferai comme je pourrai. Je vais prendre les choses de haut et tâcher de retrouver les premiers souvenirs de mon enfance. Ils sont très confus, comme ceux des enfants dont on ne développe pas l'intelligence par l'éducation.[10] (37)

The paragraph shows more than just modesty regarding Nanon's poor education or her provincial turns of phrase, since reading and writing profoundly transform the way she thinks and perceives her surroundings and imply that language itself structures memory. At the end of chapter 9, Nanon makes a striking announcement about her mastery of language:

> À présent, ceux qui m'auront lue savent que mon éducation est assez faite pour que je m'exprime plus facilement et comprenne mieux les choses qui me frappent. Il m'eût été impossible, durant tout le récit que je viens de faire, de ne pas parler un peu à la manière des paysans; ma pensée n'eût pas trouvé d'autres mots que ceux où elle était alors contenue, et, en me laissant aller à en employer d'autres, je me serais prêté des pensées et des sentiments que je n'avais pas.[11] (116–17)

Nanon's narrative, although retrospective, must follow exactly the course of her education, since her vocabulary expands with her world. The words themselves contain her thoughts and feelings of the past, thoughts whose very simplicity cannot be translated into a more sophisticated, in her words, "bourgeois," language. Even though born a peasant and illiterate until the age of twelve, Nanon progressively changes into an eloquent writer and complex thinker, as she herself remarks and as the increasingly rich vocabulary of her narrative attests.

The correlation between reading, space, and perception becomes clearer when Émilien teaches Nanon how to read in chapter 4. Sitting outside on a wide plateau and looking out on the narrow valley of her hometown for the very first time, Nanon learns the alphabet from Émilien. Afterward, she begins to notice natural beauty for the first time and, remarkably, to see the world as a function of letters:

> Je connus tout mon alphabet ce jour-là, et j'étais contente, en rentrant, d'entendre chanter les grives et gronder la rivière. . . . Le soleil se couchait sur notre droite, les bois de châtaigniers et de hêtres étaient comme en feu. . . . Ça n'était pas comme ça les autres fois. . . . Mes yeux éblouis voyaient des lettres rouges et bleues dans les rayons du couchant.[12] (70)

The new spatial perspective achieved by walking to the crest of the valley combined with what might be described as the afterimage produced from staring intently at the printed letters in Émilien's book provokes in Nanon a transformative vision, where not only rays of sunlight become colored letters, but also where everyday natural objects take on new meaning, as if she had just discovered metaphor ("tout me paraissait *drôle*"—"everything looked *funny* to me"). She notices the sounds of birds and moving water, the color of the prairie, and even compares the golden hue of the stream to the *moutier*'s statue of a virgin. Nanon then looks to the sky for a "sign" that could tell her if she will soon learn to read and is comforted by the sight of one of the thrushes that follows the couple. In a peasant version of Ruskin's pathetic fallacy, the world turns into a prophetic text to be deciphered.

After learning reading, writing, and simple arithmetic, the next subject Nanon asks Émilien to teach her is geography in order to read the maps she glimpsed at the monastery (87). Émilien, as ignorant as she, promises to teach himself geography so he can then teach it to her. Nanon later makes extraordinarily good use of her knowledge of geography and her ability to read maps, not only those of the monastery, but also a copy of the Carte de Cassini in Limoges at Costejoux's residence (149). Before traveling alone she memorizes her route, engraving, as she says, the image in her mind; she thereby internalizes a textual, cartographic space before writing her own itinerary in the spaces of central France and the space of the novel.

Though exact numbers are unavailable, Cassini maps were not best sellers. Each small section was sold separately as it was completed, over a thirty-year period beginning in 1756. Though it is not impossible for both the intellectually and geographically backward monastery and the more sophisticated bourgeois Costejoux to have owned copies of such detailed maps (and particularly Costejoux's Cassini maps), it seems rather coincidental.

In fact, the reference to these particular maps indicates that they not only serve as a mark of narrative authenticity, since the fictional places can be located on the real maps, but that a reading of the maps actually generates the space and the narrative of the novel. George Sand herself owned copies of various Cassini maps. In a letter from 1853 addressed to her son Maurice, she asks for Cassini maps of the Bourbonnais region in order to complete her collection, which she says includes maps of Nohant and part of the Creuse (Sand, *Correspondance XI,* 603–4). The narrative action in *Nanon* takes place entirely within the space represented in the maps in Sand's possession, at least as early as 1853. By paying close attention to the geographical descriptions in the novel and comparing them to the Carte de Cassini, Sand's writing process shows itself to be closely linked to her reading of the empty, uninhabited regions of the maps.

The itineraries traced by Sand in the novel coincide exactly with the spatial representation of the Cassini maps, so much so that at least once she relies on what may be a too literal interpretation of the map. On the way to liberate Émilien from prison in Châteauroux, Nanon explains, "En fait de ce que nous appelons route aujourd'hui, il n'y en avait point du tout de la Châtre à Châteauroux. . . . On s'engageait dans une grande lande où les voies se croisaient au hasard; nous faillîmes nous y perdre" (156) ("In point of fact there was nothing of what we would call today a road from la Châtre to Châteauroux. . . . We headed into a large marsh where paths were crossed haphazardly; we almost got lost").[13] According to the geographer Monique Pelletier, one of the major problems with the Cassini maps observed even at the time of their publication was the overemphasis on major routes to the exclusion of local highways, rendering small towns apparently without any connection: "Les critiques de la partie topographique de la carte de Cassini concernent surtout la figuration des chemins de terre, dont un grand nombre ont étés omis—si bien que de nombreux villages semblent ne pouvoir communiquer, ni entre eux, ni avec une grande route" (Pelletier, 226) ("The criticisms of the topographical portion of the Carte de Cassini are focused especially on the representation of roadways, a large number of which were left out—so much so that numerous villages seem to have no way of communicating with each other or with a major route"). The cartographic simplification and abstraction of space, here as elsewhere, leads to narrative complication as the novel's protagonists must find their own paths through seemingly uncharted territory.

The novel's two principal utopian spaces, Valcreux and the île aux Fades, take on a narrative significance precisely because they exist as cartographic blanks. By their very names, Valcreux being the tautological "hollow valley" and the île aux Fades "fairy island," these fictional places suggest empty and imaginary space, utopian nonplaces. Nanon situates Valcreux very precisely at various times in the novel: "J'avais vu sur la carte qu'à vol d'oiseau, le moutier était à égale distance de Limoges et d'Argenton" (154) ("I had seen on a map that as the crow flies, the *moutier* was equidistant between Limoges and Argenton"). Early on, one of Nanon's cousins exclaims that at twelve leagues, Saint-Léonard is far from Valcreux (51). Mozet asserts (*Nanon,* 28), and a quick look at the Carte de Cassini confirms, that following the novel's indications "Valcreux" would correspond to the village of Ahun, next to the Moutier d'Ahun, which counted 1,850 residents in 1793, and is strangely prominent on the Carte de Cassini for a town its size (see figure 3.1).[14] Ahun is near the geographical center of France, relatively far from any city, and utterly unremarkable except for the almost immaterial, or "hollow," quality of its name, which is composed entirely of vowel and nasal sounds.

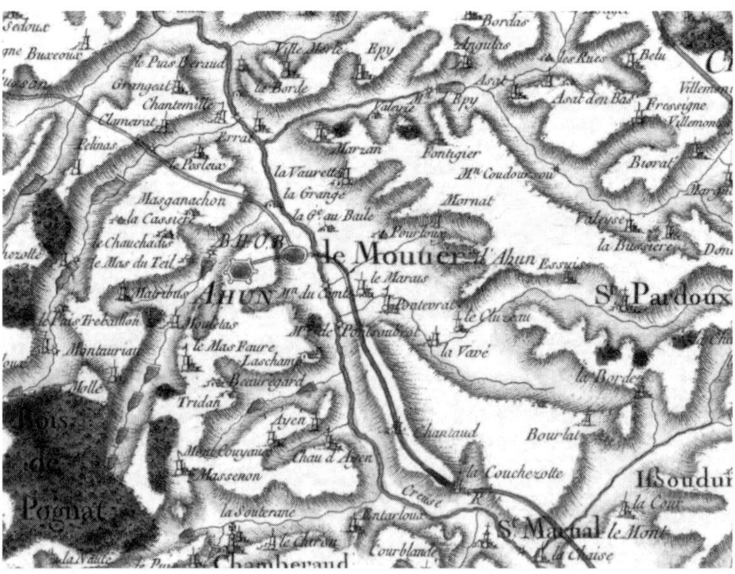

Figure 3.1. Ahun and Its Moutier. Carte générale de la France, dite Carte de Cassini, Detail of no. 12, feuille 56. Courtesy of Library of Congress, Geography and Map Division, G5830 s86 .C3 Vault.

The Cassini maps allow us to locate as well the second utopia of the novel: the île aux Fades, the refuge Nanon, Émilien, and his former servant Dumont find near Crevant in the Berry. Nanon describes the voyage from Châteauroux to this mysterious wilderness: down the Gourdon stream, through the forest of Villemort, across the Bourdesoule River, past the road leading to Aigurande, and then left into a "pays sauvage" ("wild country") (176) (figure 3.2). The uninhabited space of the map in the area indicated by Nanon's travels consists of a woods, a valley, and an oddly formed hill in the shape of a peninsula. The topographical contours of the hill (figure 3.3) inspire the isolated utopia of the île aux Fades, which Nanon compares to the island of Robinson Crusoe, complete with indigenous "savages."

If, on the level of the novel's composition, the utopias can be read as closed communities born from the blank spaces of the Cassini map, on the diegetic level the successive places of the novel all share similar narrative fates that taken as a whole suggest a direct engagement with the events of the Commune, all the while reversing its tragic outcome. Whether Nanon's uncle's cottage, the "moutier," Costejoux's apartment

Figure 3.2. The Bois de Villemort, Crevant, and the area around Sand's fictional "Île aux fades." Carte de Cassini, detail no. 11, feuille 83. Courtesy of Library of Congress, Geography and Map Division, G5830 s86 .C3 Vault.

Figure 3.3. The blank space corresponding to the "Île aux fades." Carte de Cassini, detail of no. 11, feuille 83. Courtesy of Library of Congress, Geography and Map Division, G5830 s86 .C3 Vault.

in Limoges, Émilien's prison in Chateauroux, the hut in the île aux Fades, or Émilien's ancestral castle, the places begin as enclosed fortresses, protecting their inhabitants, sometimes against their will, from the outside world. The "Grande peur" at the start of the novel forces Nanon and her family to lock themselves up in the cottage; at one point the monks throw Père Fructueux in the dungeon; Costejoux locks up Nanon in his apartment for her own safety; and at the île aux Fades the three refugees avoid all contact with strangers for fear of being discovered. It is as if the characters are continually under siege, but in almost every case the siege is only imaginary. After a few days, the "Grande peur" is shown to be based on a rumor; after the mayor puts some pressure on the monks they not only release Fructueux but make him the prior; the peasants around the île aux Fades show themselves to be just friendly peasants who are superstitious of the Druidic ruins that surround the refugees' settlement. Once the danger is seen to be illusory, or at least has passed, in every case a healthy work ethic returns and the characters set about cultivating the land for maximum productivity, always under the direction of Nanon. The enclosed spaces thus begin as defensive barriers and end up as ideal, self-contained communities. Nanon emphasizes the point by saying that Valcreux was no longer a "paroisse" ("parish") but a "commune"—a change in terminology certainly not unique to Valcreux during the Revolution, but one that had a strong resonance in 1871, since the rallying point of the Commune was to claim for Paris the same status as "commune" that other cities and towns in France enjoyed (76).[15]

The novel's cartographic intertext, the Carte de Cassini, guarantees an accurate historical and geographic reference point for the narrative's utopian places. But by exploiting the maps' empty spaces, the neutral areas devoid of place names or, in the case of the île aux Fades, topographical signs, the text superposes onto the historical space of the French Revolution an alternative space that collapses multiple times. While the novel as a whole constantly evokes the Commune of 1871, Nanon's retrospective narrative weaves back and forth not only between events in her own life, but also reaches back to the distant past. The *moutier* at Valcreux resembles a medieval monastery as much as one from the late eighteenth century; even after the Revolution, Nanon transforms the *moutier* into a communal and agrarian enterprise that combines the original functions of a monastery with nineteenth-century agricultural discourse. Likewise the île aux Fades provides refuge to Nanon, Émilien, and Dumont because the local peasants are afraid of the ancient remains left by the Druids. Nanon converts a dolmen into a shelter and begins to cultivate the surrounding land, thereby incorporating traditions of the ancient past and simultaneously disproving local superstitions. She recounts how much the area changes decades after the events she describes, now that the region has been modernized and people circulate freely across the land. Revolution in *Nanon* comes about by tracing new paths in overlooked areas, by writing in the margins of history.

Nanon, or the Neutral Subject

Like the novel's isolated communities, drawn in the interstices of the map of France, Nanon herself exists between categories. She serves as catalyst for the events in the novel and as a negotiator between the other, more ideologically rigid characters. The communities formed in the text, from her uncle's home to the "moutier," from the île aux Fades to the Franqueville château, hold together disparate, even antagonistic, individuals around a center formed by Nanon's neutrality. The novel's more theoretical or political moments all consist of long conversations between the rational and coolheaded Nanon and a more zealous, if often misguided, friend: in some of the novel's most passionate exchanges, Nanon discusses the nature of revolution, violence, and social change with her peasant uncle, Père Fructueux, the bourgeois revolutionary Costejoux, and of course her friend and husband the reformed aristocrat Émilien. Through these conversations, Nanon is able slowly to form, though not impose, a consensus, namely, that the end does not justify the means and that a lasting revolution cannot come from violence. Peasants, servants, bourgeois, monks, and aristocrats all cohabitate, sometimes more and sometimes less peacefully, in Nanon's utopian community, without losing any of their diversity of opinion or identity.

Nanon's own identity, however, does not fit easily into nineteenth-century social categories, a fact revealed by George Sand's hesitation about the novel's title. As Mozet notes, Sand refers in her letters to two different titles, "la paysanne parvenue" ("The Upstart Peasant Woman") and "la Marquise de Franqueville" (*Nanon,* 10–11), both of which focus on only one aspect of Nanon's narrative trajectory. Throughout her story, Nanon insists on her humble origins even though her financial situation and her education have her rise through the social ranks. The last few pages, narrated in the third person, confirm that the marquise still dressed in peasant attire despite her bourgeois fortune and noble title (287). Instead of remaining a simple peasant or becoming an aristocrat, she embodies all social classes at the same time as if she were an allegory for France itself. As she says describing her own education, "j'étais devenue moins paysanne, c'est-à-dire, plus Française" (234) ("I had become less of a peasant, which is to say, more French"). One is not born French, apparently, one becomes French, and Nanon's expanding knowledge of history and geography, along with her role in forming communities, make of her the ideal citizen.

While she plans her adventurous rescue of Émilien among other exploits by memorizing the complex Carte de Cassini, Nanon cannot travel freely on the roads of France. As she repeatedly remarks, it was not at all safe for a young girl of seventeen or eighteen to walk for days unaccompanied in regions far away from her own. Walking, what for Indiana constituted a mad attempt at escape (and was interpreted by Ralph as suicidal), is for Nanon not only a proof of her commitment to Émilien but also a way for her to gain firsthand knowledge of the new nation. Her walks start off relatively limited as she follows her sheep Rosette looking for pasture. Soon Émilien accompanies her and they explore the town and the region as he shares what little he knows about the world. Her first long trip, to Limoges to visit Costejoux, takes her two days on foot, and though she can intuit the way, she decides to look at the map: "J'avais dans la nuit calqué sur une carte tout le pays que j'avais à parcourir" (139) ("During the night I had traced on a map all the area I had to cover"). Already her travels are described in masculine terms, since the first day she says she walked as far as a man would (139).

Her next journey, following Émilien's carriage as he is transferred to another prison, is considerably more dangerous, as the coachmen make remarks about her beauty. Similar to the attention given to Indiana as she traveled by ship to France, Nanon's gender and her looks attract unwanted attention once she has left her native region and travels as an unknown young woman:

> Pourtant, j'avais une inquiétude pour la suite de mon voyage. La manière dont on me regardait et me parlait était nouvelle pour moi, et je m'avisais

> enfin de l'inconvénient d'être une jeune fille toute seule sur les chemins. À Valcreux, où l'on me savait sage et retenue, personne ne m'avait fait souvenir que je n'étais plus une enfant, et je m'étais trop habituée à ne pas compter mes années. . . . Je voyais enfin dans mon sexe un obstacle et des périls auxquels je n'avais jamais songé. . . . La beauté attire toujours les regards, et j'aurais voulu me rendre invisible.[16] (152)

A week later, on her next voyage to meet Émilien, she asks his former servant Dumont to accompany her, and she disguises herself as his adolescent nephew (156). For the next few chapters she succeeds at making herself almost invisible by cross-dressing as a boy named Lucas (157). Nanon's masculine attire, reminiscent of course of Sand's own youth, represents more than a simple disguise as she begins to enjoy a new freedom of movement. Later, after she helps Émilien escape from prison and they hide in the île aux Fades, she notices how self-sufficient she has become: "J'étais devenue, depuis que j'étais garçon, adroite et forte de mes mains pour les ouvrages de garçon" (179) ("I had become, ever since I started being a boy, skilled with strong hands for boy's work"). Just as she effortlessly makes the transition from peasant to bourgeoise to marquise, Nanon has no emotional or practical difficulty dressing and acting like a boy.

The paradox of Nanon's extraordinary neutrality, or even her identity as a neuter beyond gender, while suggested throughout the text, becomes explicit near the end of the novel when Costejoux declares to her: "Vous êtes une exception, vous, une très remarquable exception. Vous n'êtes ni une femme ni un homme, vous êtes l'un et l'autre avec les meilleures qualités des deux sexes" (229) ("You are an exception, you, a very remarkable exception. You are neither a woman nor a man, you are both with the best qualities of each gender"). Costejoux's statement, while obviously problematic from a feminist perspective, makes evident how Nanon as a character exists in a neutral area, since her identity is constructed in the space between categories. For Costejoux, she is "neither" woman "nor" man; the negativity inherent in her name (Na*non*) reinforces her quality as neuter (*ne-uter,* "neither one"). Nanon's protean subjectivity, in its positive dynamism emerging from negative space, is both perfectly adapted to the changing events of the Revolution and to a text that superimposes political contexts from different time periods onto the same textual space.

Nanon personifies utopia by her neutrality, by her idealistic hope of avoiding violent conflict, by her devotion to community building, and by the chiasmus of space and discourse generated from her many travels across central France. Yet the end of the novel shares with the end of

Indiana a troubling silence from the woman protagonist. While Indiana's silence at the end of that novel, as I suggest, might be interpreted as a mirroring of the hidden omniscient narrator (who in turn begins to resemble Indiana), Nanon's silence is solely political:

> Ils [Émilien and Costejoux] n'ont pas été dupes de la révolution de Juillet. Ils n'ont pas été satisfaits de celle de Février. Moi qui, depuis bien longtemps, ne m'occupe plus de politique—je n'en ai pas le temps—je ne les ai jamais contredits, et, si j'eusse été sûre d'avoir raison contre eux, je n'aurais pas eu le courage de le leur dire, tant j'admirais la trempe de ces caractères du passé.[17] (286)

Nanon's pronouncement carries her neutrality to what seems to be its extreme, abandoning all politics in order to work and in deference to the men in her life. The opposite of the *pétroleuses* (the stereotypical image of the enraged women of the Commune who, according to Versaillais propaganda, set fire to the city's monuments), Nanon refuses to give up her work for the political cause of the day, since "she doesn't have the time." As a woman involved both in negotiation between factions and dedicated to her own business ventures (*négoce* in French, *negotium* in Latin meaning business, both come from *neg-otium,* the negation of leisure), she implicitly condemns politics as leisure time. Moreover, the political passion and ideologies of Émilien and Costejoux have solidified into part of their personalities; Nanon seems to mock them gently by her fear of contradicting such caricatural figures from the "past." Politics, as the Communards argued, is not the exclusive realm of the leisure class, but belongs to all those who take part in their community. Nanon's activities such as farming the land and helping the sick and the poor constitute an extraordinary amount of labor; indeed, she dies of fatigue at the age of eighty-nine while caring for the sick during an epidemic (286). In the wake of the carnage of the Terror of 1793 (and the even greater carnage of May 1871), *Nanon*'s call for nonviolence beyond ideology and for a return to work may be not only the most politically responsible of acts but the ultimate paradox: a pragmatic utopia.

PART IV

Branching Off: Genealogy and Map in the *Rougon-Macquart*

C'est un de mes principes qu'il ne faut pas *s'écrire*. L'artiste doit être dans son oeuvre comme Dieu dans la création, invisible et tout-puissant; qu'on le sente partout, mais qu'on ne le voie pas.*

—Gustave Flaubert, letter to Mlle Leroyer de Chantepie

Moi, je tâche de travailler le plus tranquillement possible, mais je renonce à voir clair dans ce que je fais, car plus je vais et plus je suis convaincu que nos oeuvres en gestation échappent absolument à notre volonté.†

—Émile Zola, letter to Huysmans

In examining Stendhal's and Nerval's novel maps, we have seen how intensely personal and autobiographical works invent layered spaces and new subjects. Likewise, in Sand's fiction, characters imagine idealized, liberating spaces for women and men, spaces that could nonetheless exist in the real world. These works exploit a confusion between author and narrator and between real places and fictional spaces, simulating a new subject who is both preserved in an archival text and yet susceptible to the play of language. In contrast to these texts centered on individuals

*It is one of my principles that one should never *write oneself*. The artist should be in his work like God in creation, invisible and all-powerful; may he be felt everywhere, but seen nowhere.

†I strive to work the most peacefully possible, but I give up trying to see clearly into what I am doing, for the further I go the more I am convinced that our works in preparation absolutely escape our will.

who fashion space in their own image, the novels in Émile Zola's monumental series the *Rougon-Macquart* portray an entire society as it consumes itself over the course of the Second Empire. The full title of the twenty-novel series, *Les Rougon-Macquart: Histoire naturelle et sociale d'une famille sous le Second Empire* (*The Rougon-Macquart: The Natural and Social History of a Family Under the Second Empire*), underscores that each individual character must represent at the same time the family (of the Rougon or Macquart branch), a component of Second Empire society ("Histoire sociale"), and a universal or natural law ("Histoire naturelle"). Characters take on meaning not as unique individual subjects but as examples of larger social, political, economic, or biological phenomena; they are ultimately the objects of Zola's novel experiment. Characters, the "fonctionnaires" ("functionaries" or "civil servants") of the naturalist novel, emerge out of their specific milieu, they are "territorialized" by the textual spaces that produce them.[1]

If the *Rougon-Macquart*'s characters are in some sense subject to and not architects of the spaces they inhabit, if there is no "novel subject" in the series, then Zola's naturalist project seems to run counter to the novel maps of his romantic predecessors Stendhal, Nerval, and Sand. In the next two chapters, however, I argue that reading Zola's extensive notes for the series (referred to as the *dossiers préparatoires*) alongside the novels themselves exposes the artificial separation between note and novel, real document and fictional construct, author and text. The dossiers record Zola's creative process, containing the subjective and artistic origin of the "scientific" novel project and separating it from the narrative itself. Unlike earlier realists such as Stendhal, Zola did not insert a narrative "je" into his fictional texts. On a superficial level at least, no authorial presence, or even narrative stand-in, structures the fictional narrative, and yet in the dossiers Zola is everywhere present, describing his firsthand experiences, recording in detail his research, appropriating "his" characters. Just as remarkable as the abundance of "je" and "moi" in the dossiers compared to their absence in the novels, an absolute partition divides the factual origins of the novels meticulously preserved in the dossiers from the fictional novels themselves.

The author's scientific writing method along with the existence of the visual, factual dossier must be made public (in theoretical publications by Zola himself and by those select friends who saw the dossiers), but the textual, fictional novels erase their material origins as if they were spontaneous productions of the Second Empire society they represent. The *Rougon-Macquart* derives its driving force and its representational authority from the vast archive that makes up the *dossiers préparatoires*;

every observation about an aspect of society, every event, every place and character in the novel, it may be inferred, have their origin in a document somewhere in the unpublished dossiers. Inferred but not known by the reading public, since the dossiers were kept first at Zola's home, then safely stored and archived at the Bibliothèque nationale de France after his death.[2] These notes guaranteed for posterity, and even perhaps for Zola himself, an assurance of the authenticity, the reality behind his fictional works. Moreover, the dossiers were kept in excellent condition, whereas the preliminary drafts of his manuscripts were systematically destroyed.[3] The *Rougon-Macquart* exhibits, both at the level of diegesis and at the level of the novel's genesis, a severe case of "archive fever"; origins must be conserved as the foundation of authority and hidden from view to guard against the exposure of secrets and to preserve the future from the weight of the past.

In the first chapter, "Zola and the Contradictory Origins of the Novel," I take a close look at Zola's contradictions as theoretician of naturalism, as visual thinker and writer of novels, as scientific observer and literary experimenter. Drawing from Jacques Rancière's notion of the contradictions of what he terms the "aesthetic regime," I argue that the separation of visual representation from the written word reproduces itself at every level, both within the dossiers themselves and between the dossiers and the novels. In the unrepresentable gap between note and novel, and document and fiction, authorial control gives way to chance and the unpredictability of figural language. By inscribing himself so completely in the text of the dossiers, and thus on the side of fact and observation, Zola recuperates his loss of authorial control over the fiction and asserts, in vain, the novel's subservience to the dossier.

In the second chapter, "Mapping Creative Destruction in Zola," I trace how the novels reproduce the same dynamic of authority founded on hidden documents as the dossiers, their archival origin/other. Whether the desacralized cemetery of the "Aire Saint-Mittre" in the first novel or the destruction of Pascal's research on heredity in the last, whether Napoleon III's secret plan for transforming Paris in *La Curée* or his lack of battle plan in *La Débâcle,* power hinges on the successful manipulation of archives and origins, actual or invented. Like the gap between note and novel, the difference between archival referent and representation leads to speculation, in both senses of conjecture and financial gamble, as the absent documents hold simultaneously the secrets of the past and those of the future; the repressed past preserved in the archive returns in the present as a destructive force, leaving in its wake new spaces for new subjects. I show how, at the end of the novel series, the blaze that consumes all of

Pascal's genealogical notes on his family (the narrative equivalent of the *dossiers préparatoires*) spares only the indecipherable Rougon-Macquart family tree, a document that closes the cycle in a teleological confusion, since it represents the starting point for Zola's project and the end point of Pascal's hereditary research. The Rougon-Macquart genealogical tree, a figure combining textual and visual, factual and fictional elements, confirms that meaning in the novel is born from a novel map where the frontiers between reality and fiction are continually shifting.

Chapter Seven

Zola and the Contradictory Origins of the Novel

Naturalism, as Zola theorized it, merged for the first time in literary history the realist ambition of depicting social interactions with the scientific examination of what underlies those interactions. Mimesis surrenders to analysis as the naturalist novelist discovers the true cause of human behavior hidden under the surface of polite nineteenth-century bourgeois society. No longer Stendhal's mirror dragged along a muddy road, the novel, in Zola's telling, would be a precise observational tool, akin to a scientist's laboratory. The author's detailed and objective study of a given milieu supported by the laws of heredity and psychology produce a novel that can both represent the logical outcome of any narrative situation and explain its scientific necessity. When milieu, as an amalgam of space, class, and historical time (derived in part from Hippolyte Taine's "race, milieu, moment"), defines the very essence of characters, the naturalist author merely juxtaposes one milieu to another and deduces the rational dénouement. The author becomes a scientist who observes phenomena and then experiments in the language of the text. By affirming the experimental aspect of fiction writing, Zola shows that naturalism does not blindly copy or assimilate science, but practices it; carefully planned novels simulate real-life situations just as laboratory experiments selectively test one hypothesis at a time. The *Rougon-Macquart* follows the vicissitudes of one simulated family, but the laws of human behavior may be applicable to Second Empire France and beyond.

In his preface to the first novel in the series, *La Fortune des Rougon,* and so to the series as a whole, Zola announces his theory of the novel and the method to his creative process, which will be focused on the analysis of a group of individuals who appear dissimilar but who are "intimately tied together," since "heredity has its laws, like gravity" (Zola, *Les Rougon-Macquart,* 1:3). Zola's novels will try to solve the "double question of temperaments and milieus" that determine people's actions. The novels must be grounded in physiological laws and historical accuracy to reveal truths both natural and social. The recent disastrous loss of the Franco-Prussian War and the fall of the Second Empire months before the novel's publication offer proof of the validity of Zola's method and the inevitability of such a historical outcome in a world governed by natural laws (1:4). Zola claims to have collected over the preceding three years all the documents needed for such an extensive study, and thus affirms the existence of a separate archive of documents at the origin of the novels (1:3). In the two short pages of the preface Zola proclaims the theoretical foundation for his novels as a scientific and historical project spanning many years and many novels based on reliable documents in the author's possession.

Equally present, however, is the author's own signature, his ownership not just of ideas but of a world he has created. The first word, "Je," is repeated eleven times and accompanied for good measure by "mon oeuvre" and "ma pensée." Napoléon III's fall, while inevitable in Zola's estimation, was also a dramatic necessity "dont j'avais besoin comme artiste" ("which I needed as an artist") (1:4). The objects of the novelistic experiment become puppets in the author's hands:

> Et quand je tiendrai tous les fils, quand j'aurai entre les mains tout un groupe social, je ferai voir ce groupe à l'oeuvre, comme acteur d'une époque historique, je le créerai agissant dans la complexité de ses efforts, j'analyserai à la fois la somme de volonté de chacun de ses membres et la poussée générale de l'ensemble.[1] (1:3)

Zola's preface alternates between a scientific vocabulary (analysis, social group, historical period) and an artistic, even theatrical, vocabulary (actor, create, drama, artist) with the effect of subsuming the whole of his work under one artistically new and scientifically valid vision. The preface amounts to a pact offered to the reader and signed by the author, who stands by the soundness of his method and implicitly acknowledges that the novel must pass through the filter or "screen" of his vision.[2]

Gustave Flaubert, in an otherwise enthusiastic letter to Zola, criticizes his younger colleague's inclusion of the preface to *La Fortune des Rougon:* "Je n'en blâme que la préface. Selon moi, elle gâte votre oeuvre qui est si impartiale et si haute. Vous y dîtes votre secret, ce qui est trop candide, chose que dans ma poétique (à moi) un romancier n'a pas le droit de faire" (*Les Rougon-Macquart,* 1:1541) ("I only disapprove of the preface. For me, it spoils your work, which is otherwise so impartial and so lofty. You give away your secret, and that is too naive, something which in my (own) poetics a novelist has no right doing"). Flaubert neatly summarizes the difference between the two authors. *La Fortune des Rougon*, like the other novels in the series, erases all signs of authorial presence, suggesting an objectivity and a distance from what is represented. The preface attached to the work, however, reintroduces the figure of the author and allows the reader to see the cogs in the textual machine. For Flaubert, a novel's preparation, its documentation and all the evidence of the author's research, must remain a trade secret, since presumably the novel must speak for itself. But Zola's preface does not tell the reader any secrets, it makes known that there is a secret, namely, the novel's factual basis in science and history recorded in a collection of documents hidden from view.

Flaubert's negative reaction to Zola's preface and to his theories in general reflects quite accurately the critical consensus until fairly recently. When not rejecting them outright, critics spared Zola's novels only by banishing the theory behind them. Even at the time, contemporary writers were suspicious of the scientific laws Zola promoted, and they ridiculed the notion of experimentation in the novel, since the outcome of the experiment was already known by the author (which assumes that authors control the meaning of their texts). Any number of reasons can be put forth to save the novels from the potentially embarrassing (and certainly dated) science found in Zola's theory: Zola's writing practice, as shown by genetic critics, does not entirely correspond to his purported method; Zola only represented scientific knowledge of the time, however erroneous it appears today; Zola did not actually believe the theories he trumpeted, but used them as part of an ingenious marketing campaign.[3] All of these assertions are convincing, but rely on a denial of Zola's theoretical and literary innovation: a scientifically and historically researched novel series with a documentary archive as long as the novels themselves. Zola's naturalism professed, in word if not always in deed, a narrative derived not from literary history and novelistic convention but from natural history and scientific practice.

The laws of heredity and the observations of social milieu described by Zola, whether true or not (and in his notes Zola hinted at his indifference to the question), generate new narrative effects, almost mythical in their sweeping vision, that can play out in an infinite number of combinations without repeating.[4] When social history and heredity become a new narratology, the novel's very structure resembles the society it depicts; Napoleon III's fall is a social, physiological, and narrative inevitability. The textual motor, as Michel Serres described it, finds its fuel, its stock, in its own subject matter (and I would add, its reserves in the dossier), consuming itself in an inexorable, entropic blaze.[5] Only by juxtaposing Zola's theoretical impulse to the *dossiers préparatoires* and to the novels themselves can we understand the complex, even contradictory, relationship between the author's aesthetic, documentary, and scientific projects.

Rancière, Zola, and the "Mute" Dossiers

The philosopher Jacques Rancière provides a useful framework for contextualizing Zola's novel project in the literary history of the nineteenth century. Instead of proposing a chronology of successive literary movements in opposition to each other that lead inevitably to modernism and postmodernism, Rancière argues that all literature defines itself internally as a struggle between the autonomy of the written word, as the indifference of subject matter to its expression, and a more mystical equivalence of all forms of expression found in material objects. Each "new" literary movement only reshuffles the terms of the original contradiction. Beyond a conception of naturalism as a stop on the road between romanticism and modernism, Zola's naturalist theories and novelistic practices reflect an attempt to harness the latent poetic energy of things in the service of a representation of society.

In *La Parole muette: Essai sur les contradictions de la littérature* (1998) as well as in many other works, Rancière describes the paradigm shift away from a "representational regime of art" toward an "aesthetic or literary regime of art" that occurred around the end of the eighteenth century. This aesthetic revolution introduced the notion of "literature" as an art that abandons the hierarchy of representational genres and defines itself exclusively in relation to language and the act of writing. Playfully mocking his and anyone else's inability to answer Jean-Paul Sartre's question "What is literature?" Rancière shows that literature has no object, no "what," but is rather a "*mode historique de visibilité des oeuvres de l'art d'écrire*" (13) ("*historical mode of visibility of works of the art of writing*"). Literature conceptualizes the very possibility of visualizing writing as an art form. It is historical since this mode of seeing did not exist before, roughly speaking, the French Revolution.[6] Literature is therefore not some spiritual and transcendental experiment. At the same time, as it has no inherent object, no conventions governing what is appropriate to represent, it cannot be defined by any strictly social or directly political context. Refusing the extremes of Sartre's idea of literature as political engagement and Maurice Blanchot's idea of literature as the exteriority of language (a concept we will return to later in this chapter), Rancière proposes that literature functions precisely because it combines these two contradictory elements inherent to the alienating nature of language and text.

Ignoring other ways of dividing and classifying literature by movements or schools such as romanticism, symbolism, or realism, Rancière proposes a different division, that of a preliterary regime of representation and the literary or aesthetic regime of art, whose visibility depends upon a seemingly never-ending list of irreconcilable dualities. Literature's contradictions, far from being negative, are described as productive tensions; accepting Rancière's argument, it becomes apparent that the different movements, schools, and authors of the nineteenth and twentieth centuries have in fact produced more and ever-changing contradictions in their impossible search for an organic literature in harmony with society and nature. Literature becomes the art of writing beginning in the nineteenth century by renouncing the primacy of fictional representation, which Rancière links to the tradition of belles lettres in the seventeenth and eighteenth centuries. In the classical imagination, every genre has its natural subject matter and specific generic conventions; fictional representation reproduced the hierarchies that structure society. With the advent of the aesthetic regime of art and the abandonment of appropriate subjects of representation, anything can become the subject of literature; now "everything speaks" or has a voice in writing, even inanimate objects. As his primary example, Rancière cites Victor Hugo's novel *Notre-Dame de Paris,* where the subject of the fiction is not an aristocratic tragic hero or a comic peasant but a stone building. Hugo famously claims that the printing press kills or takes the place of architecture ("Ceci tuera cela"). It can only do so because the stone of the cathedral can also signify or "speak," and thereby become absorbed as the "material" of the novel.

While it allows any object to become the speaking subject of a text, this same rejection of generic boundaries promotes the unchecked, democratic circulation of meaning so abhorred by Plato. The ties between language and its referents are loosened by a "parole muette," the written word devoid of any human voice or any stable meaning. The concept of writing for Rancière becomes doubled, self-contradictory: on the one hand writing is a hieroglyph where an idea is inscribed through form, and on the other hand the word becomes "orphaned" of any body or stable meaning (14). Literature is divided between the language of forms and things and the language of ideas (174); it is both "chatty" and "mute," both symbolic of what Rancière calls "the poeticity of the world" and "floating" without any fixed meaning (172); it is caught between "the indifference of what is written and the necessity of form" (154). While his text clarifies how literature is perceived by dismissing the differences and divisions between literature's various manifestations over the last two hundred years, Rancière invents, or demonstrates how texts have invented, countless and shifting new divisions, paradoxes, and partitions, not between different conceptions of literature, but within texts themselves. At each text's origin lies the failed attempt to bridge a divide, and the failure even to represent this origin as seamless.

At the same time as he argues that literature, as framed in the nineteenth century, is intrinsically contradictory, Rancière makes the surprising claim that naturalism as conceived by Émile Zola offers the novel form a compromise between the representational primacy of fiction (in the service of a political, republican agenda) and the antirepresentational play of literary expression. Zola's novels, according to this argument, would not produce contradictions or even seek to resolve them, but rather would work to structure the text so as to hide the conflicting origins of literature. Rancière's comment on Zola comes in chapter 9 of *La Parole muette* when he contrasts Stéphane Mallarmé's negative assessment of Flaubert's *Bouvard et Pécuchet* to his favorable reception of Zola:

> La description du boudoir de Nana, comme celle des fleurs du Paradou, des étalages des Halles ou des vitraux du *Rêve* applique, dans l'"égalité' des sujets, l'identité du principe d'expression. Zola, qui ne s'est jamais posé le problème d'une poéticité de la prose, obéit encore au principe de symbolicité qui fonde la poétique romantique, il fait parler les choses à la manière de *Notre-Dame de Paris*. Et ce principe d'expressivité vient doubler sans problème la narration à l'ancienne, comme la rime de l'idéal en toute réalité. Le naturalisme donne à la forme romanesque le moyen d'être la forme du compromis: compromis entre les principes contradictoires de la poétique nouvelle, et, par là, compromis entre l'ancienne et la nouvelle poétique, entre le primat représentatif de la fiction et le principe antireprésentatif d'expression.[7] (121–22)

This rather dense passage is made all the more confusing since it is difficult to tell at times whether Rancière is expressing his own judgment or is expressing Mallarmé's, given the free indirect discourse so common in Rancière's work. If Rancière is speaking for Mallarmé, his interpretation seems skewed. At the end of the passage on Zola's compromise, a footnote refers the reader to the enthusiastic letter Mallarmé wrote to Zola on March 18, 1876, after reading Zola's *Son Excellence Eugène Rougon,* one of the few novels in the series that lacks long lists of "speaking objects" à la *Notre-Dame de Paris*. Mallarmé's letter does not entirely correspond to Rancière's appraisal. It relates how the poet read the novel twice: the first time all in one sitting, as he says "à l'ancienne," like a "theatrical play," and the second time fragment by fragment as a person would who is caught up in the speed of the modern world. The novel, according to Mallarmé, is adaptable to both styles or rhythms of reading. Instead of a compromise of contradictions, for Mallarmé the forces and drives of Zola's sweeping narrative create a modulated time, one that allows for both textual detail and mythic grandeur.

Reading the passage as Rancière's own critique, Zola's naturalism would be a double compromise, the first between the contradictions within literature, which is to say between on the one hand a poetry found within banal objects and on the other a mute language of the written word. The second compromise, related to the first, would be between the "old" narration, which I take to be one from the "representative regime of art," and a newer, literary narration that would be antirepresentational. Zola's project for the *Rougon-Macquart* is representational because it seeks to describe how the laws of heredity and milieu determine the trajectory of a family during the Second Empire, while at the same time its "poetic" descriptions of objects and milieus, which belong to the new form of literature, become indistinguishable from the old representational regime. The long lists of everyday objects, technical vocabulary, and colorful ethnographic detail, which form the evidence of the naturalist's research, inevitably take on a poetic quality of their own, independent from their representational context. As Rancière shows, Zola's journalistic pretensions to the truth take nothing away from the poetic force of his descriptions (46).

Here as elsewhere, Rancière wants to deny that Zola's aesthetic or literary compromise allows for an account or understanding of what he calls "political dissensuality," the essence of politics being the capture of a share of power by a formerly marginalized group not through consensus but through "dissensus." Political dissensuality in literature has nothing to do with a representation of the politically oppressed, but rather with how a text allows innovative reconceptualizations of what is common to all, in his terms "le partage du sensible" (the partition, division, or sharing of the perceptible). Rancière thus claims that Virginia Woolf's novels are more effective for thinking politics than what he calls Zola's "social epics."

But concretely, how does the *Rougon-Macquart* amount to a compromise? I would like to argue *against* Rancière's notion of a compromise, with its implication that Zola was simply attenuating the extreme positions of literature's opposing tendencies, and *for* Rancière's concept of literature as contradiction. Zola's compromise does not involve a resolution of the contradictions of literature, or even a hybrid novel form embracing elements of both belles lettres and literature as defined by Rancière, but rather, the displacement of representation in the form of the hidden, or "mute," *dossiers préparatoires* for the *Rougon-Macquart*. It is as if the dossiers must be silenced in order to guard against the inevitability of the mute speech of the novel's text. The dossiers, which themselves contain representational documents (notes and drawings), can be thought of as the repository for the artifacts of representation; their material, sequestered and separated from the novels, remains silent, as if Victor Hugo had actually killed the cathedral with his novel.

The dossiers form a parallel text, both representational and visual, containing their own aesthetic and their own fictions, which the novels do not always incorporate. The passage from note to novel sacrifices visual representation and the guarantee of documentary evidence in favor of the freedom of verbal expression within representation. If, as elsewhere in *La Parole muette*, Rancière is correct in saying that literature "est en son principe la séparation du voir et du dire" (165) ("is in principle/at its origin the separation of the seen and the spoken"), the separation of visual representation in Zola's notes from the literary text of his novels suggests that Zola's compromise actually generates the productive contradictions of a literature which cannot be reduced to its competing representational or poetic engagements.

Partitioning the Dossiers

Unearthing the *dossiers préparatoires* for the *Rougon-Macquart*, making the silenced or muted documents speak, exposes the contradictory origins of the novel series as a poetic and scientific project. Zola's notes, like Rancière's argument, progress through a succession of partitions that literally and metaphorically separate the poetic from the representational, and the written from the visual. The simultaneous juxtaposition and separation of contradictions only serves to heighten the contrasting elements of the literary paradox, as we will see by examining the role of the visual in the notes, and in particular the first maps found in the dossiers.

The 10,000 or so pages of Zola's *dossiers préparatoires* contain countless sketches, diagrams, maps, and lists of observations that attempt to convey a one-to-one correspondence between objects and linguistic representation. They correspond perhaps to the "base indestructible" or "des faits vrais" he mentions in his essay *Le Roman expérimental*.[8] Besides notes about plot and character development, the dossiers contain about 150 hand-drawn sketches and maps by the hand of Zola himself. There are maps of city streets (*Une Page d'amour, Germinal*), maps of the battle-field at Sedan (*La Débâcle*), and even maps of the Middle East (*L'Argent*), along with layouts of dinner tables (*Nana*), department stores (*Au Bonheur des Dames*), and countless other visual documents. These dossiers serve as the factual, observational double to Zola's novelistic experiment; they are visual, in the manner of Stendhal's ichnographic maps, compared to the novels, which are inevitably rooted in the play of language. Though Zola claimed in his preface to have amassed all the documentation necessary in the three years preceding the publication of the first novel, as the *Rougon-Macquart* series progressed, the number of notes taken for each novel increased exponentially: for *La Fortune des Rougon* there are only 111 folios, whereas for *La Débâcle* there are 1,250 (Becker, preface to Zola, *La Fabrique des Rougon-Macquart,* 1:10).

A meticulous organization evolved over the course of the project; each novel would eventually have a dossier containing notes classified into the following sections, "Ébauche" (rough outline), "Personnages" (characters), "Plans" (meaning variously outline, project, or map), then the notes documenting Zola's research. These classifications also function as divisions within the dossiers themselves, sorting out the fictional from the documentary, even as these boundaries were highly porous. In his thorough study of the visual imaginary structuring the *dossiers préparatoires,* Olivier Lumbroso argues that Zola was a visual thinker who framed reality in geometric terms.[9] According to Lumbroso, Zola's creative process habitually began with the invention of a frame ("le cadre") that not only defined the limits of a fictional place, but stratified characters, arranged the novels' chapters, and organized the dossiers themselves; furthermore, the geometric frame not only defines the places and the chapters, but extends, to use Rancière's term, to the novels' poeticity, since geometric figures abound in the novels (Lumbroso, *Zola: La plume et le compas*, 37–38). Likewise, the words on the page or the order of the chapters form visual puns, "calligrammes," where the repressed visual image returns displaced in the text (267–79). Far from imposing two distinct and noncommunicating regions, Zola's frames set up a hidden network of internal cross-references, where (fictional) word and (documented) image continually change places.

The first two sketches drawn by Zola himself in the *dossiers préparatoires* for *La Fortune des Rougon* establish the partitions between the visual and the textual and the factual and the fictional, as well as between the two branches of the same family, Rougon and Macquart. The sketches inaugurate the section entitled "Plan de la Fortune des Rougon," in which Zola wrote out a detailed outline of all the chapters of the novel. The first sketch is a map depicting the march of republican insurgents against Napoleon III's coup d'état around the fictional city of Plassans (figure 4.1) (Zola, *La Fabrique des Rougon-Macquart,* 1:249). Just as Sand's fictional village Valcreux in her novel *Nanon* was a transparent stand-in for the easily identifiable Ahun, Plassans corresponds to Zola's childhood home Aix-en-Provence. The geographical situation of the fictional towns on the map is rather approximate, since Zola rearranged them along a line and drew a road connecting them that did not yet exist, as if the narrative needed to improve the infrastructure of the region (Lumbroso, 36). Plassans, according to Henri Mitterand, shares the same geographical location as the town of Lorgues, while the layout of its streets and its history are that of Aix (*Les Rougon-Macquart,* 1:1545). On the map itself, Zola includes in parentheses beside the fictional toponyms, the real names of the towns: Sainte-Roure (Aups), Orchères (Salernes), Alboise (Vidauban), and a double referent for Plassans (Lorgues, Aix). The line of the road on the map visually links the circles representing the fictional towns, establishing a fictional spatial network even as the text of the place names in parentheses refer to a very different and real spatial configuration. The

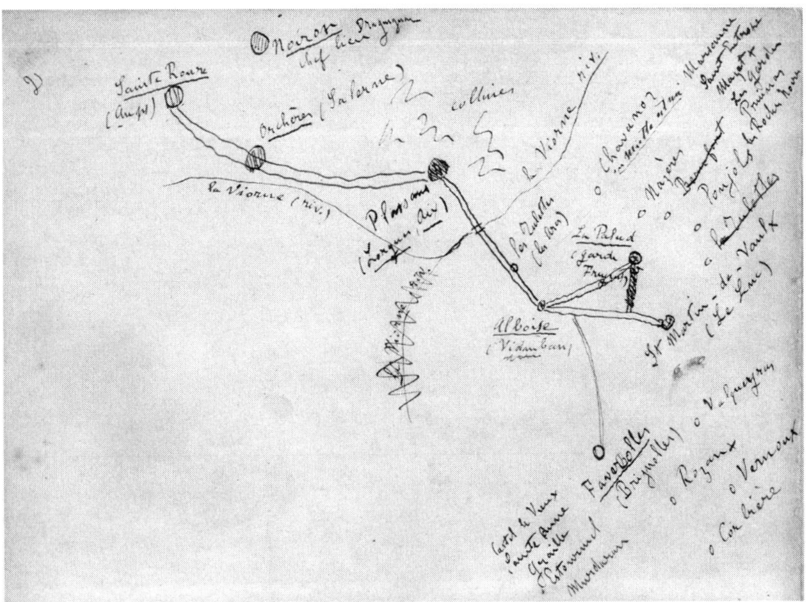

Figure 4.1. Zola's preliminary map of the region surrounding Plassans. Mss, NAF 10.303 folio 2. Courtesy of Bibliothèque nationale de France.

map captures the process of metamorphosis as the real Provence dissolves into the Plassans of the *Rougon-Macquart.*

The second sketch found in the dossiers represents a map of the "Aire Saint-Mittre," an abandoned lot at the edge of the city of Plassans (figure 4.2) (Zola, *La Fabrique des Rougon-Macquart,* 1:251). Adjacent to the lot is the property called the Jas-Meiffren where Adélaïde Fouque begat the split or double family, Rougon-Macquart. When the novel begins in 1851 right before Louis-Napoléon's coup d'état, the Aire Saint-Mittre is inhabited by gypsies; moreover, by day it is a wood yard where children come to play, and by night a favored rendezvous point for young lovers. The Aire Saint-Mittre and the cul-de-sac of the same name uncannily resemble the impasse Sylvacanne in Aix-en-Provence where Zola lived with his mother and grandparents between 1843 and 1858, which is to say the time of the novel's narration (*Les Rougon-Macquart,* 1:1545). But like the first sketch where the real Provence coincides with its fictional double, the second sketch portrays the transformation between Zola's childhood Aix and the imaginary Plassans.

The sketch makes no reference to characters or events in the novel, but the juxtaposition of places and text on the map suggests a sort of

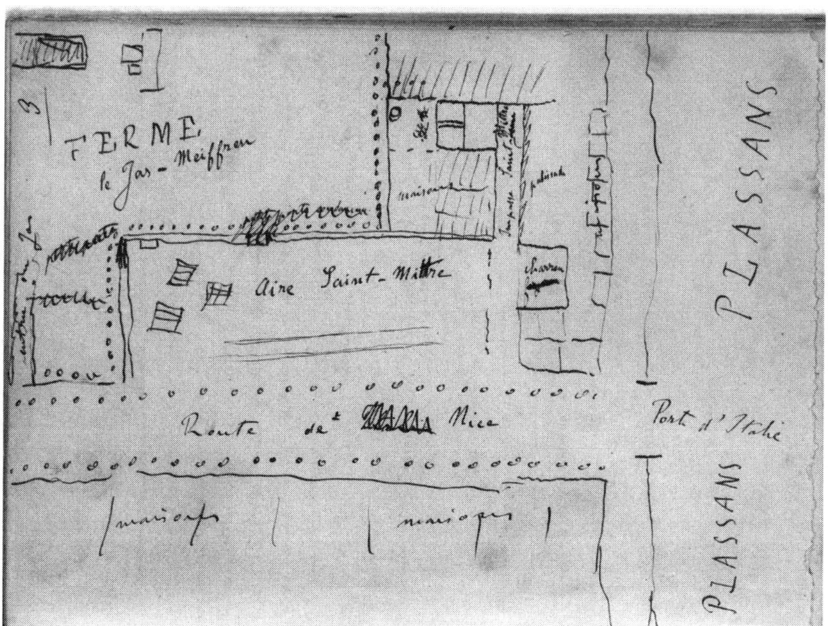

Figure 4.2. The Aire Saint-Mittre. Mss, NAF 10.303 folio 3. Courtesy of Bibliothèque nationale de France.

prenarrative. Taking a closer look at the drawing, we see that the Aire Saint-Mittre is at the southern edge outside the walls of Plassans, a liminal space. Enclosed on three sides, it is surrounded by numerous abstract marks representing trees, walls, houses, and other buildings forming square shapes and boxes within boxes. In the novel, the wall between the Jas-Meiffren and the impasse Saint-Mittre will split Adélaïde Fouque's legitimate descendants, fathered by the rough peasant Rougon, from her illegitimate descendants, fathered by the drunk Macquart, who lives in a shack on the impasse Saint-Mittre. After Rougon's death, Adélaïde and her lover Macquart build a door between the two properties, an action which the local gossips find more scandalous than the fact that she had two illegitimate children. On the sketch it is possible to make out in a few places the words "petites portes" or openings that Zola drew and then crossed out, which implies that he first thought of creating a way for the two places to communicate. By suppressing any gap in the walls, the separation between the properties becomes even more absolute and the divide between the lovers more poignant.

The other love story in the novel grows out of the same spatial complications. Adélaïde ends up living with her grandson Silvère in Macquart's hovel on the impasse, and their portion of the Jas-Meiffren is sold to a certain Rébufat. Rébufat's niece, Miette, falls in love with Silvère, and at the beginning of the novel, she climbs over the wall enclosing the Jas-Meiffren, since there are no "petites portes" in the wall, in order to meet Silvère at night. Three-quarters of the way into the novel Silvère and Miette are separated again by walls as her family tries to prevent her from seeing him. They discover, however, that the two properties share a large well, split by a wall, which the novel refers to as a "puits mitoyen" (an adjoining or shared well) (Zola, *Les Rougon-Macquart,* 1:179). By looking into the well on each side of the wall, they can see each other's reflections and hear each other's voices. The sketch hesitates between a few different locations for the well, none of them between the walls, an idea again which postdates the dossiers (Mitterand and Lumbroso, *Les Manuscrits et dessins de Zola,* 3:324). The sketch puts forth and then rejects several breaches in the partitions around the Aire Saint-Mittre, as if to seal off the "air" from circulating. As the novel describes at the end of the second paragraph: "Ainsi fermée de trois côtés, l'aire est comme une place qui ne conduit nulle part et que les promeneurs seuls traversent" (Zola, *Les Rougon-Macquart,* 1:11) ("Thus enclosed on three sides, the Aire Saint-Mittre is like a square that leads nowhere and which only strollers traverse"). The subsequent narrative in the novel invents new ways for the characters to communicate by exploiting the points of juncture between places, which is to say the very structure that divides them; Adélaïde and Macquart build a little door in the wall, and Silvère and Miette take advantage of the privacy afforded by the wall to stare at each other's reflections in the well. The novel formulates narrative out of the notes' frames.[10]

The sketch of the Aire Saint-Mittre gives no indication at all of the novel's most extraordinary invention: a hundred years before Silvère and Miette meet in the empty lot, it used to be a cemetery, a fact all but forgotten by 1851. The opening pages of the novel describe how the cemetery was desacralized and desecrated: tombs were taken down; bones were dug up and carted through the streets to a new area on the other side of the city; the cemetery's walls were torn down in an unsuccessful effort by city officials to sell the land to investors. Inexplicably, fragments of some of the tombs remain, one of which especially troubles Miette with its enigmatic epitaph: "*Cy-gist . . . Marie . . . morte . . .*" (*Les Rougon-Macquart,* 1:11) ("Here lies . . . Marie . . . died . . ."). The tombstone retains the trace of the long-dead woman, but time and the destruction of the cemetery by the city have effaced the text that could have identified her name, her place of birth, and the relevant dates. The grave of one particular woman in the past loses its specificity, its material reference, and becomes an ill omen for whoever finds it in the future; Miette fears she shares the same fate because she shares the same first name (1:208). Naomi Schor argues that the passage from cemetery to "Aire," and in particular the suspicious death of a young woman (Marie or Miette) and destruction of her tombstone, represent the secret at the origin of the Rougon-Macquart family: "the origins of the Rougon-Macquart are encoded in a half-erased message, at the same time revealed and concealed, thus literally indecipherable" (Schor, *Zola's Crowds*, 19). The bloody origins of the family, presumably in the death of a sacrificial victim, haunt the family, but the original secret stays unknowable, opening up a "hole" or "discontinuity" in a novel that ends with Docteur Pascal's attempt to map a "seamless genealogy" (19).

As I have argued, Rancière's many partitions and contradictions in literature reveal that at each text's origin is the failed attempt to bridge a divide or to represent a seamless origin. The sketch of the Aire Saint-Mittre, at what Zola called the "origin" of the *Rougon-Macquart,* presents a structure of partitions and walls that part space into noncommunicating enclosures, which in turn lead to the division of a family into opposing branches. The partitions differentiate the family members into classes as they occupy every position of Second Empire society (Hamon, *Le Personnel du roman,* 209–11). Moreover, as this sketch as well as the narrative of the *Fortune des Rougon* demonstrate, the porous walls and barriers of the text break down over time to create new divisions and new boundaries. The invention of a razed cemetery, and the idea for the gruesome details of graves being dug up and children playing with skulls, what Rancière might call the "poeticity" of the novel, was invented after the completion of the dossiers and therefore might be considered to fall outside the "representational regime"; the novel's "poeticity," then, fabricates a verbal image of its own origins without a factual or a visual equivalent in the dossiers.

At the origin of the narrative lies a divide between dossier and novel and at the origin of the family lies a spatial division between the different branches. This original division is passed down as an inheritance from the founder of the family, Adélaïde Fouque, also known as Tante Dide, in the form of the physiological and hereditary "fêlure," the "crack" or rupture she has in her brain, which manifests itself in various ways for all of her descendants. This "fêlure," this hole or discontinuity, resurfaces silently in every novel until it erupts, destroying the status quo. As Gilles Deleuze theorized it in relation to Zola's *La Bête humaine* in *Logique du sens,* the "fêlure" in Zola's works represents inheritance itself, it divides instinct from the object of desire, it is the death drive or even death, and ultimately it raises obstacles to thought that make thought possible (*Logique du sens*). From the empty grave in the Aire Saint-Mittre and the crack in Tante Dide's head flow all of the novels of the *Rougon-Macquart.* If literature emerges from its contradictions, Zola shows us, despite whatever compromises he might have made, that the art of the novel is always "fêlé."

Zola's *Fêlure*

The distinction between dossier and novel, the factual and the fictional or the visual and the verbal, creates opposing zones that are then partitioned or cordoned off from each other. The novels rely on the factual basis of the dossiers for their fictional narratives, while the supposed absence of fiction in the dossiers reinforces the narrative innovations of the novels. The unchecked circulation of meaning inherent in the written word, its "silent speech," can be given a stable meaning, a body, in the silent dossiers; in turn, the archival dossiers liberate the novels from the strictly mimetic representation of the world and allow for flights of poetic fancy. The disjuncture, the crack, that rips the two parallel works apart at their origin generates more and more text on both sides of the divide—twenty novels (instead of the original ten) and 10,000 pages of notes (beyond the original documents collected over the three years prior to the publication of *La Fortune des Rougon*).

Another rift tears the two bodies of text apart and separates them into a first-person journal of artistic creation and a fictional text with an omniscient narrator. In both senses of the word as "crack" and its more colloquial meaning of mental instability, Zola's "fêlure" protects the integrity of the authorial subject from the instability of the written word by insisting on the author's appropriation over the factual dossiers and by producing the illusion of a godly remove from the play of language found in the fictional novels. Zola's fear of his own "fêlure" as authorial subject, which is to say the abandonment of the self to the uncertainty of textual meaning, leads to a proliferation of "fêlures" that replicate themselves throughout the two bodies of text. The only way to resist the division of the writing self from the self on the page is to amplify this split, to assert the complete independence of the two.

Reminiscent of Stendhal's Brulard who feared that his autobiography would "fall into the novel," Zola's dossiers amount to a first-person account of a novelist afraid of losing control of his fictional narrative. The dossiers' autobiographical aspect exposes the alienating process of composing an independent world in a fictional text. Colette Becker detects in Zola's correspondence and in the dossiers an anguish over his inability to master the writing process (Becker, preface to Zola, *La Fabrique des Rougon,* 1:8). The very fact that the dossiers declare over and over "an affirmation of the will to power" signals Zola's profound self-doubts and hesitations (18); the phrases "je veux" ("I want") and "je voudrais" ("I would like") are among the most frequently used in the "Ébauches" of the dossiers. Continually doubting his talents as a novelist, Zola worked through his anxieties in the dossiers, using them as an escape valve for psychic pressure and as a generator of text.

While many critics have found in the dossiers proof that Zola intended to portray facets of himself in many of the characters in the *Rougon-Macquart* (most obviously Sandoz in *L'Oeuvre* and Docteur Pascal in the final novel), Zola's appropriation of his fictional creation goes beyond simple character identification.[11] Abstract concepts, such as plot turns and chapter arrangements, as well as characters and places, become possessions marked by the author's ubiquitous possessive adjectives: "ma série," "mon histoire," "mes personages," "mes chapitres." Zola creates his world ("Je crée" appears almost as frequently as "je veux") as text and story, but then imagines himself within it. In the "Ébauche" for *La Conquête de Plassans* Zola writes, "Comme marche générale dans l'oeuvre, il est temps de revenir à Plassans, où, de longtemps ensuite, je ne pourrai remettre les pieds. Vers la fin seulement" (*Les Rougon-Macquart,* 1:1648) ("For the unfolding of the work as a whole, it is time to come back to Plassans, where, for a long time afterwards, I will not be able to set foot. Only towards the end"). Likewise, the novel itself, and the events created within it, must be experienced firsthand. For his research documented in the dossiers, Zola famously descended into the mines for *Germinal,* rode with train engineers for *La Bête humaine,* and traversed the farmland of the Beauce for *La Terre.* His notes for *La Débâcle,* named "Mon voyage à Sedan," plan to have the soldiers in the narrative follow Zola's own itinerary, though in the novel itself he makes them follow the same route as an actual army corps during the war (*Les Rougon-Macquart,* 5:1379–81). While fascinating documentation of Zola's time, these first-person accounts prepare for the transition from note to novel by way of the author's "screen."

Crucially, the dossiers chronicle Zola's own transformations as the struggle to define his style, in opposition to other writers and in relation to the representational material he collected, resulted in a heightened awareness of his own thought process and his sense of self. In the fragment entitled "Différences entre Balzac et moi" included in the dossiers and written in the early stages of the project's conception, Zola summarizes the differences in style, scope, methodology, and ambitions between Balzac's *Comédie humaine* and his own vast project. But the fragment also describes their differences in temperament and their visions of the role of a novelist: "Je ne veux pas comme Balzac avoir une décision sur les affaires des hommes, être politique, philosophe, moraliste. Je me contenterai d'être savant, de dire ce qui est en en cherchant les raisons intimes" (*Les Rougon-Macquart,* 5:1737) ("I do not want, like Balzac, to have a say in men's affairs, to be a politician, a philosopher, a moralist. I will be happy to be a scientist, to say what is while studying its internal logic"). In another note probably written a little later, Zola ridicules Balzac's philosophical pretensions and conservative moralizing, all the while allowing that moralists and legislators are free to draw their own conclusions from the truth of his novel (*Les Rougon-Macquart,* 5:1740), and conceding that his novels need some sort of philosophical bent (such as "materialism") so as to liberate them from tedious metaphysical explanations (5:1744).

As the novels and the dossiers progressed, Zola's aggressively combative tone gave way to a more reflective, internal monologue. In the "Ébauche" for *L'Oeuvre,* he envisions writing a novel about his own creative process, the pains and joys of Zola the writer embodied by Claude the painter: "Avec Claude Lantier, je veux peindre la lutte de l'artiste contre la nature, l'effort de la création dans l'oeuvre d'art. . . . En un mot, j'y raconterai ma vie intime de production, ce perpétuel accouchement douloureux, mais je grandirai le sujet par le drame" (*Les Rougon-Macquart,* 4:1353) ("With Claude Lantier, I want to paint the struggle of the artist against nature, the effort of creation in a work of art. . . . In a word, I will tell in this novel the story of my personal work life, this perpetual, painful childbirth, but I will exaggerate it through tragedy"). The novel about a failed artist reflects the writing process itself, as if in a dream Zola projects himself in the unfolding of the novel as a whole as well as in each of its characters.

In the "Ébauche" for *Le Rêve,* the sixteenth novel, Zola expresses the desire to prove his artistic versatility, almost as a challenge to himself and his detractors: "Je voudrais faire un livre qu'on n'attende pas de moi. . . . Puisqu'on m'accuse de ne pas faire de psychologie, je voudrais forcer les gens à confesser que je suis un psychologue" (*Les Rougon-Macquart,* 4:1625–26) ("I would like to make a book that no one expects from me. . . . Since I'm accused of not doing psychology, I would like to force people to admit that I am a psychologist"). Here, Zola conveys his temptation to break with the *Rougon-Macquart*'s stated project by abandoning the laws of heredity for the more intimate, and classical, psychological novel. But this temptation, later in the same "Ébauche," proves to be rooted in a more personal need to understand his own creative drives: "Moi, le travail, la littérature qui a mangé ma vie, et le bouleversement, la crise, le besoin d'être aimé, tout cela à étudier psychologiquement" (*Les Rougon-Macquart,* 4:1626–27) ("Me, work, literature which has devoured my life, and upheaval, crisis, the need to be loved, all of this needs to be studied psychologically"). To write a novel, psychological or otherwise, is to confront what lies behind the need to write, the dangerous combination of self-doubt and hubris. In the end, Zola opted for "something much simpler" for *Le Rêve,* saving the tale of artistic and scientific angst for the last novel, *Le Docteur Pascal* (*Les Rougon-Macquart,* 4:1627).

In *L'Espace littéraire,* Maurice Blanchot describes how the act of writing is a confrontation with death, with the loss of self to a work whose central point is "l'oeuvre comme origine, celui que l'on ne peut atteindre" ("the work as origin, an origin that cannot be attained") (60). According to Blanchot, in the transition from first-person "je" to third-person "il" intrinsic to the fictional writing process, a writer will often begin a journal:

> Il est peut-être frappant qu'à partir du moment où l'oeuvre devient recherche de l'art, devient littérature, l'écrivain éprouve toujours davantage

> le besoin de garder un rapport avec soi. C'est qu'il éprouve une extrême répugnance à se dessaisir de lui-même au profit de cette puissance neutre, sans forme et sans destin, qui est derrière tout ce qui s'écrit, répugnance et appréhension que révèle le souci, propre à tant d'auteurs, de rédiger ce qu'ils appellent leur *Journal.*[12] (24)

To write fiction is to search for an unknowable, unattainable origin, the origin of the work in the depths of language. The author grapples with conflicting literary and existential constraints since the act of writing requires an extraordinary will to project the self on the page and a corresponding loss of self to the "solitude" of the text. A journal inscribes the author's memories in a parallel text, but mimics the very act that threatens the integrity of the self: "Le moyen dont il se sert pour se rappeler à soi, c'est, fait étrange, l'élément même de l'oubli: écrire" (24) ("the method used to remember oneself, is, strangely, the very element of oblivion: writing").

Zola shows us in the dossiers that the only cure for the torment of writing, the work which has "devoured" his life, would be further writing, an analysis of the self through text. The *dossiers préparatoires* may document the novelist's research, but they are also a journal of the abandonment of the self to the work. Zola's partition between the notes and the novel proves to be a futile attempt to protect the self from written language, all the while generating more and more text. Out of Zola's "fêlure" grew the expanding notes and increasingly inward-looking monologues in the dossiers that attest to both his terror at the independence of his creation and to the fact that with each novel finished, he approached, little by little, the very essence of literature.

Chapter Eight

Mapping Creative Destruction in Zola

In the novels of the *Rougon-Macquart,* power resides in the ability to harness the destructive force of origins—of memory, of history, of heredity. In the beginning there was only the fateful "fêlure," the crack that renders impossible a whole, univocal origin. The "fêlure" reproduces only itself as every successive generation invokes the authority of the origin's secret, but the secret is that there is no one comprehensive or comprehensible origin. As the present moment unfolds in time it splits off from the past, differentiating itself from the origin; the past determines the future, but in unknowable ways. With the past irretrievably lost and the future indecipherable, the unattainable desire for the unity of a foundational beginning generates in turn a circular movement of thought that fantasizes the existence of an image capable of fusing past and future, of sealing the fissure at the center of the self. Artistic vision, genealogical tree, philosophical musing, scientific paradigm, financial swindle, or political ideology, whatever form this image takes it can project an original harmony only by displacing difference, which is to say locating the "fêlure" anywhere else than the origin.

The most potent incarnation of this fantasy, an archive functions as the site of an imagined origin, providing the illusion of a material foundation in a localizable space. An archive derives its authority from its capacity to memorialize; therefore it must acknowledge the inevitable deterioration of memory, while maintaining the promise to guard the remains of the past for a time in the distant future when its secrets can be read. Jacques Derrida traces the forgotten origins of the word "archive" as both "commandment" and "beginning," stemming from "archontes," the magistrates in whose home ("arkheîon") official documents were kept (*Mal d'archive,* 12–13). Documents held in the archive become part of the public record, but kept secret, classified according to a "privileged *topology*" (13). An archive governs from a site and commands by virtue of silent or silenced documents, which are preserved so as not to be exposed to the outside and so that the outside is not exposed to them. As we have seen, Zola's *dossiers préparatoires* operate as a type of archive for the novels. The dossiers, Zola's record of his own writing process, safeguard his artistic development as a source of his legitimacy as author and show the fundamental truth that the novel escapes the author's control. The dossiers document the preparation behind the novels and amount to a treasure of ethnographic research, but also reveal how the novels diverge, sometimes radically, from their documented genesis.

The Rougon-Macquart family emerges from near the "Aire Saint-Mittre" as if surfacing from the cemetery to haunt Second Empire France. The founding member of the family, Adélaïde or Tante Dide, expresses the original "fêlure" first in her eccentric choice of husband, the peasant Rougon, and then her lover, Macquart. Her eldest son, Pierre Rougon, realizes early that to claim legitimacy and take hold of the family possessions, he must disinherit his younger half-siblings Antoine and Ursule Macquart. His mother's embarrassing madness incites Pierre to sequester her with his inconveniently republican nephew Silvère in what used to be Macquart's hovel. When Pierre gets advanced warning from his son Eugène of Louis-Napoléon's coup d'état, he easily manipulates public opinion and his brother Antoine's republican opposition, "saving" Plassans from disorder. During the uprising, Dide falls into a permanent catatonic state after watching her grandson Silvère's murder at the hands of a gendarme, and is sent by Pierre to spend the rest of her life at the Tulettes asylum. There Dide outlives at least sixteen of her thirty or so descendants, living in almost complete silence and dying in the final novel of the series at the age of 105. Witness to the terrible secrets of the family, Dide is carefully watched and locked away at a safe distance from Plassans. At the cracked origin of the family, she embodies the family's memory even while remaining incapable of speech, incarnating Rancière's "parole muette"; upon seeing her great-great-grandson Charles bleed to death from hemophilia, the original, awful memory of Silvère's murder returns and her final words before she herself dies are "Le gendarme!"

While the family's sordid beginnings obviously echo those of the Second Empire, "archive fever" spreads beyond the political realm to encompass every aspect of society. Archives must be visible signifiers of absent origins, while concealing the textual evidence of this original lack. Secret documents, concealed origins, and empty signifiers proliferate, granting control to those who claim to be custodians of knowledge, memory, and tradition. Eugène Rougon exemplifies the power of the new regime, but how he transformed himself from provincial petit bourgeois to imperial minister stays shrouded in mystery; tellingly, the end of *Son Excellence Eugène Rougon* finds him named "Ministre sans portefeuille" ("Minister without Portfolio"), as if his power increases when he no longer has a "portfolio" or official document detailing his specific responsibilities. A persistent trope in the series is the anonymous letter or blackmail note exposing an inconvenient truth or a threat: Florent's police dossier full of anonymous letters in *Le Ventre de Paris,* Hélène's anonymous letter to Henri accusing Juliette in *Une Page d'amour,* Mme Robert's anonymous letters to Count Muffat exposing Nana's numerous affairs, Séverine's letter to Grandmorin in *La Bête humaine.* When documents or dossiers do become public, they lead to the downfall of their owner: Florent's notes for a delusional plot to overthrow the government, Lazare's disastrous or unfinished projects in *La Joie de vivre,* Père Fouan's "donation entre vifs" (a sort of living will) in *La Terre,* Docteur Pascal's research on heredity. Specific places in the novels materialize the spatial function of the archive by situating authority and concealing origins: the neutral territory of François Mouret's property in *La Conquête de Plassans,* the enchanting garden paradise of the Paradou in *La Faute de l'Abbé Mouret,* Saccard's palatial Banque Universelle in *L'Argent.* The archival source of the novels in the *dossiers préparatoires* threatens to overtake the narrative by the ubiquity of questionable documents. Instead of confirming that genetic and class origins circumscribe the fate of each character in a project that is both a "natural" and a "social" history, the novels (and their dossiers) question the very possibility of a knowable or legitimate origin, even as they assert the need for a stable foundation.

The omnipresence in the novels of the "cracked" origin and the archives that endeavor to contain it render an exhaustive study of this structuring principle impossible in one book chapter. Instead, in what follows I focus on how textual images, "novel maps," project a synoptic view of time that attempts to encompass an illusory origin and an inscrutable future. Paris, setting for over half the novels of the *Rougon-Macquart,* inspires numerous attempts at a totalizing panorama, especially in the novel *La Curée,* for whoever can visualize the development of the city masters it. Yet a complete map of the city, in the novels and in the dossiers, proves elusive. The map or image overlying Paris hides the city's social, geographical, and temporal fractures, while it gives to its beholder the impression of seeing into the future. Similarly, the genealogical tree drawn up by Pascal at the end of the series undertakes a complete description of the family across four or more generations, tracing the transmission of hereditary traits over time. An elegant figure illustrating years of scientific research, it becomes indecipherable with the destruction of Pascal's papers.

The Absent Map of Paris

The second novel in Émile Zola's *Les Rougon-Macquart, La Curée,* describes the rapidly gained and ephemeral fortune of land speculator Aristide Saccard. Saccard owes his fabulous success to an intimate knowledge of Napoleon III's hand-drawn plan for transforming Paris. In a key scene in the novel, Saccard explains to his first wife, Angèle, Haussmann's incredible building project while overlooking Paris from Montmartre. The bird's-eye view of the city translates the map of Haussmann's urban plan into language. Saccard's panoramic vision of Paris takes the static spatial image of a map and puts it into motion, deterritorializing city space, like the flow of capital itself which exploits the inherent disjuncture between use-value and exchange-value. In the novel, speculation and creative destruction go hand in hand. The real estate speculator depends upon the fiction that he can control space and foresee the future, a control embodied in the image of a map. Zola's novel itself, I argue, attempts to ground the verbal and temporal instability of the literary text's origin in visual and spatial representations archived in the thousands of pages of his *dossiers préparatoires.* That Zola did not in fact include a complete map of Paris in his preparatory notes for the novel and that Haussmann did not in fact receive a map from Napoleon III prove that these maps are screens for the fear of the unchecked circulation of meaning, the "fêlure" at the origin of thought.

Zola's 1871 novel *La Curée,* contemporaneous with Sand's *Nanon* and usually translated in English as "The Kill" or "The Rush for the Spoil," portrays the parallel narratives of Aristide Saccard's pursuit of financial gain, or the joy of the kill, alongside the story of the semi-incestuous relationship his second wife, Renée, carries on with Saccard's son Maxime. This juxtaposition of crass materialism with sexual depravity underscores how the Second Empire eroded French society's moral foundation through what Sandy Petrey calls the "capitalization of humanity."[1] Money and human flesh circulate freely in the novel, crossing physical and moral boundaries. Renée is a stepmother who represents the absence of a mother, just as Saccard's financial transactions have little basis in the real estate he sells. Indeed, Saccard raises the money to realize his first scheme thanks to Renée's dowry; she is abandoned more or less with his consent to Saccard's son Maxime. The characters' loyalty to each other proves to be as changing as the market. In the end Saccard, as well as his son, return in another novel in the series, *L'Argent,* an even more explicit analysis of the workings of capitalism, while Renée withdraws to her father's mansion and dies.

Aristide Rougon begins the novel penniless but ambitious. Arriving in Paris with his wife, Angèle, after Napoleon III's coup d'état, he hopes to cash in on his brother Eugène Rougon's rise to political power. Eugène offers him an ostensibly low-level position working for the Hôtel de Ville as an "agent voyer" (a city surveyor), but on condition that his brother change his name. The newly minted "Saccard" (resonating with the sound of sacks of money and also one who sacks) quickly learns the intricacies of land speculation and eventually discovers the plans for the city's urban renewal projects. He concocts a simple but effective scheme to purchase property marked for demolition, inflate its value, and sell it for many times its worth:

> Le plan de fortune de l'agent voyer était simple et pratique . . . Il connaissait son Paris sur le bout du doigt; il savait que la pluie d'or qui en battait les murs tomberait plus dru chaque jour. Les gens habiles n'avaient qu'à ouvrir les poches. Lui s'était mis parmi les habiles, en lisant l'avenir dans les bureaux de l'Hôtel de Ville.[2] (*Les Rougon-Macquart,* 1:387)

Saccard knows Paris as someone who has studied it as a poor outsider, on foot through every neighborhood. Besides his methodical research of city space, what distinguishes him from his colleagues and superiors is his ability to read the future in the maps and documents scattered throughout the Hôtel de Ville: "Il en devinait plus long que ses chefs eux-mêmes sur l'avenir de moellons et de plâtre qui était réservé à Paris. Il avait tant fureté, réuni tant d'indices, qu'il aurait pu prophétiser le spectacle qu'offriraient les nouveaux quartiers en 1870" (1:387) ("He saw further than even his superiors into the future of rubble and plaster that lay ahead for Paris. He had rummaged about enough, pieced together enough clues, that he could foresee the spectacle offered by the new neighborhoods in 1870"). Saccard composes from seemingly unrelated bits of information a vision, a prophecy, of Paris fifteen or twenty years into the future. This fantastic vision, Paris as spectacle and object of speculation, has already altered how he looks at the present city, since he knows the fate of so many of its streets and buildings.

Saccard projects his imaginary map of Paris onto a view of the real city when he takes his first wife, Angèle, to dinner at a restaurant in Montmartre. Uncharacteristically romantic and tipsy, Saccard stares lovingly, not at his wife, but at the city, mesmerized by the play of light on the golden mist rising up between the Madeleine and the Tuileries (the imperial palace), which creates the illusion of gold falling on the rooftops. The giddy couple joke to each other that it is raining coins on the city.

This metaphorical vision of money recalls for Saccard his secret plan and inspires him to share it with his wife. The ephemeral, elusive golden mist reflecting immaterial light on the city rooftops evokes the paradoxical use of gold as immaterial abstraction, money or "universal equivalent," and its more or less useless material essence as shiny metal.[3] Real estate ("biens immobiliers" or "immobile goods") must too be abstracted from its materiality, put in motion, in order to convert it into money.

Just as atmospheric conditions lead to the fantastic vision of golden plunder, Saccard is able to transform a bird's-eye view of Paris into a dynamic, moving image of the city over time, as buildings make way for roads and money falls into the pockets of speculators. Saccard anticipates the violence that will be done to the city by urban planners as he gestures with his hand:

> Et de sa main étendue, ouverte et tranchante comme un coutelas, il fit signe de séparer la ville en quatre parts. . . . [then speaking to his wife] "Tiens, suis un peu ma main. Du boulevard du Temple à la barrière du Trône, une entaille; puis, de ce côté, une autre entaille, de la Madeleine à la plaine Monceau; et une troisième entaille dans ce sens, une autre dans celui-ci, une entaille là, une entaille plus loin, des entailles partout. Paris haché à coups de sabre, les veines ouvertes, nourrissant cent mille terrassiers et maçons."[4] (*Les Rougon-Macquart,* 1:389)

Like Baudelaire's book of prose poems, *Le Spleen de Paris,* which the poet claims can be chopped up into as many pieces as the reader or editor wishes in the image of the modern city, Paris here is mercilessly hacked up in the minds of speculators and the pickaxes of workers. As Saccard looks at the entire city from Montmartre, he destroys whatever organic vision he had of Paris, cutting open its veins to feast on the kill. The violent apparition of a Paris gashed, "fêlé" perhaps, by Saccard's knife or workers' shovels recalls how the Saint-Mittre cemetery was dug up in the vain hope of selling it to land developers, but also how the subsequent Aire Saint-Mittre concealed the murderous origins of the Rougon-Macquart family.

A few pages later, the reader learns why Saccard is so confident in his prophecy for the future of Paris and why he can see further than his immediate superiors:

> Saccard s'était permis, un jour, de consulter, chez le préfet, ce fameux plan de Paris sur lequel "une main auguste" avait tracé à l'encre rouge les principales voies du deuxième réseau. Ces sanglants traits de plume

> entaillaient Paris plus profondément encore que la main de l'agent voyer.[5] (*Les Rougon-Macquart,* 1:391)

Violating the sanctity of the archive, Saccard entered into Haussmann's office to sneak a peek at the map of Paris drawn up by the "august" hand of the emperor himself. The existence of this map guarantees that Haussmann's project is backed by the full might of the empire and that Saccard's vision of Paris represents the future. Moreover, the destruction of vast sections of the city will adhere to a creative, aesthetic, and ideological, albeit secret, plan. The majestic hand of the emperor guides Saccard in his quest for fortune—certainly a much more reliable one than the "invisible hand" of the market.

Zola relies in this passage on the story, spread perhaps most of all by Haussmann himself, that the emperor had drawn up a detailed plan for Paris's renewal, a plan that Haussmann only executed. In the second volume of his memoirs, Haussmann describes the moment when Napoleon III named him the préfet de la Seine and handed him an annotated map of Paris: "L'Empereur était pressé de me montrer une carte de Paris, sur laquelle on voyait tracées par Lui-Même, en bleu, en rouge, en jaune et en vert, suivant leur degré d'urgence, les différentes voies nouvelles qu'Il se proposait de faire exécuter."[6] Though Haussmann's memoirs were published after Zola's novel, the image of a map marked up with different colors is strikingly similar. While Napoleon III did indeed form a commission to draw up a new plan for Paris based in large part on his uncle Napoleon I's plans at the beginning of the century, the commission was formed before Haussmann's appointment and proposed sweeping changes rather different than what Haussmann eventually carried out (or claimed that the emperor requested).[7] Historians have convincingly argued that Haussmann invented many details of his meeting with the emperor and that the map, at least in the form Haussmann describes, never existed; it was nothing but a legend no doubt invented by Haussmann to defend himself against his many critics.[8]

The invention of this imaginary map was also in keeping with the Second Empire's uneasy relationship to politics, secrecy, and capitalism. The empire attempted to control, or at least to project the image of control, over all aspects of society, from the military to the economy. Its inability to organize the military effectively is brilliantly illustrated by Zola himself with the second-to-last novel in the *Rougon-Macquart* series, *La Débâcle*. There, during the Franco-Prussian war, the army's officers are lost within France itself, never having been given maps of their own country but only maps of Germany: "On avait distribué à tous les officiers des cartes d'Allemagne, tandis que pas un, certainement, ne possédait une carte de France" (5:472) ("Maps of Germany had been distributed to all the officers, while not one, certainly, possessed a map of France"). The empire's management of the economy was just as haphazard, vacillating between laissez-faire principles and the emperor's socialist antipauperism campaign. As David Harvey writes, "Economic liberalization . . . gradually undermined imperial power. The Empire was brought down just as much by capital as by republicanism . . . or worker opposition" (*Paris*, 88). For want of a map—of Paris, of France, of the economy—Napoleon III lost his empire.

It is possible to see in the legendary map Haussmann invented the desire to create a holistic image of modern Paris, after the destruction he unleashed with all of its competing, chaotic visions, as if knowing that a plan existed can retrospectively organize spatial meaning. Yet the second and third phases, or "réseaux" of Haussmann's plan relied on speculation from investors. His eventual downfall might be linked to his inability to harness the forces of speculation, to make the destruction adhere to his unified vision. T. J. Clark has argued in *The Painting of Modern Life* that capitalism works against a stable image of the city:

> Capital did not need to have a representation of itself laid out upon the ground in bricks and mortar, or inscribed as a map in the minds of its city-dwellers. One might even say that capital preferred the city not to be an image—not to have form, not to be accessible to the imagination, to readings and misreadings, to a conflict of claims on its space—in order that it might mass-produce an image of its own to put in place of those it destroyed. (Clark, *The Painting of Modern Life,* 36)

The Paris of modernity, born from urban planning during the First and Second Empires, nevertheless resists any image imposed on it. Instead, the city becomes itself a factory for producing images. I would argue that these images were neither the homogeneous bird's-eye views of the early part of the century, nor were they always the mass-produced ones Clark mentions, but rather heterogeneous, fragmented images in the works of poets like Baudelaire, painters like the impressionists, and eventually filmmakers like Godard.[9] While capitalism deterritorialized Parisian space by hacking it up and selling it piecemeal, the pursuit of a unified urban plan or map of the city paradoxically upsets networks of signs, speeding up the circulation of meaning, the proliferation of fragmented images.

Émile Zola's *dossiers préparatoires* for his novels show that a true panorama of Paris, a map of the city, was elusive, but that the city itself reflected the productive tension in his novel between visual representation and textual creation. Given the importance of the dossiers' role in establishing the factual basis for his novels, one would expect there to be maps of the city of Paris, perhaps an old map from before 1853 or at the least a sketch of Haussmann's overall project. In the notes for *La Curée,* however, there is no such thing. Zola took notes about finance, land speculation, and Haussmannization in general. Zola even included four detailed drawings of the Hôtel Menier on the Parc Monceau, the model for Saccard's garish mansion, as well as a drawing of the hothouse, the symbolic center of Renée's incestuous relationship. But nowhere in the notes does Zola plan the scene when Saccard looks out over the city from Montmartre. The most iconic episode in the novel has no concrete basis in visual observation, outside Zola's own imagination and his personal experience of the city as if the city's dynamism can only be conveyed in a poetic image.

Paris plays a central role in many of the series' subsequent novels such as *L'Assommoir, L'Oeuvre,* and *Une Page d'amour,* and yet these all lack a panoramic image of the city. There are, of course, hand-drawn maps of the streets around certain neighborhoods, but no view of the city as a whole. In *L'Assommoir,* after Gervaise and the wedding party visit the Louvre and the Palais-Royal, they decide to climb up the Vendôme column for the magnificent view of the city—but the staggering height of the column gives the viewers vertigo (*Les Rougon-Macquart,* 2:449–59). They look around the city, staring dumbly at the monuments, and then attempt unsuccessfully to see the wine merchant's where they will be eating later on, on the boulevard de la Chapelle, aptly named the "Moulin d'Argent" (the silver or money mill). The city's immensity, and the ignorance of its natives, render it impossible to take it in at a glance in a single image. The narrative describes a beautiful scene of a band of sunlight piercing through a gold-bordered cloud and reflecting off panes of glass, a sight similar, one imagines, to the one of money raining on the city in *La Curée,* but *L'Assommoir*'s wedding party remains indifferent to the spectacle, unable to see Saccard's vision of the future. The top of the Vendôme column, with its statue of Napoleon I, may be at the symbolic center of the empire, but affords no perspective on the city.

The dossier for *L'Oeuvre,* the story of the painter Claude Lantier's battle to create life in art, as Zola described it, contains very detailed notes taken by Zola describing the view from Montmartre and the surrounding area at sunset in the month of April; according to Mitterand, the author consulted a map of Paris from 1860 (Zola, *Les Rougon-Macquart,* 4:1377). The dossiers for the novel also contain a map drawn by Zola of the Montmartre cemetery and its surrounding streets, as well as a photograph entitled "PARIS Panorama de la Cité" taken downstream from the Île de la Cité and showing, not the entire city, but essentially the quays.[10] It would seem as if Zola had prepared for Lantier to paint a panorama of Paris from Montmartre, an artistic rendering of Saccard's speculative vision. Yet the novel itself does not contain this passage—instead, Claude obsessively paints the view of Paris from the quays, analyzing the view from below under ever-changing light conditions. Claude fails to capture time in the static images of his paintings, whereas Zola's narrative, by giving up a stable "factual" representation of Paris, allows the work of time to transform his characters; as Kenneth Cornell writes, his panoramic views of Paris demonstrate "Zola's talent for producing totality of effect from detailed descriptions" (Cornell, "Zola's City," 111).

Whereas Paris serves as a backdrop or as an object of speculative desire in *La Curée, L'Assommoir,* and *L'Oeuvre,* the city becomes something of a character in its own right in Zola's novel *Une Page d'amour.* The novel's narrative follows a Provençale, Hélène Grandjean, née Mouret, and her daughter Jeanne as they move to the very fashionable neighborhood of Passy, at the time not yet incorporated into the city of Paris. From her window in Passy, Hélène can look out and see all of Paris—each of the novel's five chapters end with a view of Paris from a different season and time of day in a reflection of Hélène's psychological state. Zola included in his notes for *Une Page d'amour* a photograph of Paris from on top of Saint-Gervais, which is to say from the exact opposite perspective of the city, as well as an engraving of a bird's-eye view of Paris from a balloon over the Champs-Elysées, to the north of Hélène's window (Zola, *La Fabrique des Rougon-Macquart,* 1:11). According to Zola himself in a later preface to the novel which responded to the many criticisms of the five descriptions of Paris as artificial, there is a different origin to the inspiration than any visual representation (*Les Rougon-Macquart,* 2:1607–8). As a young man living in Paris, the view of the city from his window accompanied him, "immobile et indifférent" in all of his hardships; when he began to write novels he vowed to make Paris itself a character, or rather to have the city serve the role of a Greek chorus. Zola claims that his apparent "furor" of description was none other than a desire to create a symphonic and human story, where the city would reflect and heighten human emotion. As for his documentation, he took notes from the elevations of Passy but was dissatisfied with the view of the northwest of the city, where the new monuments of the Opéra and Saint-Augustin rose up out of a sea of nondescript roofs. Although his novel took place before the completion of the two buildings, he decided to include them in his description anyway, "succumbing to the temptation," as he says, that these monuments could lead to a personification of the city, despite the anachronism. This rare concession to the apparent aesthetic unity of Haussmann's Paris, despite Zola's usual insistence on a strict adherence to facts, allows him to show the ever-changing aspects of the city over time, not as an organic image so much as a dramatic backdrop juxtaposed to his character's state of mind.

Claude Lantier toils away at multiple paintings of the city, lost in the never-ending variations of city time and space. Hélène Grandjean sees the transformations of her own emotional life reflected and contrasted in images of the city as the seasons pass. Zola the novelist inscribes new monuments onto a vision of the city in his youth, creating an amalgam of times and spaces, and affirming the aesthetic over the factual. While no single map of Paris exists that can capture the modern city in a holistic vision, the city produces virtual maps of itself, images which correspond to no one moment in time and no actual, concrete view of the city. Saccard sees a vision of the immediate future as he gazes out a restaurant window in Montmartre. And of course Haussmann invents a map from the past that would serve as a foundation for the city of the future. Zola shows us that speculation as well as the creative destruction known as fiction writing both rely on the ability to see past, present, and future in the spaces of the modern city.

A Figural Genealogy

There were at least four different stages in the conception of the Rougon-Macquart genealogical "tree" (*Les Rougon-Macquart,* 5:1777). While in the beginning phases of planning the series in 1869, Zola composed a simple sketch of a family named "Richaud-David," which became "Rougon-Machard" and eventually "Rougon-Macquart." The family members of the first and second generations are already established, but the third and fourth generations are not filled in until 1870 and 1871. Some characters disappear from the tree never to appear in the novels, such as a "Camoin Mouret." It remains a work very much in progress, covered in annotations and erasures. A second early tree later the same year completed more details related to dates and hereditary traits, but is still uncertain about the names of many characters and includes roughly half of the eventual members of the family (*Les Rougon-Macquart,* 5:1778–79). Only with the preparation of the first novel with its elaborate genealogical narrative did the essential details of the family take shape. Far from being a blueprint laying out in advance the foundation and structure of the ten, and then twenty, novels, the genealogical tree provides inspiration and a fairly abstract idea of narrative possibilities, while at the same time adapting to the shifting needs of the project.

Included in the eighth book, *Une Page d'amour,* in 1878, the first published genealogical tree offered the reading public a succinct outline of the family and therefore of the seven preceding novels. More important, it also provided clues about the twelve novels yet to be published; for instance, Jean Macquart is described as a soldier (though he next appears in the novel about peasants, *La Terre*). In the note accompanying the tree, Zola justifies the publication of the document and establishes the parameters for interpreting it (*Les Rougon-Macquart,* 2:799–800). It acts, first of all, as a guide for the reader, an index to help keep track of the numerous family members. The second reason for publishing it is purely promotional fabrication: "Je regrette de n'avoir pas publié l'arbre dans le premier volume de la série, pour montrer tout de suite l'ensemble de mon plan. Si je tardais encore, on finirait par m'accuser de l'avoir fabriqué après coup" (2:799) ("I regret not having published the tree in the first volume of the series, in order to show my whole plan right away. If I were to stall longer, people would accuse me of having fabricated it after the fact"). This third version of the tree was indeed fabricated after the fact, and not in 1868 as he claims, but the fiction of the dossiers and Zola's naturalist method require scientific preparation before the composition of the novels, not a parallel unfolding. Moreover, by situating the project's entire conception before the end of the Second Empire, Zola protects himself from the criticism of disguising depictions of current events and scandals under the veil of historical fiction.

The genealogical tree therefore reinforces the claims to scientific logic and historical objectivity set forth in the preface to *La Fortune des Rougon.* Because each member of the family inhabits a section of time (a generation), a social stratum, and a genetic variation, the author only has to plug in the coordinates in the resulting grid in order to produce a novel. Fiction becomes an experiment with logical results:

> Depuis 1868, je remplis le cadre que je me suis imposé, l'arbre généalogique en marque pour moi les grandes lignes, sans me permettre d'aller ni à droite ni à gauche. Je dois le suivre strictement, il est en même temps ma force et mon régulateur. Les conclusions sont toutes prêtes. Voilà ce que j'ai voulu et voilà ce que j'accomplis.[11] (*Les Rougon Macquart,* 2:799)

Zola articulates the same paradoxical authorial remove and incredible will power in the avowed composition of the novels as he did in the preface and throughout the dossiers. Conveniently, he has constrained himself to doing exactly what he wanted to do all along. The tree is a source of strength and a limiting factor, focusing his attention and channeling his energies. Yet with the publication of the genealogical tree, at least in principle he adds another constraint, since any reader will be able to see how the future novels branch off from the tree.

Finally, Zola announces in his note for *Une Page d'amour* that he will include the tree one more time at the front of the last novel, *Le Docteur Pascal,* as well as in the body of the narrative. The tree sums up all of Pascal's research and the novel cycle as a whole: "Dans ma pensée, il est le résultat des observations de Pascal Rougon, un médecin, membre de la famille, qui conduira le roman final, conclusion scientifique de tout l'ouvrage" (*Les Rougon-Macquart,* 2:799–800) ("In my mind, it is the result of the observations by Pascal Rougon, a medical doctor, member of the family, who will lead the final novel, the scientific conclusion of the whole work"). Just as the tree was the (fictional) source of the novels in 1868, it will be the scientific conclusion, the validation of the original hypothesis. The only rationale for not including all of the details Zola claims to have collected about the family, and that Pascal will expose at length in the final novel, is out of consideration for the reader, whose pleasure at discovering the various dénouements of the remaining novels must be kept intact, as he writes, "pour ne pas déflorer les épisodes futurs" ("in order not to deflower the future episodes"). Zola thus cleverly offers himself an escape route, since he had not yet planned out many of the novels to be written.

Various documents in the *dossiers préparatoires* for *Le Docteur Pascal* show the development of the tree from 1878 to 1893, when the final volume was published. Besides a copy of the tree drawn by Zola's wife Alexandrine, the dossiers contain extensive files on nearly all of the individual family members detailing their medical histories and professions, along with a list of the novels with each Rougon-Macquart who appears in them (*Les Rougon-Macquart,* 5:1562–64). One document of particular interest is an annotated copy of the 1878 tree, which records the changes to the original plan as the novel cycle closes (figure 4.3). As if pruning the tree, Zola marks which members have died ("mort" or "morte") and which continue to live ("vit") in 1874, when the last novel ends. Curiously, the family member most tied to the empire, Eugène, bears the ambiguous label "à Paris vivant défendant l'empire mort" ("in Paris liv-

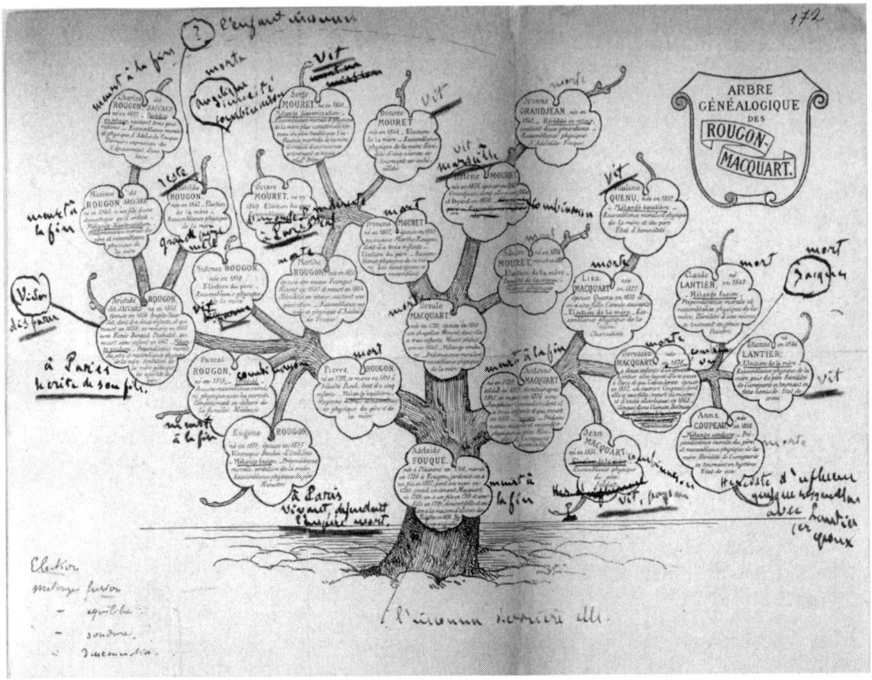

Figure 4.3. 1878 genealogical tree revised by Zola. Mss, NAF 10.290 folio 172. Courtesy of Bibliothèque nationale de France.

ing defending the dead empire"). New branches sprout (or perhaps are grafted onto the tree after the fact), such as Jacques Lantier ("mort"), son of Gervaise Macquart, who was invented for *La Bête humaine* years after Gervaise's novel *L'Assommoir.* The most significant aspect in this transitional document is that for the first time the tree inscribes the unknown onto the text: Saccard's illegitimate son, Victor, is labeled "disparu" (he disappears at the end of *L'Argent*); Clotilde and Pascal's child, nameless and here sexless, is labeled "? L'enfant inconnu" ("? the unknown child"); below the "trunk" of the tree, buried in the ground under Tante Dide, are the words "l'inconnu derrière elle" ("the unknown behind her"). The desecrated cemetery of the Aire Saint-Mittre, with its mysterious past, finally appears on the tree, the family's inscrutable origins extend beyond the madness of Adélaïde. Likewise, the fifth generation reintroduces uncertainty as the tree can no longer provide the key to deciphering the future of the anonymous child.

True to the promise he made in 1878, Zola plants the genealogical tree at the center of the narrative of the final novel. Pascal, like Zola, records significant events in the tree as he closely follows the lives of his family members; Pascal's tree has the same graphic form as the one published with the novel:

> C'était une grande feuille de papier jaunie, aux plis coupés par l'usure, sur laquelle s'élevait, dessiné d'un trait fort, un arbre symbolique, dont les branches étalées, subdivisées, alignaient cinq rangées de larges feuilles; et chaque feuille portait un nom, contenait, d'une écriture fine, une biographie, un cas héréditaire.[12] (*Les Rougon-Macquart,* 5:1006)

For the doctor, and perhaps for the novelist as well, it is the symbol and the summation of the piles of scientific dossiers. At the same time, Pascal acknowledges that it is a beautiful fiction, "où il n'y a pas un trou" ("without one hole"), that only works because it ignores the genetic input of the spouses (Mouret, Lantier, Quenu, etc.), the numerous other families who have been grafted onto the tree. It has its basis in reality, even if a selective reality, that confounds a simple mathematical logic, since genetics proves not to be strictly distributional; Charles, in the fifth generation, closely resembles his great-great grandmother Dide even though, as Pascal observes, he inherits only one twelfth of his genes from her (*Les Rougon-Macquart,* 5:1008). Full of scientific optimism, Pascal is nonetheless prudently skeptical about his own theories and the fumbling beginnings of the new discipline. Indeed, Pascal confirms what Zola's novels themselves demonstrate, that thinking through genetic origins and destinies belongs equally to the poet as well as to the scientist: "Il y a là [dans les sciences commençantes] une marge qui leur appartient [aux poètes], entre la vérité conquise, définitive, et l'inconnu, d'où l'on arrachera la vérité de demain" (5:1008) ("There is [in emerging fields] a margin which belongs to them [poets], between conquered, definitive truth and the unknown, from which will be torn the truth of tomorrow"). This poetic margin, between truth and the unknown, indicates, to those who know how to read it, the place where "solutions" are to be found (5:1008).

The tree's role as poetic text to be interpreted for possible solutions becomes clear later in the novel when Pascal himself scrutinizes it for answers. For over twenty years, the doctor carried on his research at a safe, objective remove from his subject, for he believed he was free of the family affliction, the "fêlure," despite rumors that he is a half-crazed genius, "toute cette légende de génie à demi fêlé" (*Les Rougon-Macquart,* 5:1119). The 1878 genealogical tree notes that he is "complètement en dehors de la famille" ("completely outside the family"). His obsession with work, his growing fear that someone will destroy his dossiers, and his budding passion for his niece Clotilde provoke in him a paranoid state, which he fears to be the manifestation of inherited madness. Desperately, he interrogates the tree: "Il étala l'Arbre sur la table, il continua à le considérer longuement, de son air terrifié d'interrogation, peu à peu vaincu et suppliant, les joues mouillées de larmes. Pourquoi, mon Dieu! L'Arbre ne voulait-il pas lui répondre?" (*Les Rougon-Macquart,* 5:1034) ("He spread out the Tree on the table, and continued to stare at it for a long time, with a terrified look of interrogation, little by little defeated and supplicating, his cheeks wet with tears. Why, my God!, wouldn't the Tree answer him?"). He is only cured of his temporary madness after he is assured that Clotilde will not destroy the dossiers (*Les Rougon-Macquart,* 5:1043). The incident proves to him that his illness was only an accident (perhaps "archive fever"), and so heredity played no part; the tree could provide no answers but only act as a mirror to his paranoia.

After the moving scene of Pascal's death, when he completes his own leaf and that of his unborn child on the tree, Pascal's mother, Félicité, and his servant set fire to all the papers locked in his armoire in order to destroy the archive implicating the family in countless horrors. The only remains are fragments of paper, scraps where not one page is left completely intact. The tree, at Pascal's bedside, survives despite Félicité's feverish search for it (*Les Rougon-Macquart,* 5:1197), but his years of research, his data and theories, are lost forever. At the end of the novel, Clotilde contemplates the charred remains of the dossiers and unfolds the tree, lost in a daydream. Unable to make out much of anything, the words on the page instead recall memories and emotions. A vision comes to her in the form of a living family tree: "L'Arbre montait, ramifiait ses branches, épanouissait ses feuilles, et elle s'oubliait longuement à le contempler, à se dire que toute l'oeuvre du maître était là, toute cette végétation classée et documentée de leur famille. Elle entendait les paroles dont il commentait chaque cas héréditaire, elle se rappelait ses leçons" (*Les Rougon-Macquart,* 5:1216) ("The Tree rose up, extending its branches, unfolded its leaves, and for a long time she lost herself in contemplation, telling herself that the master's entire work was there, the whole classified and documented mass of their family. She heard the words with which he explained every hereditary case, she recalled his lessons"). No longer a rigidly scientific document, the tree without its accompanying and explanatory dossiers becomes a deeply personal text, bringing back memories of Pascal and his work, though not his complete theories. The tree contains an image of the past, but also turns toward the future, reaching out its branches into the unknown with the young children of the next generation, perhaps untouched by the family illness: "Et elle-même retombait à une rêverie, devant l'Arbre prolongeant dans l'avenir ses derniers rameaux. Qui savait d'où naîtrait la branche saine? Peut-être le sage, le puissant attendu germerait-il là" ("And she fell back into a daydream, in front of the Tree, which extended its last branches into the future. Who could say where the healthy branch would be born? Perhaps the long-awaited wise, great man would germinate there?"). The Rougon-Macquart genealogical tree records a long list of atrocities, madness, crime, and imbecility, but it also inscribes on the page the rejuvenating forces of life, the eternal hope for the new.

A comparison of the 1878 genealogical tree to Pascal's definitive tree from 1893 (figure 4.4) illustrates the change of focus from origins to a concern about the future. The drawing for the 1878 tree very much resembles a traditional depiction of a tree: each family member has a label in the form of a leaf, and the earth at the tree's base is shaded and in relief, extending out into the horizon. The branches are arranged naturally, with the result that some family members appear lower than their parents, as a tree extends its branches outward as well as upward. The legitimate Rougon side of the tree appears healthier than the Macquart side, reaching upward toward the top of the page. The 1893 tree, while still retaining "leaves" for each family member, becomes much more abstract. Branches extend far out horizontally and only go up. Each leaf lines up exactly with those from the same generation and is roughly the same size, regardless of the amount of information contained. The ground is much less developed and does not convey the sense of horizon, but blades of grass adorn what was once barren dirt. While still having fewer members than the Rougon side, the Macquart branches are just as healthy. Less "arborescent" and more "rhizomatic," the Rougon-Macquart genealogy spreads outward in unpredictable ways, like blades of grass. Jean Macquart's robust peasant children and Pascal and Clotilde's nameless boy have equal chances for brilliance or decadence. The tree branches out and continually upward, drawing the eye to the top of the page and to the future.

The title in both cases is placed in the corner within a form reminiscent of a family crest. As a coat of arms, it bears only the words "Arbre généalogique des Rougon-Macquart," and the name of the family is inscribed on a ribbon that is folded in on itself. If one were to imagine unfolding the paper, the names of each branch of the family would be on opposite ends, just as the two branches are split at their origin and their family members destined to occupy separate economic and social realms. The fold in the ribbon brings the two branches together, juxtaposed to each other on the page, but not repairing the original break, like the tree itself which

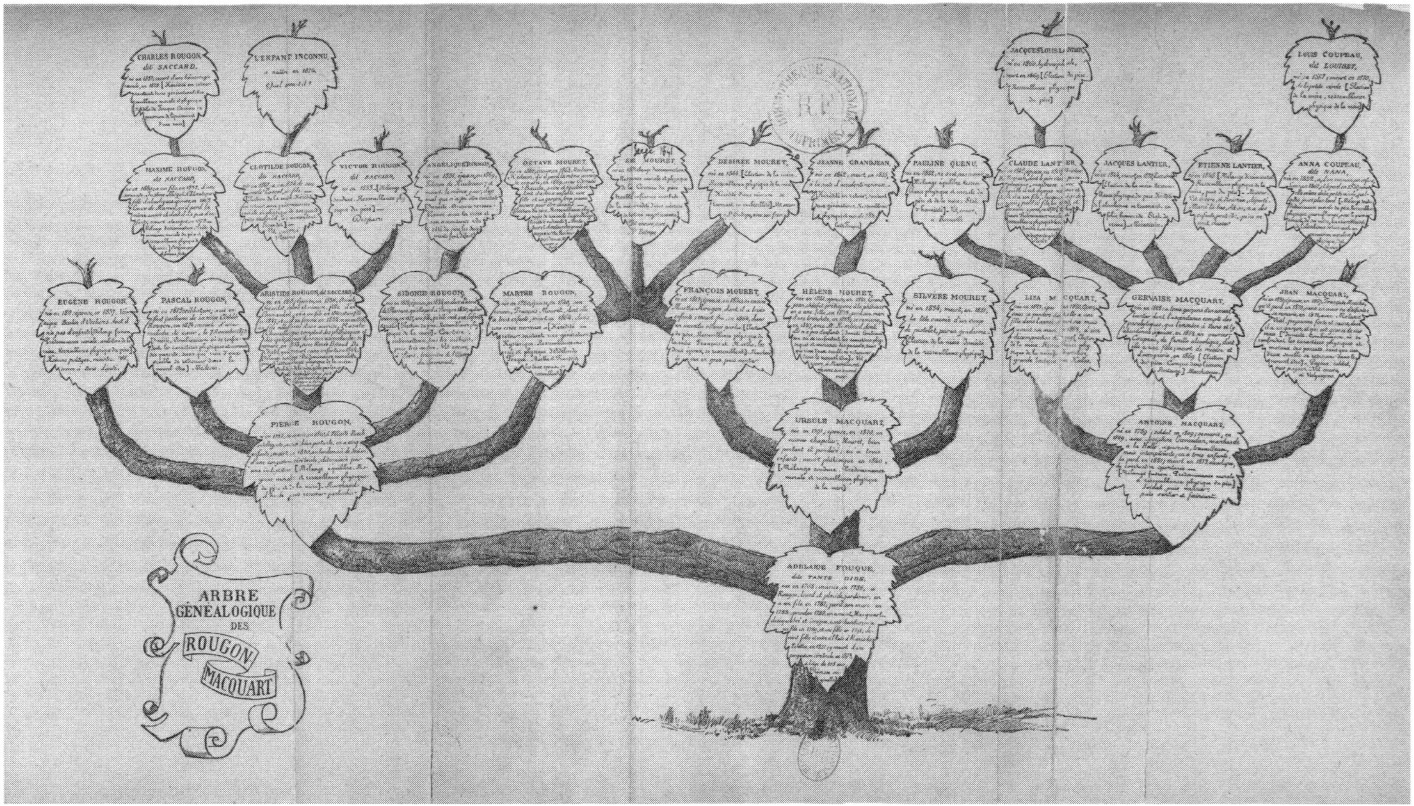

Figure 4.4. Definitive genealogical tree for the Rougon-Macquart. LLA, NQ-C-034532. Courtesy of Bibliothèque nationale de France.

points to a common though unknowable origin. The ribbon itself makes a vaguely circular movement as the Rougon, always on top, turns down to make the fold out of which the Macquart begin to ascend.

Even more than Saccard's mental map of Paris, one image in particular crystallizes the will to locate a simulated origin in the space of a text. The successive genealogical trees drawn up for the *Rougon-Macquart* fuse the "natural" history of the family to its "social" history in a single iconic representation, since genetic traits are inscribed alongside class markers across all social strata and four or five generations. Expanding as the family swells along with the number of novels, the genealogical tree, no matter how much it grows and changes, must continue its role as surrogate origin, documenting what little is known of the past while inventing what may exist beyond the immediate present. The explicit point of juncture of the *dossiers préparatoires* and the fictional narrative, the genealogical tree fantasizes an impossible synthesis of origin and termination, birth and death, cause and effect: it transforms a novel series into the *Rougon-Macquart* cycle.

PART V
Proust's Double Text

L'espace fond comme le sable coule entre les doigts. Le temps l'emporte et ne m'en laisse que des lambeaux informes . . .*
—Georges Perec, *Espèces d'espaces,* 180

Marcel Proust's monumental novel *À la recherche du temps perdu* captures the struggle to write the self in the spaces of the text, fictionalizing the process of the formation of textual subjectivity found in Stendhal's and Nerval's autobiographical texts, as well as the anguish of Sand's fictional characters and of Zola in his *dossiers préparatoires.* Stendhal employed the autobiographical form to gain perspective on the self; the subject was enclosed and controlled by a mapped text. The rigid mathematical and Cartesian mapped self inscribed in the *Vie de Henry Brulard* proves to be incompatible not only with a self that changes over time, but also with a text that produces a multiplicity of meanings through the very ambiguity of fictional autobiographical narrative. Though the problem of time and change is partially resolved by Stendhal through the bird's-eye-view maps evenly spaced in the text, his objective study of the self fails to satisfy the dual necessity of communicating the particulars of subjectivity while maintaining the integrity of the self. The *Vie de Henry Brulard* ends abruptly in order to save the self from certain death in and by the text.

Instead of mapping subjectivity as Stendhal had done, Nerval's works seek to envelop the self in the places it inhabits to the extent that the self becomes indistinguishable and inextricable from its environment. The Oriental Gérard, the Gérard of the Valois, or the universal Gérard of

*Space melts like sand runs through the fingers. Time carries it away and only leaves me with shapeless fragments . . .

Aurélia and of the "Généalogie" are situated in extra-temporal places that would seem to protect the self from the adverse effects of change. Nerval does not prematurely end the narrative to ensure the integrity of the self as Stendhal's text had done, but rather has others die in his place in order to fulfill the death inherent in narrative's dénouement. Only in *Aurélia* will an equivalent to Stendhal's bird's-eye view emerge in the form of the "double aspect." The simultaneous presence and superposition of a sane or conscious narrator with a dreaming or unconscious narratee reintroduces the element of time, which had been repressed by the Nervalian subject. Time changes the self and transforms it into another, a double. The "double aspect" of Nerval's narration suggests at the end of *Aurélia* that the text can, as Stendhal had wished, provide a means to see oneself as other through a textual image, a novel map that collapses spaces and times to reveal the becoming of the self.

Sand's *Indiana* and *Nanon* convey the dangers and advantages of textuality for nineteenth-century women, the need to invent new models of subjectivity in the utopian spaces and hypothetical time of the novel. Similar to Proust's novel, her works engage with and ultimately transcend the realist tradition. Zola's division of his text into dossiers and novel, unified by the *Rougon-Macquart* genealogy, becomes an integral structuring principle in Proust's novel. The *Recherche* is a double text unifying Zola's split or parallel texts: at once the journal of one man's long and painful path to becoming a writer and the novel that man eventually writes.

Proust's novel tells the story of what happens when Stendhal's autobiography falls definitively into the novel. The autobiographical simulacrum (that the "I" of the present coincides with the "I" of a text) becomes a simulated autobiography where the two components of subjectivity (the self and its relation to the other) are copies without originals, since "Marcel" is not Proust. The other is an exteriorized image of the self, and the self proves to be absent from the text. Just as Zola's and Nerval's genealogies marked the impossible coincidence of the self across time and especially of the writer with the written, Proust's circular novel connects the novel's conclusion (the narrator decides to write a novel) with its beginning (the narrator is inscribed as text). The death of the writing subject in text, feared by Stendhal, Nerval, and Zola as well as Sand's fictional characters, is in Proust reversed as the only true life is now one lived in literature. But the cost of this textual life amounts to a hollowed self, written in time and not space as a perpetual becoming in text, in language, and actualized by readers who use the novel as an instrument to see themselves.

The cyclical structure of the novel calls for a cyclical reading where the key to its interpretation as a novel about time is revealed retrospectively. A first reading, chapter 9, considers the text as the story of a failed autobiography where the narrator progressively loses his identity in the spaces of his imagination, until the final revelation that his true vocation is that of a novelist. The second reading, chapter 10, considers the text as the successful novel about time, or the story of the success of literature in forming what Nerval called a "passable subject." The novel in its entirety forms a novel map: instead of a referential illusion confusing a space outside the text with the space of the text, the (material) novel (in the reader's hands) about the becoming of a writer coincides at every point with the (hypothetical) novel the writer claims to write in the future (in the reader's imagination).

Chapter Nine

The Law of the Land

In Search of Lost Place

At the familiar beginning of *À la recherche du temps perdu* one finds in contradiction to the novel's title, not a search for lost time, but the frantic search for a lost place. The narrator, writing in the ambiguous tense of habit, the imperfect, relates the trouble he has going to sleep and the even greater trouble he has of finding himself again upon waking. The anonymous *je,* who for a long time put himself to bed early, floats in and out of sleep, in and out of consciousness in an unspecified time and place. Improbable identities are assumed and discarded as the reading *je* turned dreamer becomes whatever subject of the book happened to be on the page when consciousness was lost: "Il me semblait que j'étais moi-même ce dont parlait l'ouvrage: une église, un quatuor, la rivalité de François Ier et de Charles Quint" (*CS I,* 3) ("It seemed to me that I was indeed what the work was talking about: a church, a quartet, the rivalry between François I and Charles V").[1] The subject of any text can manifest itself as the textual subject: *je*'s consciousness is invaded by the image of whatever he is reading, be it a person, a church (reminiscent of Rancière's idea that Victor Hugo was the first to make a building the subject of a novel), or even an abstract concept such as a rivalry. When he first wakes, the images persist in confusing his identity, since the dreamed text has absorbed the narrator's awareness of himself. Even the pronoun varies from *je* to *il* and *on,* as the narrative moves between the particular anonymous first person to the general third person. Just as Nerval began *Aurélia* with a dreaming subject, free from the conditions of time and space, who reformulates the Cartesian experience of doubt into the liberating experience of dream, the opening of Proust's novel explores the liminal space between consciousness and unconsciousness, dream and "reality," perception and illusion.

After the initial description of an identity confused by the textual images of the books he reads, the narrating *je* restates the experience in general terms, as a law. The second formulation is an ontological theory that displaces the original cause of confusion—reading—onto what is now described simply as deep sleep: "il suffisait que, dans mon lit même, mon sommeil fût profond et détendît entièrement mon esprit" (5) ("it sufficed that, in my very bed, my sleep was profound and entirely relaxed my mind"). The shift from the persistence of textual images to deep sleep implies that the experience of the "dormeur éveillé" ("wakened sleeper") is a universal human condition, and not one restricted to avid readers; as we will see, however, subjectivity in the *Recherche* is profoundly tied to the reading of literature. On a narrative level, the displacement of reading prepares the way for the separation of the narrating *je* and the narrated, and therefore textual, *je*, since the text will reflect the past of the narrating subject instead of the unfolding of a present in the text, as in Stendhal's self-discovery in *Vie de Henry Brulard*, or Zola's in his *dossiers préparatoires*.

The "dormeur éveillé" scene emphasizes the spatial component of identity and memory. The dreamer is able to move freely between different times and different worlds; once he awakens, his power to travel across time and space diminishes and he must remember his location. If the sleep is too deep, the awoken sleeper is faced with the terrifying proposition of not knowing where he is and therefore who he is:

> Un homme qui dort, tient en cercle autour de lui le fil des heures, l'ordre des années et des mondes. Il les consulte d'instinct en s'éveillant et y lit en une seconde le point de la terre qu'il occupe, le temps qui s'est écoulé jusqu'à son réveil; mais leurs rangs peuvent se mêler, se rompre . . . Mais il suffisait que, dans mon lit même, mon sommeil fût profond et détendît entièrement mon esprit; alors celui-ci lâchait le plan du lieu où je m'étais endormi, et quand je m'éveillais au milieu de la nuit, comme j'ignorais où je me trouvais, je ne savais même pas au premier instant qui j'étais; j'avais seulement dans sa simplicité première, le sentiment de l'existence comme il peut frémir au fond d'un animal; j'étais plus dénué que l'homme des cavernes; mais alors le souvenir—non encore du lieu où j'étais, mais de quelques-uns de ceux que j'avais habités et où j'aurais pu être—venait à moi comme un secours d'en haut pour me tirer du néant d'où je n'aurais pu sortir tout seul; je passais en une seconde par-dessus des siècles de civilisation, et l'image confusément entrevue de lampes à pétrole, puis de chemises à col rabattu, recomposaient peu à peu les traits originaux de mon moi.[2] (5–6)

Once again, like Balzac's *La Peau de chagrin*, Stendhal's *Vie de Henry Brulard*, and Nerval's *Aurélia*, Proust's novel grafts the experience of an anonymous subject onto the model of Descartes's cogito. The *je* finds itself in a dark bedroom, deprived of any sensation except that of existence itself. For Descartes, the knowledge of existence, proven by the simple act of thought, was sufficient to guarantee being; for Proust's awakened sleeper, mere existence is not enough; it is his essence, here connected to a place, that must be found. Proust's anguished narrator, in the pitch-black darkness of his bedroom, does not even have the dim light of Plato's cave dweller to project an image of his identity onto the wall.

Descartes was granted the assurance of the truth of his perception by the miraculous presence of God to his consciousness; no less miraculous for Proust's *je* is the "salvation from above" of the memory of the bedrooms where he has lived. Memory is not a part of the subject and cannot be accessed at will; the narrator's passing over "centuries of civilization" reinforces the concept of a universal memory of which our personal memory is only a part. The impersonal character of memory suggests that we do not remember ourselves, but only the places where one of our many selves may be found (just as the view of Rome recalled all of Stendhal's life as well as all of Roman history, and as Nerval attempted to regain his childhood memories by returning to the Valois).

The narrator's consciousness uses memory to link identity to place, with the assumption that the subject is contiguous with an unchanging place in the external world (Bersani, 21). Blocks of space-time, in the form of bedrooms, offer the subject a multiplicity of selves from which to choose. The act of taming a hostile room, described here and later in the first scene of the Grand-Hôtel in Balbec, terrifies the narrator not because of the newness of the room, but because one self must cede to another. Habit, a form of inattentive memory, is the process that creates a new self in response to an unfamiliar place; habit renders a place inhabitable by projecting a stability onto place and masking its inevitable movement and change in time. Yet habit creates an illusory stability, since places, and therefore identity, are anything but stable: "Peut-être l'immobilité des choses autour de nous leur est-elle imposée par notre certitude que ce sont elles et non pas d'autres, par l'immobilité de notre pensée en face d'elles" (6) ("Perhaps the immobility of things around us is imposed on them by our certitude that it is these same things and not others, by the immobility of our thought confronting them"). As will be argued in chapter 10, movement and mobility are essential to the understanding of time and identity in the *Recherche*. The miraculous, involuntary memory of the many bedrooms and the attentive memory of intellect required to choose from among them the bedroom of the present counter the immobilizing effect of habit or inattentive memory: "Toujours est-il que, quand je me réveillais ainsi, mon esprit s'agitant pour chercher, sans y réussir, à savoir où j'étais, tout tournait autour de moi dans l'obscurité, les choses, les pays, les années" (6) ("Still is it that, when I would wake up in this way, my mind casting about, without success, trying to know where I was, everything would turn around me in the darkness: things, countries, years"). The active attention of the mind forces places into movement and reveals time's relation to place and identity.[3]

The shock created by the search for identity in the bedrooms of the past, while short-lived, has lasting effects. The first effect is a temporary solution to the problem of identity: after a few seconds, certitude has settled in, and a bedroom is chosen. The furniture of the bedroom is put "approximately" in its place, and the present identity of the subject is assured. The last sentence of "Combray" questions the very notion that remembered places are stable. The narrator definitively awakens only to find that the immobility he imposed upon the bedroom furniture was illusory; the light of dawn sets everything in motion as it rectifies the error of the narrator's memory: "La demeure que j'avais rebâtie dans les ténèbres était allée rejoindre les demeures entrevues dans le tourbillon du réveil, mise en fuite par ce pâle signe qu'avait tracé au-dessus des rideaux le doigt levé du jour" (184) ("The dwelling I had rebuilt in the shadows was to join up with the dwellings glimpsed in the whirl of waking, made to flee by this pale sign which the raised finger of daylight had traced above the window curtains"). The end of "Combray" is thus another revelation that places and identity cannot be accurately remembered, but instead must be created.

The narrator's search for place and identity at the beginning of "Combray" leads directly to the active remembering of the events recounted in the text, which flows from the insomnia caused by the disruption of habit. Since the mind of the narrator has already been set in motion, he can no longer fall back to sleep as the memories of past places, selves, and stories unsettle the stability and immobility of the localized self:

> Mais j'avais beau savoir que je n'étais pas dans les demeures dont l'ignorance du réveil m'avait en un instant sinon présenté l'image distincte, du moins fait croire la présence possible, le branle était donné à ma mémoire; généralement je ne cherchais pas à me rendormir tout de suite; je passais la plus grande partie de la nuit à me rappeler notre vie d'autrefois, à Combray chez ma grand'tante, à Balbec, à Paris, à Doncières, à Venise, ailleurs encore, à me rappeler les lieux, les personnes que j'y avais connues, ce que j'avais vu d'elles, ce qu'on m'en avait raconté.[4] (8–9)

The nostalgic reminiscence of Combray, Balbec, Paris, Doncières, and Venice introduces the reader to the dominant places of the novel and lays the foundation for the narrator's identity as it will appear in the text. Like Stendhal's declaration "After so many general remarks, I am going to be born," the Proustian narrator's awakening and reminiscence creates both a *je* that narrates in the present and a narrated or remembered *je* of the past anchored in the text in an autobiographical simulacrum occurring after the agonizing analysis of the self across many times and many places. The *Recherche* will tell the story of how the narrated *je* becomes the narrating *je,* and the two will reunite at the end of *Le Temps retrouvé.*

The memories that directly follow the sleepless night form the basis of "Combray I," which is centered around the famous "goodnight kiss" scene. Despite the vivid recollection of the scene, the narrator is incapable of recalling anything but one distinct place and time of day: "comme si Combray n'avait consisté qu'en deux étages reliés par un mince escalier et comme s'il n'y avait jamais été que sept heures du soir" (43) ("as if Combray had only consisted of two stories joined by a narrow staircase and as if it was only ever seven o'clock in the evening"). The past contained in Combray cannot be remembered in full and is therefore dead to the narrator, as is, by extension, the narrator's past self. Just as a miraculous intervention in the form of the memories of past bedrooms saved the awakened dreamer from his identity crisis, the sensation and ensuing involuntary memory provoked by the madeleine create the greater world of "Combray II," and suggest the possibility of existence beyond death. Though the involuntary memory stimulated by the taste of the madeleine also involves the movement of consciousness, it differs from the initial active remembering of bedrooms in that it is an act of creation:

> Je pose la tasse et me tourne vers mon esprit. C'est à lui de trouver la vérité. Mais comment? Grave incertitude, toutes les fois que l'esprit se sent dépassé par lui-même; quand lui, le chercheur, est tout ensemble le pays obscur où il doit chercher et où tout son bagage ne lui sera de rien. Chercher? pas seulement: créer. Il est en face de quelque chose qui n'est pas encore et que seul il peut réaliser, puis faire entrer dans sa lumière.[5] (45)

Proust's famously long sentences become suddenly terse as the narrator's mind or consciousness (*l'esprit*) grapples with the enigma of the madeleine and searches desperately within the interior space of the self ("le pays obscur") to create a connection between past and present. The present and the past taste of the cake dipped in tea are both found in the narrator's *moi,* but it is the task of his mind to invent the link between the two that will bridge the vast distance in time that separates the two sensations. As Gérard Genette has shown in "Métonymie chez Proust," the madeleine scene begins with a creation that bridges two times through metaphor, and then continues with an opening up of the place of Combray through metonymy in order to begin the narrative (*Figures III,* 63). After the false start of "Combray I" which introduced the difference in narrating and narrated subject, the madeleine episode, through the vertical axis of time (metaphor) and the horizontal axis of space (metonymy), creates the places of the text and lays the foundation of identity, which will continue until the final revelations of *Le Temps retrouvé.* The narrative, therefore, relies on places, and by extension space, to create identity. Yet how are the places of the *Recherche* inscribed in the space of the text?

Place Names and Name-of-the-Father

Instead of Stendhal's or Sand's visual maps, Nerval's mythical genealogies, or Zola's geometries, Proust's novel uses as its structuring principle the places conjured up in the evocation of a proper name—*le Nom.* The titles of volumes and subsections sufficiently reveal the role of place and name in organizing the *Recherche:* "Combray," "Nom de pays: Le nom," "Nom de pays: Le pays," *Le Côté de Guermantes,* and *Sodome et Gomorrhe.* For Proust, a name is already an essence distinct from, yet inextricably related to, the object it designates. Names hold within their syllables the secret of places, and by pronouncing a name, by exploring the resonance of its sound, the narrator unfolds place and essences contained in it. The names of persons or families, and especially noble families whose names are "toujours des noms de lieux" ("always names of places"), prove to be just as spatial as the names of places.[6] Proper names have the power to capture an essence, and everything contingent with it, because of the illusion that they refer to only one object, as opposed to common words which designate interchangeable objects (Barthes, "Proust et les noms," 124). Places, likewise, are supposed to be unique and not interchangeable;[7] yet the very oneness of names and places means that place names are paradoxical. The essence, or place, contained in the name is far greater than that of the "real" place itself, with the result that the two are incompatible. Names, for Proust, are already places, and two places cannot occupy the same space; names are also signs, and every sign indicates the absence of its object (in the words of Mallarmé in "Crise de vers": "Je dis: une fleur! . . . l'absente de tous bouquets"—"I say: a flower! . . . the one absent from all bouquets"). A place name and the place it designates are inextricably but arbitrarily linked; they form two separate regions that cannot overlap.

The tension between a proper name and its object fuels the novel's narrative as the young hero first acquires the imagery of names, then experiences the disillusionment of places, and finally discovers the redemption of literary creation. For Roland Barthes, in "Proust et les noms," the "accident" that allows the passage from Proust's earlier writing attempts to the *Recherche,* the event that imposes a unifying system to the novel, is the invention of proper names: "L'événement (poétique) qui a 'lancé' la *Recherche,* c'est la découverte des Noms" (124–25) ("The (poetic) event that 'launched' the *Recherche* is the discovery of Names"). Proper names, as Barthes suggests, are "voluminous signs" that call to be interpreted by the narrator, or "apprentice," as Barthes names him following Deleuze (125). The work of the novelist is to explore the relationship, not between the object and its form or the sign and its referent, but rather between the signifier and the signified, to explore the depths of signs (133). Barthes is correct in expanding Deleuze's conception of the Proustian sign to account for the crucial role of proper names, but he fails to account for the spatial dimension of names or their relation to identity as outlined by Proust himself. Toponyms provide the unifying system of the novel by structuring it *spatially.*

"Combray" introduces the narrator, and the reader, to the names of the *Recherche,* and in "Combray" names are received from the father. Of all the narrator's family members, it is perhaps the father who appears to play one of the smallest roles in the text;[8] after the episodes of "Combray" he is hardly mentioned at all, in contrast to the mother and the grandmother who continue to dominate the affective life of the narrator.[9] The father's minor part in the narrative reduces him to a caricature. He becomes the figure of fatherhood, all the more so because he himself lacks a proper name (conversely, the mother's lack of a proper name keeps her more intimate, especially since she is often called "Maman," while the father is only called "Papa" once, presumably after he has died, at the end of *Le Temps retrouvé*). Combray may be a matriarchy led by Tante Léonie that often reveals the father to be ridiculous or arbitrary in his actions, but it is through this very arbitrary domination that he involuntarily teaches his son the power of names.

As the beginning of *Le Côté de Guermantes* declares, "Les Noms [nous offrent] l'image de l'inconnaissable que nous avons versé en eux" (*CG II,* 310) ("Names [present us] the image of the unknowable that we have poured into them"), and in the sketch of the same episode published in the 1954 version of *Contre Sainte-Beuve,* a name is "une urne d'inconnaissable" (272) ("an urn of the unknowable"). A name is only magical for the narrator if he can project onto it, or pour into it, the unknowable. The name of someone or something already known is as banal as a common word. The narrator mocks the grandmother when she claims that her friend Mme de Villeparisis is a Guermantes: "Comment aurais-je pu croire à une communauté d'origine entre deux noms qui étaient entrés en moi, l'une par la porte basse et honteuse de l'expérience, l'autre par la porte d'or de l'imagination?" (*JF II,* 58) ("How could I believe in a communality of origin between two names which had entered my mind, one by the lowly and shameful gate of experience, the other by the golden gate of imagination?").

The father's reflex in raising his son is to say "no," and in so doing, he denies the narrator an immediate experience of the world. Often incapable of leaving the house, the narrator projects onto names his desires for knowledge, for travel, and for sex. In "Combray I," following the suggestion of the grandfather, the father sends the narrator to bed without the ritual kiss from the mother (*CS I,* 30–36); this denial of motherly affection sets in motion a pattern of desire that is repeated continuously until *Albertine disparue.* The father, against the grandmother's wishes, forbids the narrator from taking evening walks in the rain, instead asking him to read in his room (*CS I,* 11). He disapproves of the grandmother's reading choices for the young child (*CS I,* 39). He habitually and arbitrarily breaks the "pacts" that the mother and grandmother make with the narrator, since "il ne se souciait pas des 'principes' et qu'il n'y avait pas avec lui de 'Droit des gens'" (*CS I,* 35) ("he was not concerned with 'principles' and there were no such things for him as 'Rights of Man'"). The father's persistence in snubbing Swann and his wife only adds to their prestige in the eyes of the narrator; their greater social distance fills the name of Swann with wonder and contributes to the narrator's budding love for Gilberte (*CS I,* 98 and 142–43). At the end of *Le Côté de chez Swann,* in the section titled "Noms de pays: Le nom," the narrator dreams of traveling to Balbec or to northern Italy and wonders three separate times whether his parents will allow him to go. When his father, checking the barometer and confirming the weather, finally agrees to a voyage to Italy, the son's excitement is so great that he falls sick; the doctor, another father figure, especially if we take into account that Proust's father was a physician, forbids the narrator both to travel to Venice and to go to the theater to see la Berma (*CS I,* 382–86). The desire to know Venice, repeatedly prevented because of Albertine, is not satisfied until *Albertine disparue.* Because of his father, the narrator is unable to experience firsthand the objects he desires; he therefore maintains the distance between name and place or object needed to transform a name into a place of desire. The father's "negative influence" on the narrator succeeds in nourishing his rich imaginary world and in filling names with the mystique of the unknowable.

The father is instrumental in another key way: he lays out the mental and physical geography for the novel. It is the father who leads the family walks through Combray, and he is a master of the terrain. On moonlit nights, he would lead the family on long walks: "Mon père, par amour de la gloire, nous faisait faire par le calvaire une longue promenade, que le peu d'aptitude de ma mère à s'orienter et à se reconnaître dans son chemin, lui faisait considérer comme la prouesse d'un génie stratégique" (*CS I*, 113) ("My father, out of love of glory, would take us on the ordeal of a long walk, which my mother's ineptitude at orienting herself and recognizing what road she was on made her regard as the feat of a strategic genius"). The family would be so disoriented that the father could lead them directly behind their home without the rest of the family recognizing the back door of the house (114). In the eyes of the narrator, the father controls perspective and mysteriously navigates the space of Combray.

It is the father who teaches the son, inadvertently, that the two "côtés" ("ways") are so opposed that one cannot walk both of them on the same day:

> Car il y avait autour de Combray deux "côtés" pour les promenades, et si opposés qu'on ne sortait pas en effet de chez nous par la même porte, quand on voulait aller d'un côté ou de l'autre . . . Comme mon père parlait toujours du côté de Méséglise comme de la plus belle vue de plaine qu'il connût et du côté de Guermantes comme du type de paysage de rivière, je leur donnais, en les concevant ainsi comme deux entités, cette cohésion, cette unité qui n'appartiennent qu'aux créations de notre esprit . . . Cette habitude que nous avions de n'aller jamais vers les deux côtés un même jour, dans une seule promenade, mais une fois du côté de Méséglise, une fois du côté de Guermantes, les enfermait pour ainsi dire loin l'un de l'autre, inconnaissables l'un à l'autre, dans les vases clos et sans communication entre eux, d'après-midi différents.[10] (132–33)

The habitual activity of taking either one "côté" or the other on any given afternoon (an activity presumably dictated by the father) seals each path off from the other definitively, which creates in the mind of the narrator two "vases clos" ("sealed vessels") that can never communicate.[11] Because the father would speak about each "côté" in superlatives and, for the son, in apparently contradictory terms, the narrator conceived of them as absolutes that structured spatial relations and therefore organized mental categories. They are united in the narrator's mind only because they share the same quality as classifying places. People, as well as other places, are defined throughout the rest of the novel in relationship to one or the other "côtés," as shown by the titles of two volumes, *Du côté de chez Swann* and *Le Côté de Guermantes.* The narrative is written as the narrator follows the two divergent paths and explores the world from the two perspectives of Combray.

The father literally and figuratively misleads his son. During the family walks he manipulates space to reveal the view of the home as an unfamiliar place. As the narrator discovers later, the father arbitrarily separates the two "côtés"; thus the narrator's future experience (and consequently the structure of the narrative) is mapped in advance according to the father's conception of Combray's places. The mapping of the novel through Combray manifests the more general paternal role: the production of the symbolic. He imposes on his son, albeit without knowing it, a dichotomy between the symbolic world of names and the world of experience. Jacques Lacan, in "Fonction et champ de la parole et du langage," has described this process in psychoanalysis as the "Nom-du-père" ("Name-of-the-father"): "C'est dans le *nom du père* qu'il nous faut reconnaître le support de la fonction symbolique qui, depuis l'ordre des temps historiques, identifie sa personne à la figure de la loi" (*Écrits I,* 276) ("It is in the *Name-of the-father* that we must recognize the foundation for the symbolic function which, since the beginning of history, identifies its person to the figure of the law"). Lacan argues that the father, or more accurately the already dead symbolic father, establishes himself as the figure of the law through his *nom* (and its homonym *non*). The law the Name-of-the-father founds is that of the symbolic order. The Symbolic, for Lacan, constitutes a structure like language, where a symbol or signifier is not fixed to any one signified (Laplanche and Pontalis, *The Language of Psychoanalysis,* 440).

In the *Recherche,* the father inscribes the law of signifiers, thereby defining the social interactions of his son. Within the narrative, the narrator is constantly defined by the notoriety of his father, and specifically by his father's name. When the narrator first meets Odette, in her incarnation as *la dame en rose,* she recognizes him as the image of his mother, at which point his uncle Adolphe corrects her: "Il ressemble surtout à son père" (*CS I,* 76) ("He especially resembles his father"). In *À l'ombre des jeunes filles en fleurs* Mme de Villeparisis is impressed by his last name (*JF II,* 59). Suspecting that the father of the narrator is traveling with her longtime companion Norpois, she asks him, "Est-ce que vous êtes le fils du directeur au ministère? . . . Il paraît que votre père est un homme charmant. Il fait un bien beau voyage en ce moment" (61) ("Are you the son of the department head at the ministry? . . . It seems that your father is a charming man. He is having a beautiful trip at the moment"). The other characters in the novel are much more concerned about the father's status than is the narrator. That the narrator should lack a family name in the text only reinforces the transgression of the written text. The narrator, without a proper name and thus without a proper place in the text, wanders the places of the text whose borders were drawn by the Name-of-the-father.

The law of the Name-of-the-father reigns over the symbolic order, over the names and therefore the places of the text. The father institutes the uniqueness of names and places, legislating identity as a function of the two "côtés." There is a law of the land, inscribed by the father, that prevents the narrator from moving from one place to another, from redefining his identity, and from changing or writing his name. Michel de Certeau, in *L'invention du quotidien 1. Arts de faire,* makes a distinction between space and place that elucidates the relationship between space, place, and identity in the novel:

> Au départ, entre espace et lieu, je pose une distinction qui limitera un champ. Est un *lieu* l'ordre (quel qu'il soit) selon lequel des éléments sont distribués dans des rapports de coexistence. S'y trouve donc exclue la possibilité, pour deux choses, d'être à la même place. La loi du "propre" y règne: les éléments sont les uns *à côtés* des autres, chacun situé en un endroit "propre" et distinct qu'il définit. Un lieu est donc une configuration instantanée de positions. Il implique une indication de stabilité.[12] (172–73)

Place is defined as an order of distribution of relationships based on juxtaposing objects without superposing them. The stability of places relies on the "loi du 'propre,'" its uniqueness, in the same manner as proper names. The law of place, the law of the land, stabilizes identity through an ordered classification of signs.

There is thus a fundamental link in the *Recherche* between the system of signs imposed by the father's law and the system of places that structure the novel. The narrator's apprenticeship of signs and the revelation of his vocation as writer is, in essence, an apprenticeship in the transgression of the law of places and in the power of literature to create new signs. For Certeau, space is the necessary counterpart to place: "Il y a *espace* dès qu'on prend en considération des vecteurs de direction, des quantités de vitesse et la variable de temps. . . . À la différence du lieu, il n'a donc ni l'univocité ni la stabilité d'un 'propre.' En somme, *l'espace est un lieu pratiqué*" (173)[13] ("There is *space* as soon as directional vectors, quantities of speed, and the variable of time are taken into consideration. . . . Unlike place, it has neither the univocity nor the stability of the 'proper.' In short, *space is a place put into practice*"). Space, in Certeau's definition, is mobile; it accounts for movement and time with the effect that it disrupts the apparent stability and immobility of place (in a similar way to the movement given to the narrator's consciousness in his search for a stable identity). Through its multiplicity, its disrespectful disruptions, space disobeys the law of place. Space as practice of place is transgression or "délinquance." All narratives contain a spatial component since they describe an itinerary or a succession of places over time (171); for Certeau, then, narrative itself is delinquent: "Si le délinquant n'existe qu'en se déplaçant, s'il a pour spécificité de vivre non en marge mais dans les interstices des codes qu'il déjoue et déplace, s'il se caractérise par le privilège du *parcours* sur l'*état,* le récit est délinquant" (190) ("If the delinquent only exists by moving around, if he has as his specificity living not at the margins but in the interstices of the codes which he foils and shifts, if he characterizes himself by the privilege of the *path* over the *state,* narrative is delinquent"). The nameless, placeless, narrator, in the interstices of the text, crosses the places of the text and transgresses the law of the land as established by the father. The *Recherche* itself tells the story of how, through his transgression of paternal law, the narrated *je,* defined by the stability of place, is transformed into the narrating *je* of transgressive space and transformative time. He changes from being subject *to* the text to being the subject *of* the text. A new conception of subjectivity will emerge as a function of the narrator's relation to place through the slow apprenticeship of signs and the final discovery of his vocation.

Places Lost, Time Regained

A comprehensive study of the narrator's disillusionment with place is beyond the scope of this chapter, since the bulk of his apprenticeship of signs, names, and places covers over 2,500 pages, roughly from the end of *Du côté de chez Swann* to the beginning of *Le Temps retrouvé.* However, by focusing on a few key passages, the trajectory of the narrator's path toward the final revelation of his vocation as writer can be traced. "Nom de pays: le nom" ("Place Names: The Name" or "Name of the Country: The Name"), at the end of *Swann,* expands and theorizes the narrator's infatuation with the power and place of names; it is there that he develops his love for Gilberte and her name and his obsession with Balbec and

Venice. The logical counterpart to this initiatory section of the *Recherche* is found in the second half of *À l'ombre des jeunes filles en fleurs,* titled "Nom de pays: le pays" ("Place Names: The Place" or "Name of the Country: The Country"). At Balbec the narrator encounters for the first time the deception of place names and the impossible coexistence of the essence of a name and the experience of place. "Nom de pays: Le pays" sets in motion the forces that unravel the system of names and places that structure the narrator's world.

The Balbec of his dreams, as detailed in "Nom de pays: Le nom," is a synthesis of various descriptions given to the narrator by Swann and Legrandin: Balbec has a magnificent beach and a church that is both Romanesque and Norman Gothic, "on dirait de l'art persan" (*CS I,* 377–78) ("one could say Persian art"). The narrator envisions Gothic architecture mixed with a sea storm (378). Nothing, of course, could be further from the reality he comes across when he arrives there with his grandmother by train. He imagines that certain city names, like Chartres and Bourges, "servent à désigner, par abréviation, leur église principale" ("can designate, as an abbreviation, their principal church"), and therefore that the cities themselves take on in the imagination the same architectural style as the church itself (*JF II,* 19). The name Balbec, by its synthesis of stormy beach and Persian, Gothic, and Romanesque architecture, should radiate onto everything connected to it the uncanny combination of a Norman seascape with an Oriental flair. The first deception happens on the train when the unity of the Balbec name is sectioned into different train stations: Balbec-le-Vieux, Balbec-en-Terre, and Balbec-Plage. The locals are confused when the narrator asks to find a slope where he can view only the church and sea at the same time. Not only is it a sunny day with no storm in sight (in fact, his lasting memories of Balbec will be those of sunny afternoons), but Balbec church is very far from the sea. No view can encompass what turn out to be contradictory elements contained in the false unity of the name Balbec.

The narrator discovers that his synthesis of church and sea was based on a misreading of guidebooks and an inattention to the conversations he had with Swann, Legrandin, and Norpois. Like Nerval's Oriental voyager, who was misled by an overly enthusiastic reading of guidebooks and ancient texts, the narrator projects meaning onto the letters and syllables of names. He mistook the colorful architectural metaphors of guidebooks for geographical indications:

> C'était bien de falaises battues par les flots qu'avait été tirée la pierre de la nef et des tours. Mais cette mer, qu'à cause de cela j'avais imaginée venant

> mourir au pied du vitrail, était à plus de cinq lieues de distance, à Balbec-Plage, et à côté de sa coupole, ce clocher que, parce que j'avais lu qu'il était lui-même une âpre falaise normande où s'amassaient les grains, où tournoyaient les oiseaux, je m'étais toujours représenté comme recevant à sa base la dernière écume des vagues soulevées, il se dressait sur une place où était l'embranchement de deux lignes de tramways, en face d'un café qui portait, écrit en lettres d'or, le mot "Billard"; il se détachait sur un fond de maisons aux toits desquelles ne se mêlait aucun mât. Et l'église . . . faisait un avec tout le reste, semblait un accident.[14] (*JF II,* 19)

Materially, Balbec church is built out of the rocks from the sea cliffs. Metaphorically and metonymically, the steeple resembles the cliff out of which it is made. It shares its name with Balbec-Plage, and can therefore assimilate some of the essence of the beach. Around its steeple, seabirds hover. The unity of the church's stones and structure constitutes a place that evokes the sea, and yet the church itself has been displaced. It has apparently been banished to the very landlocked Balbec-en-Terre, where the imaginary church has been "en-terrée" ("buried"). Instead of the steady crash of waves against the rocks, tramways disturb the unity of place by shuttling passengers between places. The gilded letters above the café mock the sanctity of names, as they designate the common game of billiards and not what the narrator considers as the holy and unique name of Balbec. The configuration of the place of Balbec has no meaning as its constituent parts are randomly juxtaposed. Balbec is not the unique manifestation of an essence, but a mere accident.

The narrator vainly attempts to revive the dying image of Balbec church by repeating to himself the uniqueness of place: "C'est ici, c'est l'église de Balbec. Cette place qui a l'air de savoir sa gloire, est le seul lieu du monde qui possède l'église de Balbec" (20) ("It is here, this is Balbec church. This place, which seems to know its glory, is the sole place in the world that possesses Balbec church"). He wants to believe that the statues in front of him at Balbec are somehow more, because unique, than the countless photographs and descriptions that had filled his imagination before his voyage. Instead of being more than the sum of the images it has inspired, the church is much less. The narrator comes to this realization when he grasps that he occupies the same space as the church, that he can measure its statues. He could permanently alter the physical appearance of the site by simply writing his signature over the soot crusted on the stone, disfiguring the unique, and only, statue of the Virgin of Balbec. The essence of eternal beauty incarnated in the statue changes into "une petite vieille de pierre" (21) ("a little old lady made out of stone"). Graffiti operates by crude appropriation through the superimposition of the narrator's name over the statue: the now materialized art object loses its own name, which is replaced by that of the narrator. He leaves the church in dismay, but for the moment at least, blames himself and bad circumstances for his inability to see in the church what he imagines is expressed in its name (21).

While the metaphors found in guidebooks can lead astray the traveler who knows of places only through their names, the narrator learns later during his stay at Balbec that metaphors created by a work of art can free objects of their names and alter our everyday perceptions of them. The work of the painter Elstir, one of a series of artists in the *Recherche,* imposes on the narrator the need to manipulate the perspective of place through metaphor in order to counter the debilitating effects of habit. When the narrator first enters Elstir's studio in Balbec, he is disappointed that the majority of paintings there are only "marines" ("seascapes") inspired by local views. Yet what at first appear to be clichéd paintings of the sea turn out to be unexpected transformations that represent true impressions instead of the constructions of intelligence:

> J'y pouvais discerner que le charme de chacune [des marines] consistait en une sorte de métamorphose des choses représentées, analogue à celle qu'en poésie on nomme métaphore et que si Dieu le Père avait créé les choses en les nommant, c'est en leur ôtant leur nom, ou en leur donnant un autre qu'Elstir les recréait. Les noms qui désignent les choses répondent toujours à une notion de l'intelligence, étrangère à nos impressions véritables et qui nous force à éliminer d'elles tout ce qui ne se rapporte pas à cette notion.[15] (*JF II,* 191)

The metaphors expressed by Elstir's paintings are epitomized by his view of the port of Carquethuit where the artist reverses the viewer's intellectual expectations by only using for the town "des termes marins" ("sea terms") and for the sea "des termes urbains" ("urban terms"). Elstir's metaphors teach the narrator that names signify only a concept dictated by intelligence and that truth lies in our impressions. Elstir practices a blasphemous re-creation of the world by removing or changing the names that God *the father* created. Elstir reveals not only that the father's symbolic order is an illusion, he also teaches how to perceive the truth beyond the illusion of space: "Mais les rares moments où l'on voit la nature telle qu'elle est, poétiquement, c'était de ceux-là qu'était faite l'oeuvre d'Elstir" (*JF II,* 192) ("But the rare moments when we see nature as it really is, poetically, Elstir's work was made of those"). The narrator is only able to put theory into practice after the revelation of his literary vocation. When Julia Kristeva, in *Le Temps sensible,* asserts that "Proust ne cesse de 'déchiffrer,' mais son monde n'est pas fait de 'signes.' En tout cas, ce ne sont pas des signes-mots ni des signes d'idées, encore moins des signifiants ou des signifiés" (307) ("Proust never stops 'deciphering,' but his world is not made of 'signs.' In any case, not word-signs or signs of ideas, even less signifiers and signifieds"), she works backward from the novel's conclusion without taking into account how the narrator arrives there. If the world of the narrator (Proust's world is presumably our world, whereas the world of the narrator is the text) is made up of impressions, as the passage quoted above suggests and as Kristeva argues (252), impressions themselves can only be revealed and communicated by the displacement of signs, by the process of renaming proper to metaphor. Proust's text never argues that signs do not exist, but rather argues for their continual reformulation through art.

The collapse of the system of places and of names that started with "Nom de pays: Le pays" continues as the narrator discovers the vacuity of aristocratic society, the deterritorialized cities of the plain (since homosexuality is ubiquitous), and the impossibility of sequestering a loved one (in his words "un être de fuite" or "a being of flight"). This slow destruction of places of the novel, and thus of the identity of the narrator, speeds up exponentially at the end of the cyclical novel, in *Albertine disparue* and *Le Temps retrouvé.* The two "côtés" change forever as they too are destroyed and delocalized, not by God the father, but by World War I and the experience of the narrator. After his return from Venice, he learns that Gilberte Swann and Robert de Saint-Loup-en-Bray are engaged. Their marriage indicates a possible link between the two "côtés," since each represents for the narrator one of the two paths. A few pages from the end of *Albertine disparue* Gilberte, now married, invites the narrator to her home, Tansonville, near Combray, where he has been absent since childhood. The return to Combray leads to a succession of discoveries for the narrator. He and Gilberte take long moonlit walks, not unlike the ones that the narrator's family would take in his youth, but now the countryside has no effect on him. The actual geographical places no longer have anything in common with his memories of them. Gilberte tells him that they could walk to Guermantes in less than fifteen minutes (*AD IV,* 268). There is thus an end to the Guermantes Way, but it retains the mystery of its name:

> C'est comme si elle m'avait dit: "Tournez à gauche, prenez ensuite à votre main droite, et vous toucherez l'intangible, vous atteindrez les inattingibles

> [*sic*] lointains dont on ne connaît jamais sur terre que la direction, que—ce que j'avais cru jadis que je pourrais connaître seulement de Guermantes, et peut-être, en un sens, je ne me trompais pas—le 'côté.'"[16] (*AD IV*, 268)

The "côté de Guermantes" as well as the name Guermantes first acquired their mystique because the destination of Guermantes was unreachable, the contents of the place, unknowable. The only tangible, attainable aspect of Guermantes was the name and the path, or the "side," that led to the mysterious place. The narrator maintains that, in a sense, he was correct in believing that he could never reach Guermantes, the place, because it only exists in his imagination as a name, a path, and a family. A reversal has happened, where the importance now lies in experience, in the tangible as opposed to the imaginary. The syntax of the sentence reinforces the narrator's discovery, since the word "côté" has been removed to the end of the sentence, which indicates that the path is an end in itself.

Gilberte's next stunning geographical revelation, already prepared by the narrator's apathy to the places of his childhood, is the fact that the most agreeable way to walk to Guermantes is to take the Méséglise path ("Swann's way"). The two "côtés" connect in space, as they have already done socially through the marriage of Gilberte (Swann) and Robert (a Guermantes). The discovery of the paths' unity "boulever[sait] toutes les idées de mon enfance" (*AD IV*, 268) ("shattered all the ideas from my childhood"), as it unravels all the mental geography of Combray inscribed by the father, the mental geography upon which is based the entire novel. Yet Combray and his memories of it are already dead to the narrator, who no longer shows any interest in his past or even life itself. The destruction of the places that structured his world encourages him further in his self-imposed isolation (he will spend most of the war in a "maison de santé"). Gilberte makes one final disclosure that ends both *Albertine disparue* and, in a sense, the errors and wanderings of the narrator: the secret desires that he held for Gilberte at their first meeting were shared, if not surpassed, by Gilberte herself, as she had tried to show him with an indecent gesture (271–72). What he desired so much during his walks in Combray, what he felt to be attainable only in his imagination, had always been possible, indeed would have been realized had it not been for his investment in the imaginary. He had desired only what he thought he could not have (Gilberte, Guermantes, and the power of names detached from places); yet it was the obstacle of the imaginary that obscured the possibility of experience. The structure of places, founded upon the desire for an essence contained in a name, completely collapses through Gilberte's revelations.

The passages devoted to the First World War in *Le Temps retrouvé* complete the destruction of the system of place set up in "Combray." History erupts to sweep away the illusion of the permanence of place. Like the "blank" Proust praises in Flaubert's *L'Éducation sentimentale* which separates Frédéric's horror at the murder of Dussardier from his return to Paris years later, the narrator abandons society for health reasons for an untold number of years, the minute details of his observations suddenly disappear, his quest to be a writer abandoned. The narrator finds himself in a "maison de santé" (ambiguously "nursing home" or "mental home") far from the social and political upheavals in Paris brought on by the war. The asylum functions as an absence of place and desire; nowhere does the narrator indicate why he is there, where it is located, or what it looks like. On a strictly narrative level, his stay at the asylum provides a distance, both in time (over many years) and space, from both the social world of Paris and the places of Combray; this distance allows the narrator sufficient perspective to understand the momentous changes in society after the war (Shattuck, 61–64). By severing the link with the past, the war disrupts the effects of habitual memory and permanently transforms the geographical and mental places of the text. Yet the "maison de santé" also marks the complete failure of the narrator to make the names which fill his imagination coincide with the places he occupies. Recovering from what may be a nervous breakdown, he exists nowhere, he writes nothing.

Only the lack of medical personnel during the war forces the narrator to leave the asylum briefly to travel to Paris. He describes a transformed city where the skies above are filled with warplanes and underground in the metro social classes are mixed while seeking shelter. The social hierarchy is shifted by the war, as it had been earlier by the Dreyfus Affair. Mme Verdurin ascends to the top of the social ladder, and Charlus, because of his Germanophilia, loses his prominence.

The war transfigures Combray even more than Paris. In a letter to the narrator, Gilberte describes her experiences at Tansonville in the middle of the fighting: "Vous n'avez pas idée de ce que c'est que cette guerre mon cher ami, et de l'importance qu'y prend une route, un pont, une hauteur" (*TR IV*, 335) ("You have no idea what this war is my dear friend, and the importance that a road, a bridge, an elevated site can take"). The Germans destroyed Méséglise, blew up the bridge over the Vivonne, and fought all along the "côté de Méséglise," where over 600,000 men died (335). Names are created to reflect military realities: the end of the Méséglise Way becomes infamous as the "côte 307" ("hill 307"). The war performs the same metaphorical transformations as Elstir's paintings, temporarily imposing a military perspective on the countryside. The Vivonne stream, the place of the narrator's childhood fascination, becomes a strategic battleground that divides Combray into French and German territories. The nostalgic *lieu de mémoire* of childhood is now a national *lieu de mémoire.* Gilberte is correct in emphasizing the new importance of Combray's places, but the war has changed their role. Instead of constituting identity through stability, places during the war become a function of strategy and instability; war transgresses the places of Combray and creates indeterminate identities that change rapidly depending on the location of enemy territory.

Charlus, in a conversation with the narrator, provides another blow to the system of places set up in "Combray": Combray's church, serving as a German observatory, was destroyed by the French and the English troops (*TR IV,* 374). The Combray church, when it first appears in *Du côté de chez Swann,* is described in human terms: it is a "simple citoyenne de Combray" (*CS I,* 62); the steeple looks over the whole town, giving meaning to the affairs of Combray's inhabitants (64). The church is not simply a symbol for the town, but its organizing principle (just as the two "côtés" organize the narrator's world). The Combray church used to stand for the very presence of time incorporated in place:

> Un édifice occupant, si l'on peut dire, un espace à quatre dimensions—la quatrième étant celle du Temps—déployant à travers les siècles son vaisseau qui, de travée en travée, de chapelle en chapelle, semblait vaincre et franchir non pas seulement quelques mètres, mais des époques successives d'où il sortait victorieux.[17] (*CS I,* 60)

The church, however, does not survive the modern epoch victorious; its destruction during the war indicates the inability of places or persons to resist the work of time. The church is built in the space of a few meters and is built in time across the centuries, but it is never outside of time nor immune to time's effects. The final sentences of the novel will return to the idea that being is subject to time more than it is to space. However, instead of the "four-dimensional" church which symbolized the people of Combray in a few meters and over many centuries, it is people themselves who occupy a disproportionately greater place in time than they do in space.

After the war is over, after the places and symbols of the narrator's youth have been destroyed, the narrator despairs of ever being capable of writing a novel or even of acting in a meaningful way. The places that formed the basis of his identity have vanished; he no longer believes in the father's symbols that had mapped out his world. Without a preexisting discourse, even an oppositional one, no place exists for the narrator to inscribe himself in space. He can no longer decide between the magic of names and the disappointing experience of places. The complete rejection of external space, the hollowing out of the narrator himself, coupled with the five successive incidents of involuntary memory before the "bal de têtes" at the Princesse de Guermantes's lead to the revelation that the narrator's vocation is to write a novel about time. Instead of the narrator's inevitably flawed perception of places conforming to the imaginary world formed by evocative place names, instead of looking for truth in deceptively legible external signs, the narrator must look inward toward the space of the unconscious.

For Proust's narrator, the unconscious is a text composed of signs engraved by the impressions of reality: "Ce livre, le plus pénible de tous à déchiffrer, est aussi le seul que nous ait dicté la réalité, le seul dont l'‘impression' ait été faite en nous par la réalité même" (*TR IV*, 458) ("This book, the most painstaking of all to decipher, is also the only one that reality has dictated to us, the only one whose ‘impression' was made in us by reality itself"). The unconscious text is to be deciphered with difficulty by the artist, who must search within the self for the truth of external reality.[18] The reading of this text can only be accomplished through an act of creation, through the writing of another text, which would be the translation of the "livre intérieur de signes inconnus" (*TR IV*, 458) ("the interior book of unknown signs"). The composition of a book about time that would translate the "unknown signs" of subjective interiority necessarily reconfigures the paternal signs that founded the law of places. This new book would set the "paternal" places in motion through narrative and would thus create unexpected connections between places and between signs. Instead of the hierarchical law of the land imposed by the narrator's father, the narrator's book about time would represent the transformation of signs over time and according to the interpretation of each new reader.

An understanding of the self through a reading of the "inner text" allows the narrator to perceive himself and others as they really are. Art and literature in particular are the only means of making us "sortir de nous" ("leave ourselves"), by transporting us to different places, re-creating the temporal experience of involuntary memory and communicating it to others (474). Only through literature can we perceive our own essence in its relation to time. In this way, real life is, paradoxically, a life of literature: "La vraie vie, la vie enfin découverte et éclaircie, la seule vie par conséquent pleinement vécue, c'est la littérature" (474) ("True life, life finally discovered and understood, the only life consequently fully lived, is literature").

Chapter Ten

Creating a Space for Time

Proust Paradox

The end of the *Recherche* leaves the reader with an unanswerable question. Is the novel the narrator is about to write the novel the reader is about to finish, or is it a virtual novel, existing somewhere beyond the reader's imagination and the theoretical projections of the aging narrator? Many indications within the text itself favor one or the other interpretation: Proust's text most often calls itself a story or "récit," which distinguishes it from the "ouvrage" ("work") that the narrator will write (Landy, 127); on the other hand, the *Recherche* is so unquestionably a masterpiece that it would be difficult to label it a simple *mémoire,* and perhaps even more difficult for the reader who has finished many thousands of pages to accept that the narrator does not succeed in his vocation. Critics have tended to make a clear choice for one or the other possibility.[1]

As I noted in chapter 9, the experience of confusion upon waking (and later of involuntary memory) suspends the narrator's consciousness between different times, places, and identities. Perhaps the reader of the *Recherche* can and should find the same joy in indecision and suspend decision not only about her or his own identity upon reading (as the text seems to solicit), but also about the identity of the very text that is read. At any one moment the reader could interpret the narrative *je* as either the narrator of a story about a writer (who may or may not ever finish a novel) or as a meta-narrator, one who narrates the story of his own coming into narration. Paul Ricoeur, in *Temps et récit II,* argues that throughout the *Recherche,* until the very last moments of revelation at the "bal de têtes," the voice of the narrator is practically indiscernible from that of the hero, or narrated *je;* at the end of the novel, the two voices become one (or rather the narrator drowns out the hero), as they were the same presumably in the first few pages when the narrator floats between time, space, and multiple identities (Ricoeur, 252–53). The functions of the two narrative voices are distinct, but it is difficult at any one instant to declare which voice speaks through the *je*.

Gérard Genette in "Proust Palimpseste" (*Figures I*) argues that since the *Recherche* is a double text, the reader feels an imperative to reread:

> En effet chaque moment de l'oeuvre est en quelque sorte donné deux fois: une première fois dans la *Recherche* comme naissance d'une vocation, une deuxième fois dans la *Recherche* comme exercice de cette vocation; mais ces "deux fois" nous sont données ensemble, et c'est au lecteur, informé *in extremis* que le livre qu'il vient de lire reste à écrire . . . qu'il échoit de remonter jusqu'à ces pages lointaines . . . et qu'il doit maintenant relire.[2] (62–63)

But if the *Recherche* is a "practice of this vocation" the careful reader will be capable of reading the text for the elements of its style that reflect or anticipate the final revelation about time, even if the reader is not informed in extremis of the dénouement. Paul Ricoeur argues that there are signs in the text that hint to the final revelation. He compares the *Recherche* to an ellipsis with "deux foyers" ("two foci"): one the apprenticeship of signs, as described by Deleuze, and the other the final revelation of the narrator's vocation. The *Recherche* tells a "fable about time" because it relates these two incompatible "foci." Ricoeur's focus on the structural level of the novel leads him to emphasize only the aspects of time that reveal the extra-temporal and the past. As will be seen later in this chapter through a close reading of the image of time itself, time in the *Recherche* is not only what reveals the past, but what allows us to see the work of time through text.

The *Recherche* is a work that projects backward from the final revelation to the beginning of the novel, a sort of "futur dans le passé" (Ricoeur, 257). The conditional mode is nothing other than a verbal form of the future in the past; the novel itself can be taken as a conditional text. If the reader chooses to read for the plot that leads toward the final revelation of the narrator's vocation, then, as in chapter 9, the novel ends as a failed autobiography that looks toward the future and the creation of a literary work not yet written. However, if the reader chooses to read (presumably in a second reading of the *Recherche*) as if the work itself were the novel written by the narrator, then, as in chapter 10, the text appears to be the writing of its own past, its own becoming. In this second conditional statement, the literary theories of the eventual narrator or the diegetic author of the novel would be apparent, not in what the narrated *je* says (since he is not yet the writer of the novel), but rather in the form and style of the writing itself.

À la recherche du temps perdu is both a work about the role of place, where time is kept at bay, and a novel about the role of time against the stability of places. It is both a work obsessed by places where time appears, literally, as an afterthought only in the last two hundred pages, and a novel where the image of time is infused in every single sentence. The *Recherche,* because of the very impossibility of deciding one absolute condition for its reading, becomes a virtual text, actualized differently with every successive reading.

Spatial Time: Movement and Metaphor

If the *Recherche* may be read (also) as a novel about time, then it can only be so despite its own plot. As chapter 9 demonstrated, the novel portrays the narrator as a character obsessed with the connection of places, names, and identity, to the exclusion of time. The novel form, while possessing an element of time (one reads over time), is structured by the places of proper names and the spaces of the written page.[3] The narrator, in his literary apprenticeship, spends the greater part of the novel (all but the last few hundred pages) deceived by these spatial elements of his textual world. In the same way as he becomes aware, retrospectively, of the role time has played in his life, the enlightened reader of the *Recherche,* who presumably reads the novel for a second time, perceives time everywhere in the text. Time must be in some relation to place and to space, and yet also must remain hidden to the narrator until the end of the novel. The act of reading the *Recherche* (as the novel about time) becomes a search for the time lost in the text. Such a reading requires a willful inattention to the troubles of the narrator and the plot, and necessitates an active focus on the language of the text and in particular metaphors as manifestations of the creative force of time revealed by involuntary memory.

Time, on the level of each sentence, in the *Recherche* is expressed through a relation to or a practice of place. As I argued in chapter 9, the law of place relies on the stability of ordered relations represented in one moment of time. A unified system of places, such as that imposed by the father's law, would negate time and becoming because it would prevent movement across places and across the instants of time. The negotiation of place, the practice of place (by a walker, by narrative, or by transgression) constitutes space, "space is a place put into practice" (Certeau, 173). Space is at the crossroads of mobile place ("l'espace est un croisement de mobiles"—"space is a crossing of moving objects/motives," 173), and forms destabilized, and therefore temporalized, place. Time manifests itself in space as movement since it is the motion of places that make up space. Once places are set in motion, the ordered, fragmented, and chronological time expressed in the law of place yields to the flux of true time experienced as duration. The *Recherche* is a novel about time and duration because it is a novel about movement.

The text creates movement through narrative, through metaphor, through involuntary memory, and through literal representations of motion (such as the description of automobiles). Narrative inscribes movement in the text because it describes the changing relationships of places to each other and to the characters. The narrator as character distinguishes himself from the narrator as writer of the novel because he is subject to the law of places while the writing narrator continually upsets the law of places. The narration of the novel is a transgression of the (father's) law of places, a creation of space, and a revelation of time through motion. However, a reading that strictly analyzed the plot would follow the first-person character's attempts to fix identity in place and would consequently miss the more fundamental revelation of time through the movement of metaphors, which threaten his sense of immobile places. Metaphors bridge the distance between places; they translate impressions and shuttle meaning.

Movement in the form of metaphor exists at every level of the text, from individual words, to sentences, and to entire episodes. The monumental scale of Proustian sentences multiplies the possible implications of a metaphor, sometimes over many pages. The narrator's world becomes increasingly complex and marked by speed as technological advances (the telegram, the telephone, the train, the automobile, and the airplane) allow movement and communication to cross previously impossibly distant places in ever shorter time increments; in a literal way movement is a sign of the times, an indication of a changing society.[4] The technological analogy of harnessing movement would be the ordered regulation of train schedules that attempts to neutralize any unexpected event; both Swann and Marcel in their jealousy use train schedules to trace the flight of their elusive beloveds (Carter, 26). Though metaphor takes two different objects and "les enferm[e] dans les anneaux nécessaires d'un beau style" (*TR IV,* 468) ("encloses them in the necessary links of a fine style"), the movement of metaphor, as a function of time, invariably creates something new and unexpected. An accelerated cycle of movement occurs where a dangerous movement necessitates the control of metaphors, which in turn create a new movement requiring even more metaphors. The play of meaning in a text cannot be stopped by the writing of more text.

The "moments bienheureux" ("happy or felicitous moments") caused by involuntary memory, the most famous of which is of course the madeleine scene in "Combray," provide the inspiration for literary creation at the end of the novel by revealing the role of metaphor, and so any analysis of movement in the text must account for movement in the various "moments bienheureux" scattered throughout the novel. Roger Shattuck's classification of these episodes in *Proust's Binoculars* remains the most complete analysis. He counts eleven "moments bienheureux," but notes that Samuel Beckett names them "fétiches" and includes a few other, incomplete, episodes; Shattuck also writes that Howard Moss names them "mnemonic resurrections" and counts eighteen of them (*Proust's Binoculars,* 149–50). Shattuck recognizes six stages in a basic but variable pattern: (1) a preexisting state of mind (usually depression), (2) an intense sensation (like the taste of the madeleine), (3) an inner feeling (pleasure, exaltation, or sadness), (4) recognition of a past sensation, (5) presentiment of the future, and (6) some result (like the revelation of Marcel's literary vocation) (*Proust's Binoculars,* 70). Shattuck's most original insight is the role of the fifth stage, that of presentiment. Involuntary memory not only recalls a past sensation, but very often announces the future, or at least the future of the text: the madeleine scene announces the composition of the episode of Combray; the steeples of Martinville announce "la réalité pressentie" ("a premonition of reality") (*Proust's Binoculars,* 75) and also another "moment bienheureux," the three trees in Hudimesnil; Vinteuil's septet announces the possibility of joy in the afterlife; and the sequence of five episodes in *Le Temps retrouvé* announces Marcel's vocation and the future composition of his book (70–75). The involuntary memory of a past sensation calls forth images of the future and therefore creates a movement between the individual instants of the past and the text as a whole. Involuntary memory does not arrest time, but sets in motion images that manifest time. The images describe the past of a sensation, the present, and a future in a block of time where creation (the literary text) can emerge.

Movement also exists in the emergence of the sensation of involuntary memory. In the madeleine episode, the narrator, after tasting the madeleine soaked in tea and undergoing an intense sensation, attempts to repeat the sensation by drinking more tea, to no effect. He understands finally that the sensation is not in the object, but within himself. He must force his mind to travel deep into his memory in order to find the original sensation. Finally, after emptying his consciousness and tasting the madeleine again, the past sensation is unleashed and moves to the surface of the present:

> Je sens tressaillir en moi quelque chose qui se déplace, voudrait s'élever, quelque chose qu'on aurait désancré, à une grande profondeur; je ne sais ce que c'est, mais cela monte lentement; j'éprouve la résistance et j'entends la rumeur des distances traversées. Certes, ce qui palpite ainsi au fond de moi, ce doit être l'image, le souvenir visuel, qui lié à cette saveur, tente de la suivre jusqu'à moi.[5] (*CS I*, 45)

The narrator attempts a few more times to re-create the sensation and search his memory, always using a vocabulary of movement: "arrivera-t-il jusqu'à la surface?" ("will it arrive all the way to the surface?"), "l'attraction d'un instant identique" ("the attraction of an identical instant"), "soulever tout au fond de moi" ("to lift up everything from deep within me"), "il est arrêté, redescendu peut-être; qui sait s'il remontera jamais de sa nuit?" ("it stopped, went down again perhaps; who knows if it will ever ascend again out from its darkness?") (46). The image or visual memory attached to the taste of the tea-soaked madeleine moves upward from the depths of his memory and causes another sensation of shivering, different from that of taste. He is unable at first to make out the image since it becomes confused in the "insaisissable tourbillon des couleurs remuées" (46) ("the elusive whirlwind of shifting colors"). The image of memory is in movement as it translates the time of the original sensation to the present.

The episodes of involuntary memory, while describing motion, often portray the narrator himself in motion, a "movement of movements" as Bergson would say (Deleuze, *Cinéma 1*, 37). Shattuck counts five of the eleven episodes where the narrator moves while experiencing a "moment bienheureux": at Martinville and at Hudimesnil he is in a carriage; in Paris with Saint-Loup he descends a staircase; after a dinner at the Duc de Guermantes's he again travels in a carriage and "[il s'agitait] dans la voiture, comme une pythonisse" (*CG II*, 840) ("[he wiggled about] in the car, like a prophetess"); he is on a train going to Paris in an episode at the beginning of *Le Temps retrouvé*. The narrator's movement multiplies perspective and destabilizes place. His privileged perspective becomes a-centered, which seems to disrupt his habitual repression of the past and obsession with immobile places.

The first and quintessential episode of a "mobile" "moment bienheureux" is that of the "steeples of Martinville" near the end of "Combray." During a family walk on a late afternoon, he despairs, already as an adolescent, that he has no talent for letters. As it is getting late, his family accepts a ride home in a neighbor's carriage; the narrator takes the seat next to the coachman. The unusual speed of the coach, the winding turns in the road, and the changing light of sunset provoke in him "ce plaisir spécial qui ne ressemblait à aucun autre" ("this special pleasure that resembled no other"): the two Martinville steeples appear to change places and then seem to be right next to the Vieuxvicq steeple, which is separated from them by a hill and a valley (*CS I,* 177–78). The experience so preoccupies the narrator that he borrows pencil and paper, and, without sensing the analogous relation between the pleasure of this new perception and "une jolie phrase" (179) which he will understand much later, he decides to compose a short prose description right in the carriage, despite the rattling motion. The young narrator's passage is cited directly in the text, but the details are more vivid and the metaphors more startling than in the first description. The steeples are now anthropomorphized, and their apparent motion is given intentionality. At one point they remind him of three legendary young girls. He is very attentive to the passing of time, as if the scene were a race between the steeples and the coach: "Les minutes passaient, nous allions vite et pourtant les trois clochers étaient toujours au loin devant nous . . . Puis le clocher de Vieuxvicq s'écarta, prit ses distances . . . je pensais au temps qu'il faudrait encore pour les atteindre" (179) ("The minutes passed, we traveled quickly and yet the three steeples were always far ahead of us . . . Then the Vieuxvicq steeple moved away, took its distance . . . I thought about the time still needed to catch up with them"). The movement in this "mobile shot" changes the relationships the steeples have between each other and with the observer: first there are two steeples, then a third; for a while they are immobile, then one moves away; they wave a sign of good-bye, and return again only to be transformed into three painted flowers and then three girls; finally, after the sun sets, they close in on one another to compose one black form that disappears into the night (179–80). The movement of the carriage ride changes the spatial relationships of the steeples and thereby creates changing perspectives and changing images. In these images each steeple expresses duration and transformation in a unique manner, just as time, in the form of old age, expresses itself differently in the faces of the "bal de têtes." Though the narrator is unaware of it when he composes his sketch, the joy he feels upon observing the movement of the steeples is related to an experience of true time expressed through the succession of transformed steeples. He is so relieved to have rid himself of the intense moment through writing, that after singing like a chicken who has just laid an egg (180), he promptly forgets about the whole episode.

This early writing experiment contains all the elements of involuntary memory and metaphor that will appear a few thousand pages later in *Le Temps retrouvé*. The episode at Martinville illustrated early that movement proliferates perspectives and images of change. While the young narrator's writing of the episode converted his experience into metaphor, and thus textual movement, it also immobilized the experience through this very writing. He quickly forgets about the episode and the passage because the act of writing temporarily captured or immobilized the moment. Because the narrator forgets the "steeples of Martinville" episode, the significance of the role of time and writing remains hidden to him throughout his long apprenticeship. He continues to wander the progressively more mobile places of the novel but cannot navigate his increasingly changing social world. After the places of Combray and the social relations of Paris are both transformed by the war, he again falls into a state of despair about his literary career much greater than he had felt at Martinville.

The five final episodes of involuntary memory, which occur before the narrator enters the Princesse de Guermantes's "matinée," serve a crucial role in that they teach Marcel how to convey his experience through art. Only metaphor can bridge the distance between two distant images in the way that involuntary memory bridges two distant times. Metaphor is spatial and temporal since it sets places in motion and therefore changes their relation to each other. Metaphors are the textual replacement of involuntary memory, since they fill the void between intermittent "moments bienheureux" and ensure that perceptions remain unstable.

Yet the narrator expresses hints of doubt about the supplemental nature of metaphor in the novel. He observes that in the work of art which he is ready to create there are nevertheless "great difficulties," since it would have to consist of "une matière en quelque sorte différente" ("a material in some sort different") from that of memory (*TR IV*, 449). Literary metaphors as the "spiritual equivalent" (458) of involuntary memory can only work by the transference of the quality of one object into another; however, the presence of metaphors does not guarantee anything about the work itself: "le rapport peut être peu intéressant, les objets médiocres, le style mauvais, mais tant qu'il n'y a pas eu cela, il n'y a rien" (468) ("the relationship may be of little interest, the objects mediocre, the style bad, but without it [metaphor], there is nothing"). Metaphor, and by extension movement, have limits that involuntary memory does not have: an uninteresting comparison, mediocre objects (could there be anything more mediocre than a madeleine?), and bad style. Movement, as an expression of time and not time itself, can express duration in varying degrees. The degrees vary so much that the narrator himself is incapable of perceiving the true nature of time in movement until the very end. The length of the *Recherche* extends metaphors to their limit and reveals that, while metaphor and movement consistently express time, they also can lead dangerously astray as the narrator tries to rein in their excess.

Movement presents an indirect representation of time mediated by space. Marcel's book of places represents time through movement in space. Yet time is indivisible, as Bergson proposes, whereas space can always be measured and divided into separate places. If the text narrates, or sets in motion, stable and isolated places, does it not also reproduce the spatialization of time (time as measured and divisible) present in Stendhal's ichnographic maps, Nerval's portrayal of the Valois, and the system of signs laid down by Marcel's father? According to Georges Poulet's *L'espace proustien,* the various, divisible episodes of the text would thus not depict a continual movement, but rather juxtaposed moments without any connection (135). For Poulet, since the *Recherche* describes a fragmented space, it cannot accurately be considered a book about time.[6]

The Image of Time

Movement and metaphor consistently present an indirect image of time as duration throughout the *Recherche.* Through metaphor and movement, the novel can claim to be the book about time and of time that the narrator decides to write at the end of his literary apprenticeship. The momentum of movement and metaphor accelerates after the death of Albertine with an increase in the appearance of telephones, telegrams, automobiles, and airplanes. The First World War invades Paris with warplanes and total mobilization, in the literal and metaphorical sense. Though he has intellectualized the relation between time and psychology after the death of Albertine, the narrator continues to fear the effects of time and tries to insulate himself from it at the "maison de santé." His complete desperation forces him to abandon his isolation, to return to Paris, and to accept the princesse de Guermantes's invitation at a "matinée." As we have already seen, the five miraculous "moments bienheureux" allow the narrator to regain his faith in his literary career and to learn the valuable lesson that metaphor translates time through a textual movement.

But the series of five involuntary memories, in notable contrast to the madeleine scene, prevents the metonymic reflection of place that persisted in many of the other episodes and forces the narrator to focus on the temporal aspect of the experience. As with the earlier "moments bienheureux," movement displaces memories that then rise to the surface of consciousness: in the first moment he trips over stones in a courtyard, literally jogging his memory; in the second moment a servant strikes a spoon against a plate; in the third he wipes a starched napkin over his mouth; in the fourth water moves in a pipe; and in the fifth the opening of George Sand's *François le Champi* creates a chain of countless memories that "sautaient légèrement d'eux-mêmes" (*TR IV,* 463) ("jumped lightly from one to the other"). The succession, or as Poulet would say the juxtaposition, of these moving images brought on by involuntary memory finally compel the narrator to investigate within himself not just the particular moment of the past linked to a particular sensation, but the more pressing issue of why this experience should cause him so much joy.

The narrator concludes that the "moments bienheureux," because they force a past moment to coexist for an instant with a present one, offer the experience of being extra-temporal or outside of time (450). However, the meaning of "extra-temporal" is qualified a page later when he elaborates on his thesis of memory; an involuntary memory satisfies the imagination because it is a past and absent sensation, and satisfies the imagination further because it is also a present sensation which provides "un peu de temps à l'état pur" (451) ("a little bit of time in a pure state"). The images set in motion by involuntary memory allow Marcel to isolate a fragment of pure time, duration itself. The new self glimpsed for "la durée d'un éclair" (451) ("the duration of a lightning flash") is extra-temporal because it is outside of habitual or chronological time, although very much in the true or pure time of duration. As Maurice Blanchot writes: "Proust . . . a pressenti que ces instants où, pour lui, brille l'intemporel, exprimaient cependant, par l'affirmation d'un retour, les mouvements les plus intimes de la métamorphose du temps, étaient le 'temps pur'" (*Le livre à venir,* 33) ("Proust . . . had a premonition that these instants, when, for him, the extra-temporal [or "intemporal"] shines, expressed however, by the affirmation of a return, the innermost movements of the metamorphosis of time, they were 'pure time'"). The isolated moments of involuntary memory manifest two different aspects of time, since the extra-temporal is both outside of (the chronological flow of) time and the heightened image of time itself ("extra" temporal), where the work of time as metamorphosis can finally be glimpsed in an instant.

Instead of the "impure" time of metaphor and juxtaposition where the effects of time are seen indirectly through spatial configurations, this image of "pure" time appears directly as a return of a past coinciding exactly with the present, the enfolding of the total subject across time, and therefore the superposition of two incompossible states of the same subject (because occurring in two different moments in time) reveals in an instant the work of time that produces difference and change. This image of time, which occurs in involuntary memory, functions like Nerval's double perspective: the imagination grasps the past, and thus absent sensation, while the senses can add to the imagination "l'idée d'existence" (*TR IV,* 451) ("the idea of existence"). The "trompe-l'oeil" effect of the dual perspective only lasts a moment and leads the narrator to doubt his very existence, though without the anguish of the opening pages of the novel in the bedroom scene (452). The involuntary memory does not bring back an echo or a memory of the past sensation, but the very sensation itself, and the sensation, in turn, causes one place to erupt into another:

> La sensation commune avait cherché à recréer autour d'elle le lieu ancien, cependant que le lieu actuel qui en tenait la place s'opposait de toute la résistance de sa masse à cette immigration dans un hôtel de Paris d'une plage normande ou d'un talus d'une voie de chemin de fer . . . Toujours, dans ces résurrections-là, le lieu lointain engendré autour de la sensation commune s'était accouplé un instant, comme un lutteur, au lieu actuel. Toujours le lieu actuel avait été vainqueur; toujours c'était le vaincu qui m'avait paru le plus beau . . . Et si le lieu actuel n'avait pas été aussitôt vainqueur, je crois que j'aurais perdu connaissance; car ces résurrections du passé, dans la seconde qu'elles durent, sont si totales qu'elles n'obligent pas seulement nos yeux à cesser de voir la chambre qui est près d'eux pour regarder la voie bordée d'arbres ou la marée montante. Elles forcent nos narines à respirer l'air de lieux pourtant lointains, notre volonté à choisir entre les divers projets qu'ils nous proposent, notre personne tout entière à se croire entourée par eux, ou du moins à trébucher entre eux et les lieux présents, dans l'étourdissement d'une incertitude pareille à celle qu'on éprouve parfois devant une vision ineffable, au moment de s'endormir.[7] (453–54)

The law of places, what Certeau called "la loi du 'propre'" (173), the law instilled by the father in "Combray," unravels through the force of a past sensation breaking through the present. The consciousness occupies two places simultaneously, outside of chronological time and fixed identity; places are not put into "practice" to form a space, as with metaphor, but occupy the same position in the consciousness as if coupled, not just playing with but obliterating the specificity inherent to the law of places and also of identity. For a brief moment, the past place resurrects the past (and thus dead) self, inhabiting the present self not only with the sensations of the past (the smell of the air, the visual aspect of the surroundings) but with an entire state of mind (the "projects" or plans one had in the past).

The "I" of the present and the "I" of the past grapple with each other, never quite fusing, but occupying the same position. That the narrator seems to substitute places for the self throughout the passage (it is after all the places that grapple with each other) seems to emphasize the inability of consciousness to comprehend the work of time. The effect of a prolonged "moment bienheureux" would make someone "lose consciousness," as the barrage of contradictory choices of moments in time and of identities surpasses the ability of the conscious mind to process the information.[8] Similarly, the text itself forces the narrator as writer of the novel and the narrator as first-person character to occupy the same subject position, the paradoxical *je* whose indeterminacy allows the work to be read as either (simulated) autobiography or novel. Thus the passage theorizes or renders visible ("theory" originally meaning a mental viewing) the image of time, which functions in a text as an impossible coincidence of origin and final result, in the same way that Zola's genealogy of the Rougon-Macquart family was the supplemental image of the novel's absent origin in the dossiers.

Just as the past returns to haunt the present and the consciousness, when experiencing an involuntary memory, turns within itself, the passage near the end of the novel marks a return to the beginning and the inscription of the novel self within the bedrooms of the past. By connecting the multiple experiences of "moments bienheureux" to the moment of falling asleep, Proust's narrator brings the reader back to the first page of the *Recherche,* where it seems to him "que j'étais moi-même ce dont parlait l'ouvrage" ("that I was myself what the work was talking about"). At the beginning of the text, the cause of the waking sleeper's confusion is replaced by a "deep sleep"; the impact of literature on the self is repressed until it resurfaces here near the very end of the text. The narrator, now outside of space and time, inhabits literature as a writer and as a textual subject. As Nerval's double perspective bridged the distance between the conscious and the unconscious self, the Proustian narrator decides to write a book that would prolong his experience about time and offer the possibility of sharing it with others through art.[9]

The theoretical moment of insight becomes exteriorized, rendered into narrative, and confirmed by the "bal de têtes" scene. After his five "moments bienheureux," Marcel is led into the Guermantes salon, what he calls the "bal de têtes," where his newfound perspective on time is challenged. There, through a series of recognitions and discoveries, he is able to see the image of time itself, unmediated by movement, not just within himself during an involuntary memory but in the faces of long-forgotten acquaintances. He struggles to recognize many faces because time has transformed their features. Even names are unable to aid him because they no longer refer to the same people: names and titles are passed down across generations, while social hierarchies are in constant upheaval. The "loi du 'propre'" of names, as with places, has no jurisdiction over him: "les noms avaient perdu pour moi de leur individualité" (*TR IV*, 510) ("names lost for me their individuality"). Eventually the recognition of old acquaintances forces Marcel to change his perspective on himself; for the first time he understands that he is no longer a young man. Blinded by habit, he had not been able to notice the passing of time within himself:

> Et maintenant je comprenais ce c'était que la vieillesse—la vieillesse qui de toutes les réalités est peut-être celle dont nous gardons le plus longtemps dans la vie une notion purement abstraite, regardant les calendriers, datant nos lettres, voyant se marier nos amis, les enfants de nos amis, sans comprendre, soit par peur, soit par paresse, ce que cela signifie . . . Je comprenais ce que signifiaient la mort, l'amour, les joies de l'esprit, l'utilité de la douleur, la vocation, etc. . . . Sans doute la cruelle découverte que je venais de faire, ne pourrait que me servir en ce qui concernait la matière même de mon livre. Puisque j'avais décidé qu'elle ne pouvait être uniquement constituée par les impressions véritablement pleines, celles qui sont en dehors du temps, parmi les vérités avec lesquelles je comptais les sertir, celles qui se rapportent au temps, au temps dans lequel baignent et changent les hommes, les sociétés, les nations, tiendraient une place importante.[10] (*TR IV*, 510)

The discovery of the meaning of old age, or the visible effects of time on the body, has finally allowed Marcel to grasp the role of the work of time as change in death, love, and life. This "cruel discovery" tempers the joy of his recent extra-temporal experience, but is infinitely more valuable. His book project is modified to incorporate this new understanding of time as it is really lived. Instead of a work based solely on the rare moments of involuntary memory, his novel will also comprise the time in which men, societies, and nations are immersed.[11]

The culmination of the novel, the final image of time that leads the narrator finally to begin his novel, occurs at the end of the "bal" when the narrator meets Gilberte and Robert's daughter, Mlle de Saint-Loup-en-Bray. Because she comes both from the "côté de Méséglise" and from the "côté de Guermantes," she synthesizes all the other characters and events in the novel. With a remarkable thoroughness, the narrator links her to every place, every major person, and every event in his life. He reasons that the effect of any one acquaintance has repercussions on every other aspect of our lives: "Quels êtres avons-nous connus qui, pour raconter notre amitié avec eux, ne nous obligent à les placer successivement dans tous les sites les plus différents de notre vie?" (*TR IV*, 607) ("What beings have we known who, in order to tell the story of our friendship with them, oblige us to place them successively in all the most different sites of our lives?"). Mlle de Saint-Loup holds a special place in the narrative, as she unites the two "côtés" and therefore recalls, in a youthful form, all of the now-destroyed Combray. Instead of being a unique individual, with a unique name and from a unique place, she has both her father's and mother's features. She is not fixed in any one place, but is rather a crossroads of places:

> Comme la plupart des êtres, d'ailleurs, n'était-elle pas comme sont dans les forêts les "étoiles" des carrefours où viennent converger des routes venues, pour notre vie aussi, des pointes les plus différents? Elles étaient nombreuses pour moi, celles qui aboutissaient à Mlle de Saint-Loup et qui rayonnaient autour d'elle. Et avant tout venaient aboutir à elle les deux grands "côtés" où j'avais fait tant de promenades et de rêves.[12] (606)

She offers an allegory of identity across places, based on intersections and not barriers. The stable places that structured the novel have given way to a practice of place, an identity of movement like in the metaphorical movement of a changing identity and the literal movement across space. Not only is Mlle de Saint-Loup the model for a new conception of place and identity, she also presents a youthful counterpoint to the aging faces at the "bal." The narrator's past is reincarnated in the sixteen-year-old girl, as she is the very image of himself in time: "pleine encore d'espérances, riante, formée des années mêmes que j'avais perdues, elle ressemblait à ma jeunesse" (609) ("still full of hope, cheerful, formed from the very years I had lost, she resembled my youth"). Quite literally she embodies both the lost time the narrator has been looking for and the very material of his future novel, since "tous ces matériaux de l'oeuvre littéraire, c'était ma vie passée" (478) ("all the material of my literary work was in my past life"). The novel he plans to write at the end of the text and which the reader is about to finish incorporates the vision of time and identity offered by Mlle de Saint-Loup.

With Mlle de Saint-Loup's appearance, the narrator vanishes from the "matinée." He offers no account of leaving the Hôtel de Guermantes; he simply disappears. His lack of place realizes his new vision that identity is in time. The remaining fifteen or sixteen pages are devoted to the composition of his future novel and to the fear that imminent death will prevent him from its completion. The novel to be written in the future or that has just come to a close, as the translation of the narrator's "inner book," disseminates the metaphors created from the "moments bienheureux" and therefore allows others, as readers, to experience life in two places, intermittently outside of chronological time. The apparent danger of the excess of metaphors, embodied by Albertine's incessant movement, has now been harnessed into a cyclical text, which sets the narrator himself in motion.

At the end of the novel, the narrator returns to the state in which he found himself at the beginning of the text, where he floats in an indeterminate place and where he is free to move across time and space. The passage from the end of the text to its beginning shuttles the reader to alternative interpretations of the text. The narrator of the end of the novel becomes the writer of the book at the start of a second reading, just as the novel obsessed with space becomes the book about time. The two "opposing" sides of a hypothesis or a paradox (the book about time/place, the narrated/narrating *je*) occupy the same space, the text of the *Recherche,* but take place in two different times of reading. Proust's novel is a book about time because it forces the reader to experience time through the cycles and apparent paradoxes of the text. The metaphors and the circular structure ensure perpetual movement and continual change as time manifests itself in the novel with each new reading. The *Recherche* transforms both its author and its readers by revealing that we *are* because we are in time.

Conclusion

Now and Then: Virtual Spaces and Real Subjects in the Twenty-First Century

In nineteenth-century French literature, the self was written in text as a subject of space in works that upset the traditional generic boundaries of novel and autobiography. This subject of space emerging from the play of language in text projected an origin outside the text, in an autobiographical self inhabiting real-world places. Maps in the novel (Stendhal's ichnographic projections, Nerval's genealogy, Sand's reference to the Cassini maps, Zola's maps of Plassans, Proust's opposing "ways") delimit textual space and the textual subject and provide a material foundation for the self as text. But the spatialization of self in text inevitably fragments it, partitions it within discrete moments of time, at once isolating it, in vain, from the instability of language and obscuring the change and difference wrought by the work of time. In order to maintain the illusion of self in text, in order to simulate the becoming across time of a changing self within and outside of the text, an image synthesizing different places in space and specific moments in time conceals the missing unity of an "I" divided between the "here" of the page and an imaginary "there." This image, the novel map, both new and fictional, supplements and surpasses the maps in the novel, creating a synoptic and textual image of the self beyond the page and the present of writing.

In this book I have argued that what I term the novel map, such as Stendhal's bird's-eye view of Rome, Nerval's double perspective of himself as other, Sand's character Indiana's confusion of Paris and the Île Bourbon, Zola's genealogy of the Rougon-Macquart, and Proust's entire work as a double text, attempts to imagine a new, textual subjectivity, one that could renegotiate the relationship between the self and the oppressive spaces of a modern society.

In our own iteration of modernity or postmodernity at the beginning of the twenty-first century, the ever-accelerating speed of communication and transportation technologies coupled with the omnipresence of new forms of surveillance have shrunken space and arrested time. As Paul Virilio has argued in *L'Inertie polaire* (1990) and elsewhere, real space has ceded to real time through the acceleration of technology, leading Virilio to the paradoxical conclusion that the state of modernity is not a greater freedom of movement in space, but rather a state of inertia. When it becomes possible to communicate instantaneously with someone anywhere on the planet, when inconceivably large amounts of data exist in an unlocalizable network, when international news is projected live twenty-four hours a day, the specificities of regions and the importance of place seem almost meaningless. And yet satellite technology, global positioning systems (GPS), and mobile telephones have combined to make the slightest movements of anyone instantly knowable and traceable, leading to the bundling of spatial information sold for marketing purposes, but eventually, one supposes, available for the formulation of political and military strategies. While the spatial imagination has contracted and the acceleration of movement and information has slowed the flow of time, our connection to real places and to materiality has been severed. Cinema is in the process of abandoning celluloid film for digital, screens are replacing paper, online social networks stand in for public meeting places.

The rapid pace of change renders any cultural response necessarily delayed and displaced. Whether an Amélie Poulain nostalgia for an era when contact with others was authentic and meaningful or a morbid fascination with the unpredictability of the everyday manifested in "reality" television, unprogrammed chance encounters in real-world spaces now seem to belong to the realm of fiction. Proust's "livre intérieur" ("inner book") that inscribed the real within us may have been replaced by the "inner book" of our genome, whose code is readable by all and which in the popular imagination formed by vapid journalistic exposés would seem to predetermine our actions and our fate. Proust may have anticipated discoveries in neuroscience, but literature's specificity lies in its ability to heighten intuition, to create new sensations and form new perceptions.

While the writing of a novel map created the fiction of a self both situated in the space of a text and ubiquitous, both material and extra-temporal, the ultimate goal of virtual reality is to lose all consciousness of the physical world and the present moment. Conversely, the ideal vacation for many today is to travel someplace outside the range of cell phone towers, to "go off the grid" only to find oneself cut off from one's own identity as a subject of technology. A more interesting tactic involves using Internet communication or GPS playfully to transform lived space; from the first flash mobs to the current Foursquare, satellite surveillance can be subverted to assert the potential of the masses to converge or at least to reinvest in the importance of place. And yet there remains something undeniably predictable, mechanical, in these ephemeral games that denies a sense of the becoming of an individual across time and across space.

The barrage of the factual launched by our information society, where everything is already recorded and quantified, needs to be answered by the counterfactual of literature. The obsession with the instantaneous and with the contraction of the global into the "glocal" must be opposed by the unique perspective of the novel map, where the past, present, and future coexist and where space is opened up to the infinite. Writing the self would then operate a movement across identities that would transcend the limits imposed by historical conditions toward the material actualization of the imaginary as text.

NOTES

Introduction

1. Honoré de Balzac, *La Comédie humaine,* vol. 10 (Paris: Gallimard, 1979).

2. "I do not know, in truth, whether to attribute to the wine and the punch this kind of lucidity that allows me to survey instantaneously my whole life like a single painting where the figures, the colors, the shadows, the light, the halftones, are all faithfully rendered. . . . Seen from a distance, my life appears contracted by a moral phenomenon."

3. "I thought that it was necessary that . . . I reject as absolutely false everything in which I could imagine the least doubt . . . I wanted to suppose that there was nothing that was as we have imagined it . . . I resolved to feign that everything that had ever entered my mind was no more true than the illusions of my dreams . . . that I had no body and that there was no world or no place where I existed."

4. David Harvey, *The Condition of Postmodernity: An Enquiry into the Origins of Cultural Change* (Cambridge, Mass.: Blackwell, 1990), 250–54.

5. Henri Lefebvre, *La Production de l'espace,* 4th ed. (Paris: Anthropos, 2000), 386.

6. The scholarship that has developed to explain the temporal shock of modernity, especially in relation to Baudelaire, is too vast to elaborate here. Some of the best works are Ross Chambers's *The Writing of Melancholy,* Fredric Jameson's *The Seeds of Time,* David Harvey's *The Condition of Postmodernity,* and Elissa Marder's *Dead Time: Temporal Disorders in the Wake of Modernity.* Wolfgang Schivelbusch's *The Railway Journey: The Industrialization of Time and Space in the 19th Century* shows how the new technology of speed not only warped conventional views of time and space, but also forced into the public consciousness an acceptance of personal danger and mass disaster for the sake of progress.

7. Louis Marin, "The Autobiographical Interruption: About Stendhal's *Life of Henry Brulard,*" *Modern Language Notes* 93, no. 4 (1978): 597–617.

8. Jacques Rancière, *Le Partage du sensible* (Paris: La Fabrique, 2000), 12.

Part I

1. "Le fil du récit n'étant pas rompu, ces ouvrages [*Journal, Souvenirs d'égotisme, Vie de Henry Brulard*] en dépit de leur ton et de leur variété présentent alors une sorte de biographie continue de Stendhal" (Henri Martineau, "Avertissement," in Stendhal's *Oeuvres intimes,* 8) ("The narrative thread unbroken, these works [*Journal, Souvenirs d'égotisme, Vie de Henry Brulard*] despite their styles and their variety represent a sort of continuous biography of Stendhal").

2. The citations from the *Vie de Henry Brulard,* the *Journal,* and the *Souvenirs d'égotisme* are taken from the Pléiade edition of *Oeuvres intimes,* edited by Martineau in 1955. The more recent, two-volume edition edited by V. Del Litto in 1981 integrates Stendhal's marginalia after 1821 to form a virtual *Journal.* Citations from this edition will be referenced as *Oeuvres intimes I* or *II.*

3. Michel Crouzet considers Brulard to be the portrait of Stendhal as a novel hero ("La *Vie de Henry Brulard :* La moins 'puante' des autobiographies? III," *Stendhal Club,* 135: 249).

Chapter 1

1. "After the *discourse* of generalities, 'I' will *then* write the *narrative* of singularities [604] . . . The writing of the narrative-text would be a sort of ontological argument: I cause myself to exist as text. Consequently, I do not yet exist, but I am going to be born as text. But don't I already exist as text because I have already written some general considerations? No, in fact, because general considerations are discourse whereas narrative—and only narrative—can make me come about [*ad-venir*], (de-)negatively, as an autonomous textual identity" (Marin, "The Autobiographical Interruption," 605).

2. "I found that my life could be summed up by these names, the initials of which I wrote in the dust, like Zadig, with my cane . . . : Virginie /Kubly/, Angela /Pietragrua/, Adèle /Rebuffel/, Mélanie /Guilbert/, Mina /de Griesheim/, Alexandrine /Petit/, Angeline, whom I never loved /Bereyter/, Angela /Pietragrua/, Métilde /Dembrowski/, Clémentine/, Giulia/. And finally, for a month at the most Mme Azur whose given name I have forgotten, and imprudently, yesterday, Amalia /B/. The majority of these charming beings have not honored me with their favor; but they have occupied my entire life to the letter. My works have followed them."

3. "One of her last actions was, one night when I was reading on my aunt Elisabeth's commode, at the spot marked H [on the accompanying sketch], the *Henriade* or the *Bélisaire* that my grandfather had just lent me, Séraphie cried out: 'How could someone give such books to this child! Who gave him this book?'"

4. "However, oh my reader, the whole problem lies in these five [*sic*] letters: B, R, U, L, A, R, D that form my name and concern my self-esteem. Let's suppose I were to write *Bernard,* this book would no longer be like *The Vicar of Wakefield* (its emulator in all innocence), only a novel written in the first person."

5. "Of the seventy-three epigraphs in the novel [*Le Rouge et le noir*], only fifteen are correctly attributed. Moreover, of these fifteen, two are inaccurately reproduced" (Jefferson, 109).

6. Stendhal may be referring to this passage of Sterne: "I declare I have been at it these six weeks, making all the speed I possibly could—and am not yet born" (Sterne, 37). *Tristram Shandy* is a first-person novel that privileges above all else the detours of narrative and lived time opposed to chronological time. Its manifold fragments prevent any possibility for closure (Christie McDonald, "Fractured Readers," 844). Shandy as narrator is present in language and text even before he is born, and thus is a subject only insofar as he is subject to language and text. The reference to *Shandy* renders closure impossible for Brulard,

as he is now an imitation of another text, itself the quintessential intertextual novel. As Nerval, in his narrator's own self-reflexive moment in *Angélique,* writes: "—Vous avez imité Diderot lui-même./—Qui avait imité Sterne . . ./" (Nerval, *Oeuvres I,* 239) ("—You have imitated Diderot himself./—Who imitated Sterne . . ./"). And of course the epigraph to Balzac's *La Peau de chagrin* is a visual citation of Captain Trim's drawing in the sand from *Tristram Shandy.*

7. Michael Sheringham, in his chapter on Stendhal in *French Autobiography: Devices and Desires,* groups the 170 sketches under the name "diagram" as a graphic and verbal representation (71). According to John Bender and Michael Marrinan in *The Culture of Diagram,* "a diagram is a proliferation of manifestly selective packets of dissimilar data correlated in an explicitly process-oriented array that has some of the attributes of a representation but is situated in the world like an object" (7). The term "diagram" is certainly appropriate, conveying the tension between the "dissimilar data" of the visual and the verbal, but it fails to recognize the spatial component of a map (which also exists in the world as an object). Beyle's drawings overwhelmingly depict spatial relations between himself and others in the past.

8. Béatrice Didier, preface to *Vie de Henry Brulard,* 14.

9. Twenty engravings of mostly Italian paintings are scattered throughout the manuscript, and are taken from the same collection as those found in the *Lucien Leuwen* manuscript. They are not included in most of the standard editions. There has been much debate as to whether the engravings placed apparently haphazardly throughout the manuscript were "intended" for publication, with most experts affirming that they are only simple partitions between chapters (Sheila M. Bell, "Stendhal's *Vie de Henry Brulard:* The Engravings—A Public or Private Matter?" *Modern Language Review* 93 [1998]: 356–69). Since the text clearly anticipates a posthumous publication, it is impossible to distinguish the "public" from the "private," authorial intention from textual significance.

10. In his essay "Ce que disent les enfants" (*Critique et Clinique*), Gilles Deleuze explores the relationship between a child's relationship to space and to parents: "Or les parents aussi sont eux-mêmes un milieu que l'enfant parcourt, dont il parcourt les qualités et les puissances et dont il dresse la carte" (82) ("Parents are also themselves a place that the child explores, the qualities and powers of which he explores and for which he draws up a map").

11. Deleuze, in *Foucault,* proposes that in all knowledge there exists a power play between visual representation and expressed language, best captured by the figure of a diagram (46–47). The tensions created by the "short-circuiting maps" expose the more general tensions between the "mathematical" representation of Brulard and Brulard's subjective self-knowledge.

Chapter 2

1. This is not meant to imply that there is an actual connection between this type of map and the works of Descartes himself, but rather a link between the function of these maps and Cartesian logic in *Brulard.*

2. "I found myself this morning, October 16, 1832, near San Pietro *in Montorio,* on the Gianicolo Hill, in Rome, there was a magnificent sun. A light

sirocco breeze, which was hardly perceptible, made a few small white clouds float above Mount Albano, a delightful heat dominated the air, I was happy to be alive. I made out perfectly Frascati and the Castel Gandolfo, which are four leagues from here, the Villa Aldobrandini where there is the sublime fresco of Judith by Domenichino. I see perfectly the white wall that marks the repairs made lately by Prince F. Borghese, the same one I saw at Wagram, colonel of a regiment of armored cavalry, the day when Mr. de Noue, my friend, had his leg carried off. Much further in the distance, I see the rock of Palestrina and the white house of Castel San Pietro, which used to be its fortress. Below the wall against which I lean are the large orange trees of the capuchin orchard, then the Tiber and the Priory of Malta, a little further on the right the tomb of Cecilia Metella, Saint-Paul, and the Cestius Pyramid. In front of me I see Santa-Maria-Maggiore and the long lines of Monte Cavallo Palace. All of ancient and modern Rome, from the Appian Way with the ruins of its tombs and its aqueducts to the magnificent Pincio gardens built by the French, is laid out to view."

3. "San Pietro in Montorio. I admire yet again the view; it is *without comparison* the most beautiful in Rome: one sees everything admirably well and one sees Mont Albano and Frascati, Cecilia Metella, etc. There has to be a day with sun and clouds chased by the wind; then all the domes of Rome are one by one in the shadows and in the light."

4. "I have seen houses in ruins elsewhere, as well as statues of gods and men: these are still men. All this is true: and yet, despite it all, I cannot often enough see the tomb of this great and powerful city without admiring and revering it. Caring for the dead is recommended to us; now, I have been nourished since my childhood with these here; I knew the affairs of Rome long before those of my own house. I knew the Capitol and its plan before I knew the Louvre, and the Tiber before I knew the Seine. The conditions and fortunes of Lucullus, Metellus, and Scipio fill my head more than those of anyone of my own country. They are all dead. So is my father, as entirely dead as they, and has become as distant from me and my life in eighteen years as they are in sixteen hundred."

5. "Both [Montaigne and Freud] appeal to cartography to bring forward some pervasive and unsettling effects of psychogenesis. The birth of the subject, what is tantamount to a universal experience of life, is situated in a specific topography. The birth of the subject is always likened to an overlay of city-views of Rome" (Tom Conley, "A Suckling of Cities: Montaigne in Paris and Rome," 168).

6. "When a memory reappears to the consciousness, it has the effect for us of a ghost whose mysterious apparition requires explanation by special causes. In reality, the adherence of this memory to our present state is entirely comparable to that of unperceived objects to objects that we perceive, and the *unconscious* plays in both cases the same type of role."

7. Representation is, of course, problematic in Stendhal's realist novels. Commenting on Stendhal's famous formulation of the novel as a mirror led through a muddy road, Lawrence Schehr remarks that "the mirror is the locus of the imaginary . . . before the mirror reflects the same, and before it creates the simulacrum in which writing repeats the world, the mirror marks the unrep-

resentable" (Schehr, 46). In Stendhal's autobiography, however, the author can no longer hide behind the textual mirror as he did in the novel since the text is supposed to reflect the author himself.

8. "I see images, I remember the effects on my heart, but as for the causes and the physiognomy [defining characteristics], nothing. It is always like the frescoes of the [ ] in Pisa, where one can see quite well an arm and the portion next to it representing a head has fallen. I see *very clearly* a series of images, but without physiognomy except for whatever one they had related to me. What is more, I only see this physiognomy by the effect it had on me."

9. "God [in English] grants me the following: . . . Article 7. Four times a year, he can change himself into whichever man he wants. . . . Thus, the privileged man will be able to, four times a year, and for an unlimited period each time, occupy two bodies at once."

Part II
Chapter 3

1. In *Orientalism,* Edward Said sets Nerval apart from his contemporaries: "his Orient untied itself from anything resembling an Orientalist conception of the Orient, even though his work depends on Orientalism to a certain extent" (183). But even this dependence on the "Orientalist canon" is subverted: "His *Voyage* incorporates numerous pages copied out of Lane's *Modern Egyptians,* but even their lucid confidence seems to dissolve in the endlessly decomposing, cavernous element which is Nerval's Orient" (183).

2. Richard Holmes sees the mental breakdown of 1841 as the year Nerval's personality split into a public, literary persona (Nerval) and a private, familial one (Labrunie) with the systematic use of his pseudonym Nerval (242).

3. To his father, from Constantinople, August 19, 1843: "Ce voyage me servira toujours à démontrer aux gens que je n'ai été victime, il y a deux ans, que d'un accident bien isolé" (*Oeuvres I*, 935) ("This trip will serve forever to demonstrate to people that I was only the victim, two years ago, of a very isolated accident").

4. Gerald Schaeffer's *Le Voyage en Orient de Nerval, étude des structures* provides an exhaustive study of this spiral structure. For an account of circuitous and spiral journeys during the Romantic era, see M. H. Abrams's *Natural Supernaturalism.*

5. The words "narrator" and "Gérard" will be used to denominate the first-person pronoun of the text, distinct from yet undeniably related to the author Labrunie/Nerval.

6. "Hearing this word *leben,* I remembered that in German it means *life.* Lebanon also traces its name to this word *leben,* and owes it to the whiteness of the snow which covers the mountains, and which the Arabs, crossing the enflamed sands of the desert, dreamed of from afar as milk, as life!"

7. "It is a painful impression, as we travel further along, to lose city by city and country by country, this whole beautiful universe we have created for ourselves in our youth, through readings, paintings, and dreams. The world thus formed in the mind of the child is so rich and so beautiful, that it is hard to say

if it is the exaggerated result of learned ideas, or if it is the return of a memory of a prior existence and the geography of an unknown planet."

8. "Egypt is a vast tomb, that is the impression it had on me upon reaching the beach at Alexandria, which, with its ruins and little hills, presents to the eyes tombs scattered on a cindered earth. Shadows draped with bluish shrouds circulate amid the ruins. . . . I would have preferred the memories of ancient Greece, but all of that is destroyed, razed, unrecognizable."

9. One of the principal objections to Said's argument is that it does not allow the possibility for dialogue between the (Western) subject and the (Oriental) object (Michael Richardson, "Enough Said," 16). If Orientalists have created their own language for describing the Orient, then the "Oriental" subject is lost in the aporia between his or her own experience and the language of the Orientalist expert. As we will see, Nerval progressively loses any ties with Orientalist discourse as he "goes native" and slowly learns the language of experience, especially from his female slave Zeynab.

10. For an exhaustive analysis of allegory, see Angus Fletcher, *Allegory, The Theory of a Symbolic Mode* (Ithaca, N.Y.: Cornell University Press, 1964).

11. "It is a word that, depending on the intonation given to it, means all sorts of things; yet it cannot be compared to the English *goddam,* except to mark the difference between a people who are very polite and a nation who are at best very policed. The word *tayeb* means variously: *very well,* or *that's fine, that's perfect,* or *at your service,* the tone and especially body language add infinite nuances."

12. "I asked her name . . . I was buying her name as well, naturally. '*Z'n'b!,*' said Abd-el-Kerim. '*Z'n'b*' repeated Abdullah with a big effort at a nasal contraction. I was unable to understand that the sneeze of three consonants could represent a name. It took me some time to guess that it could be pronounced Zeynab."

13. "I like to lead my life like a novel, and I will voluntarily put myself in the position of one of those active and resolute heroes who at all costs want to create around themselves drama, the narrative knot, interest, action in a word. Chance, as powerful as it is, has never brought together the elements of a passable subject, and at most has it laid out the setting; thus, if we leave it to chance, everything fails despite the most perfect arrangements. Since it is conventionally understood that there are only two sorts of dénouements, marriage or death, lets us aim at least at one of the two . . . given that until now my adventures have almost always ended at the expository scene."

14. Scott Carpenter, in *Acts of Fiction,* places translation at the center of Nerval's preoccupation with otherness (111). He notes, in particular, that Gérard fires his dragoman in Cairo for manipulating his translations, yet affirms the same conduct for himself when he performs the role of dragoman for the reader, translating the "Histoire de la Reine du matin" (112).

Chapter 4

1. The heading Nerval himself gave was "Généalogie d'après des renseignements pris à Francfort, le plus récemment vers 1822" ("Genealogy based on

research conducted in Frankfort, most recently around 1822"). The manuscript is found at the Institut de France, in the Collection Spoelberch de Lovenjoul, D 741, folio 78. It measures approximately 12 cm by 21 cm. The other half of the manuscript page lists numerological facts about Napoleon's life. The "Généalogie" (without the accompanying life of Napoleon) was first reproduced in Aristide Marie's *Gérard de Nerval; Le poète—l'homme* in 1914, and then transcribed by Jean Richer in *Nerval: Expérience vécue & Création ésotérique* in 1987.

2. Deleuze and Guattari insist that the arborescent and the rhizomatic are not polar opposites that would divide up the world into good and bad, or in Nerval's case sane and insane: "Il y a des noeuds d'arborescence dans les rhizomes, des poussées rhizomatiques dans les racines" ("There are knots of arborescence in rhizomes, rhizomatic shoots in roots") (Deleuze and Guattari, 30–31).

3. "Race (or family) < eye hand foot > country."

4. As Marcel Proust writes about *Sylvie* in *Contre Sainte-Beuve:* "Ce retour dans un pays qui est plutôt pour lui un passé qui existe au moins autant dans son coeur que sur la carte" (158) ("This return to a countryside which is a past existing as much in his heart as on a map").

5. "The Dream is a second life. Never have I been able to penetrate without shuddering the doors of ivory or of horn that separate us from the invisible world. The first instants of sleep are the image of death: nebulous numbness seizes our thought, and we cannot determine the precise instant when the *ego,* under another form, continues the work of existence. It is a vague underground that is lit little by little, and where out of the shadows and the darkness emerge pale faces, solemnly immobile, which inhabit the abode of limbo. Then the scene comes together, a new brightness illuminates these bizarre apparitions and makes them play; the world of Spirits opens itself to us. Swedenborg called these visions *Memorabilia,* he owed them to daydreaming more than to sleep; the *Golden Ass* by Apuleius, Dante's *Divine Comedy,* are the poetic models of these studies of the human soul. I am going to attempt, by their example, to transcribe the impressions of a long illness which occurred entirely within the mysteries of my mind; and I do not know why I use the term illness, for never, concerning my own self, have I felt in better health. Sometimes, I would feel my strength and my activity to be doubled; it seemed I knew everything, understood everything, my imagination brought infinite delights. When I recovered what men call reason, do I have to regret having lost them? . . . This *Vita Nuova* had two phases for me. Here are the notes related to the first."

6. "Two gates for ghostly dreams there are: one gateway/ of honest horn, and one of ivory,/ Issuing by the ivory gate are dreams/ of glimmering illusion, fantasies,/ but those that come through the solid polished horn/ may be borne out, if mortals only know them" (Homer, *The Odyssey* 19, cited in Harry Levin's *The Gates of Horn*).

7. "Sleep takes up a third of our lives. . . . After a few minutes of numbness a new world begins, freed from the conditions of time and space, and perhaps similar to the one that awaits us after death. Who knows if a link does not ex-

ist between these two existences and if it is possible for the soul to tie it right away?"

8. "Here began for me what I will call the effusion of dream into real life. From this moment on, everything took at times a double aspect, and that, without my reasoning ever lacking logic, without my memories ever losing the slightest detail of what was happening to me."

9. "Lying down on a cot, I heard the soldiers talking about an unknown prisoner like me and whose voice had rung out in the same room. By a singular effect of vibration, it seemed to me that this voice resonated in my chest and that my soul doubled itself so to speak, distinctly split between vision and reality. One instant, I had the idea of turning myself with difficulty toward the man in question, then I shuddered in remembering a tradition well known in Germany, that says each man has a *double* and that, when he sees him, death is near."

10. "I entered into a vast room, where many people were gathered. Everywhere I found again recognizable faces. The features of deceased relatives I had mourned were found reproduced in others, who, dressed in costumes from older time periods, gave me the same familial welcome. They seemed to be assembled for a family banquet."

Part III

1. George Sand, *Indiana,* ed. Béatrice Didier (Paris: Gallimard, 1984); George Sand, *Nanon,* ed. Nicole Mozet (Saint-Cyr-sur-Loire: Christian Pirot, 2005).

2. Cohen argues that "realist codes did not appeal to women writers . . . because of the complex interaction between the construction of gender in specifically literary and more broadly social contexts" (*The Sentimental Education of the Novel,* 14). She enumerates three aspects of the construction of gender and genre: Balzac and Stendhal's "campaigns to masculinize the novel in realist poetics as well as polemic," "the pervasive gendering of sentimentality as feminine," and, more generally, women's status within literary institutions (14).

3. Janet Hiddleston, in *George Sand and Autobiography,* argues that in the nineteenth century, "writing one's own life-story rather than that of a fictional character was perhaps more difficult for women . . . since such a project implied a self-confidence and even a presumption which could be thought unfeminine, as well as a certain celebrity and experience of public life" (5). Nancy Miller, in *Subject to Change: Reading Feminist Writing,* proposes that women's autobiography in the nineteenth and early twentieth centuries has to be read in the context of Rousseau's shadow, and that "the decision to go public is particularly charged for the woman writer" (50).

4. Philippe Lejeune cites Georges Picon's declaration that George Sand's *Histoire de ma vie* is "le plus romanesque de ses romans" ("the most novel-like of her novels") (*L'autobiographie en France,* 28).

5. As Nancy Miller argues, "the fact of [a male writer's] gender is given and received literarily as a mere *donnée* of personhood, . . . the canon of the autobiographical text, like the literary canon, self-defined as it is by the notion of a human universal, in general fails to interrogate gender as a meaningful category of reference or of interpretation" (57).

6. Germaine Brée (in "Autogynography") and Domna Stanton (in *The Female Autograph*) propose the term "autogynograph" to assert the difference of female autobiography, to make the female "I" visible: "Creating the subject, an autograph gave the female 'I' substance through the inscription of an interior and an anterior" (Stanton, 14); "at this symbolic moment the female signature, unlike the generic fixation, had liberating rather than constraining effects" (16). Similarly, Shari Benstock and Sidonie Smith claim that a female "I" destabilizes autobiographical discourse: "the self that would reside at the textual center is decentered—often absent altogether—in women's autobiographical texts" (Benstock, 9); "as 'inappropriate' subjects, women . . . become agents for autobiographical change in a double sense. They change their own lives and they change the discursive regime of autobiographical 'truth' itself" (Smith, 46).

Chapter 5

1. George Sand, *Histoire de ma vie II,* ed. Damien Zanone (Paris: GF Flammarion, 2001). "The newspapers all spoke of Mr. *G. Sand* with praise, insinuating that a woman's hand must have slipped in here and there to reveal to the author a certain sensitivity to the heart and mind, but declaring that the style and opinions were too masculine not to be a man's."

2. "People did not neglect to say that *Indiana* was me and my story. That's not it at all. I presented two types of women, and I think that when one has finished reading this portrayal of the impressions and reflections on my life [*Histoire de ma vie*], it will be clear that I have never depicted myself in feminine guise. I am too romantic/novelistic to have seen the heroine of a novel in my mirror."

3. "A long time after having written the preface to *Indiana* under the influence of what remaining respect I had for social norms, I was still trying to resolve this unsolvable problem: *how to reconcile the happiness and dignity of individuals oppressed by this same society, without changing society itself.*"

4. "Certain journalists, who have established themselves as representatives and guardians of public morals . . . declared sternly their opposition to the tendencies of my poor tale, and gave it, by presenting it as a tract against the social order, an importance and a sort of renown it would otherwise not have had."

5. "A man who speaks of love with wit is not particularly in love. Raymon was an exception; he expressed passion with art, and he felt it with fervor. Only, it wasn't passion that made him eloquent, it was eloquence that made him passionate."

6. "[He] is one of the men who has had the most authority and influence on your thoughts, whatever may be today your political views. You have devoured his political booklets, and often you have been led astray, while reading newspapers of the time, by the irresistible charm of his style and the gracefulness of his courtly and urbane logic."

7. "One would have said, upon seeing the immobility of the two characters in front of the hearth, that they were afraid of upsetting the immobility of the scene; fixed and petrified like two heroes from a fairy tale, the slightest word, the smallest movement would make the walls of a fantastic city crumble on top of them."

8. "The two panes of glass which reflected Noun's image to infinity seemed to be peopled with a thousand phantoms. He [Raymon] saw in the depths of this double reverberation a finer form, and he seemed to hold onto, in the last vaporous and confused shadow that Noun reflected, the slender and supple waist of Mme Delmare [Indiana]."

9. "She walked down the quay from the Institut de France all the way to the Corps Législatif; but she forgot to cross the bridge, and continued along the river, absorbed in a stupid reverie, in a meditation without ideas, pursuing the pointless act of walking straight ahead. Imperceptibly she found herself on the water's edge, which swept ice cubes across her feet and crushed them on the rocks of the riverbank with a dry, cold crack. This greenish water held an attractive force over Indiana's senses. One can get accustomed to terrible ideas; just by letting them cross the mind, one ends up taking pleasure in them. For a long time the example of Noun's suicide had appeased the hours of her despair that she had considered suicide as a sort of tempting sensual delight. . . . When she felt the biting cold water which was already bathing her shoe, she woke up as if in a state of sleepwalking, and, looking around at where she was, she saw Paris behind her, and the Seine, which was fleeing under her feet, carried away in its oily mass the white reflection of houses and the grayish blue of the sky. The continuous movement of the water and the immobility of the ground became mixed up in her clouded perception, and it seemed to her that the water was sleeping and that the earth was receding. In this moment of vertigo, she supported herself against a wall, and leaned over, fascinated, towards what she took for a solid mass."

10. "Occasionally, she would take the clouds from the coast for strange forms: sometimes she saw a white blade rise up over the flows and describe a gigantic line which she took for the façade of the Louvre; sometimes it was two square sails that, emerging abruptly from the mist, suggested the memory of Notre Dame's towers, when the Seine exhales a compact fog that hugs their base and makes them seem suspended in the sky; at other times it was pink wisps of cloud that, in their changing forms, displayed all the architectural whims of an immense city. This woman's mind fell asleep in the illusions of the past, and she would tremble with joy at the sight of this imaginary Paris whose realities had indicated the most unfortunate time of her life. A strange vertigo then took over her head. Suspended high above the coast, and seeing recede under her very eyes the gorges which separated her from the ocean, it seemed to her that she was thrown into this space by a rapid movement, and that she walked on air toward the prestigious city of her imagination. In this dream, she held onto the rock which supported her; and for whoever might have observed her avid eyes, her breast heaving in impatience and the frightening expression of joy spread on her face, she seemed to present all the symptoms of madness. And yet those were her hours of pleasure and the only moments of well-being she looked forward to all day. If her husband's whims had suppressed these solitary walks, I don't know what thoughts she would have lived on; because, for her, everything was related to a certain power of illusions, to an ardent as-

piration towards a point which was neither memory nor expectation, neither hope nor regret, but desire in all its devouring intensity."

11. "Out of these fortuitous encounters [of fire and rock] result bizarre games, hieroglyphic impressions, mysterious characters, which seem thrown there like a signature from a supernatural being, written in cabalistic letters. I stayed a long while under the childish pretension of looking for a meaning in these unknown figures. This useless investigation made me fall into a profound meditation during which I forgot the time which flew by."

12. We will further explore Rancière's definition of literature as "silent speech" in chapter 7.

Chapter 6

1. In her letters from 1871, Sand expresses a range of opinions and emotions about the meaning of equality after the Commune. Writing to Charles Poncy on May 25, 1871, she declares, "La voilà vaincue, cette chimérique insurrection. . . . C'est un malheur pour ceux qui aiment l'égalité et qui ont cru aux nobles instincts des masses, et j'étais de ceux-là!" (*Correspondence XXII,* 390) ("That chimerical insurrection has finally been defeated. . . . It is a misfortune for those who love equality and who believed in the noble instincts of the masses, and I used to be one of them!"). But to Gustave Flaubert, she wrote just a few weeks earlier: "Pour moi l'ignoble expérience que Paris essaye ou subit ne prouve rien contre les lois de l'éternelle progression des hommes et des choses, et si j'ai quelques principes acquis dans l'esprit, bons ou mauvais, ils n'en sont ni ébranlés, ni modifiés" (370) ("For me the ignoble experiment Paris attempted or suffered proves nothing against the laws of the eternal progress of men and things, and if I had some definite principles in my mind, good or bad, they have been neither shaken nor changed").

2. Alain Badiou uses the Paris Commune to think through the questions of singularity, site, and event: Alain Badiou, "Logic of the Site," *Diacritics* 33, nos. 3–4 (Fall-Winter 2003): 141–50.

3. Henri Lefebvre offers an hour-by-hour account of the events of March 18, 1871, in *La Proclamation de la Commune* (Paris: Gallimard, 1965).

4. Kristin Ross describes the Commune as "antihierarchical" and "horizontal"; through an analysis of Marx's *Communist Manifesto,* she argues that "political emancipation means emancipation from politics as a specialized activity. . . . The *means* through which the Commune was possible was simply its sustained attack on the divisions of labor that render administrations and government 'mysteries, transcendent functions only to be trusted to the hands of a trained caste.'" Kristin Ross, *The Emergence of Social Space: Rimbaud and the Paris Commune* (Minneapolis: University of Minnesota Press, 1988), 24–25.

5. Sand's letters during the Commune repeatedly remind her Parisian friends that the conservative provinces distrust Paris. Moreover, Parisian radicalism only serves to alienate the provinces from the republic: "Paris fait les républiques, nous le savons, mais c'est lui aussi qui les perd et les tue" (353) ("Paris makes republics, we know that, but it's also Paris that loses and kills them").

6. "I know, from having heard people around here deplore them, that it's the common people of Paris and of the big cities who push and lead you, because intellectual people like you stay in the cities. You think you understand peasants when you know workers from the suburbs or city neighborhoods, and among the workers who are half peasant and half artisan, you only pay attention to those who yell and agitate."

7. The creation of the *départements* can be directly linked to the Carte de Cassini: "The inspiration [for the division of national space into *départements*] was cartographic. The prime mover on the constitutional committee, Abbé Sieyès . . . explained that he would begin 'by obtaining the great triangulated map of Cassini, which has without dispute the most exact positions; I would divide it first of all geometrically'" (Michael Biggs. "Putting the State on the Map: Cartography, Territory, and European State Formation," *Comparative Studies in Society and History* 44, no. 2 [April 1999]: 389.)

8. Edmund Burke, *Reflections on the Revolution in France* (London: Apollo, 1814), 158–59. Quoted in Biggs, 390.

9. "La figure utopique est donc un objet de discours, non pas sans référent, mais à référent absent, comme son nom le signale: elle n'est pas le sans-lieu, voire le lieu imaginaire, irréel, mais le non-lieu, le lieu sans détermination, la figure du neutre" (Marin, *Utopiques*, 251) ("The utopian figure is thus an object of discourse, not without a referent, but with an absent referent, as its name indicates: it is not the without-place, or even the imaginary, unreal place, but the nonplace, the place without determination, the figure of the neuter").

10. "I do not know if I will be able to tell the story in writing, me who, at the age of twelve, still did not know how to read. I will do as I can. I am going to start things from the top and try to find the first memories of my childhood. These memories are very confused, as are those of children whose intelligence has not been developed through education."

11. "Now, those who will have read me know that my education is complete enough so that I may express myself more easily and understand better the things that happen to me. It would have been impossible, over the course of the narrative so far, not to have spoken a little like a peasant; my thinking would not have found other words than those in which it was then contained, and, by letting myself use other words, I would have given myself thoughts and feelings that I did not have."

12. "I learned my whole alphabet that day, and I was happy, coming home, to hear the thrushes singing and the stream rumbling. . . . The sun was setting on our right, the chestnuts and beach trees were as red as fire. . . . It had never been like that before. . . . My dazzled eyes saw red and blue letters in the rays of the setting sun."

13. In an endnote in her 2005 edition of *Nanon,* Nicole Mozet points out that Nohant is on the road between La Châtre and Châteauroux and that in *Histoire de ma vie* Sand writes of getting lost as a child on the way from Châteauroux to Nohant (291n). Sand's childhood memory of losing her way reinforces the impression that there were no clear paths from the two towns.

14. The École des Hautes Études en Sciences Sociales (EHESS) maintains a website dedicated to the Carte de Cassini that also lists demographic information from the eighteenth century: http://cassini.ehess.fr.

15. "*Paris n'aspire qu'à se renfermer dans son autonomie, plein de respect pour les droits égaux des autres communes de France*" ("*Paris only aspires to withdraw into itself autonomously, being respectful of the equal rights of the other communes of France*"). From a manifesto written by the Commune's Commission Exécutive on April 6, 1871, quoted in Lefebvre's *La Proclamation de la Commune,* 136.

16. "However, I was worried about the rest of my journey. The way in which everyone looked at me and spoke to me was new for me, and I finally became aware of the inconvenience of being a young woman all alone on the open road. In Valcreux, where I was known to be well-behaved and reserved, no one would have reminded me that I was no longer a child, and I was all too accustomed to forgetting my age. . . . I saw in my gender an obstacle and dangers of which I had never dreamed. . . . Beauty always attracts looks and I would have liked to make myself invisible."

17. "They [Émilien and Costejoux] weren't duped by the July Revolution [of 1830]. They weren't satisfied by the February [1848] one either. As for me, not having anything to do with politics for a long time now—I don't have the time—I have never contradicted them, and, even if I could be sure of being right, I wouldn't have the courage to tell them, so much I admired the caliber of these characters from the past."

Part IV

1. "Le personnage, ici, est 'fonction,' voire 'fonctionnaire,' plutôt que fiction, est personnel plutôt que personne" (25) ("The character, here, is a 'function,' or a 'functionary,' more than fictional, personnel more than person"). "Mais ce sont surtout des localisations dans des espaces 'réalistes' soigneusement nommés, balisés et circonstanciés qui définissent le personnage. Le personnage, chez Zola, est d'abord et avant tout un habitant, un 'assigné à résidence'" (208) ("But it is especially localizations in 'realist spaces,' which are carefully named, charted, and detailed, that define the character. The character in Zola's work is first and foremost an inhabitant, someone who is 'under house arrest'"). Philippe Hamon, *Le Personnel du roman: Le système des personnages dans les "Rougon-Macquart" d'Emile Zola* (Geneva: Droz, 1983).

2. Portions of the dossiers have been published as scholarly apparatus, notably in Henri Mitterand's Pléiade edition of the *Rougon-Macquart.* Mitterand and Olivier Lumbroso have published selections of the dossiers along with Zola's drawings from the dossiers in a three-volume work, *Les Manuscrits et dessins de Zola; Notes préparatoires et dessins des "Rougon-Macquart"* (Paris: Éditions Textuel, 2002). Colette Becker has undertaken the herculean task of publishing a diplomatic edition of the entire dossier and has completed four volumes, or roughly half of the total: Émile Zola, *La Fabrique des Rougon-Macquart: Éditions des dossiers préparatoires,* ed. Colette Becker and Véro-

nique Lavielle, 4 vols. (Paris: Honoré Champion, 2003). For the novels themselves and textual content in the dossiers, I will refer to the Pléiade edition (Émile Zola, *Les Rougon-Macquart,* ed. Henri Mitterand, 5 vols. [Paris: Gallimard, 1960–67]) with a volume number and page number, and for visual documents contained in the dossiers, I will refer either to the Mitterand and Lumbroso or to the Becker.

3. "Nous ne possédons, en effet, que quelques pages de brouillons . . . Or il est sûr que les manuscrits donnés à l'imprimeur sont le résultat de versions antérieures. . . . Zola a détruit cette étape du corps à corps avec l'écriture pour ne laisser que le travail de construction, témoignage de sa 'méthode'" (Becker, preface to Zola, *La Fabrique des Rougon-Macquart* 1:17) ("We only have, in fact, a few pages of the drafts [. . .] It is certain that the manuscripts given to the printer are the result of previous versions. [. . .] Zola destroyed this stage of the confrontation with writing, only leaving the work of construction [the dossiers] as testimony to his 'method'").

Chapter 7

1. "And when I hold all the strings, when I have in my hands a whole social group, I will show this group at work, as actor of a historical period, I will create it acting in all the complexity of its efforts, I will analyze at the same time the willpower of each of its members and the general movement of the whole group."

2. Well before the *Rougon-Macquart* Zola proposed his theory of "écrans" (filters or screens) in a letter to Antony Valabrègue in 1864: "Toute oeuvre d'art est comme une fenêtre ouverte sur la création; il y a, enchâssé dans l'embrasure de la fenêtre, une sorte d'Écran transparent, à travers lequel on aperçoit les objets plus ou moins déformés, souffrant des changements plus ou moins sensibles dans leurs lignes et dans leur couleur. . . . Nous voyons la création dans une oeuvre, à travers un homme, à travers un tempérament, une personnalité" ("Every work of art is like a window open onto creation; there is, set in the window frame, a sort of transparent Screen, through which objects appear more or less deformed, as they undergo more or less perceptible changes in their lines or their color. . . . We see creation in a work, through a man, through a temperament, a personality"). Cited in Colette Becker, *Zola: Le saut dans les étoiles* (Paris: Presses Sorbonne Nouvelle, 2002), 233–34. See Naomi Schor, "Zola: From Window to Window," *Yale French Studies* 42 (1969): 38–51.

3. David Baguley's introduction to his *Critical Essays on Émile Zola* (Boston: G. K. Hall, 1986) gives a succinct overview of the history of Zola criticism. In another study of the naturalist movement, Baguley shows how Zola (and naturalism in general) was motivated as much by strategic positioning within the literary and economic fields as by purely aesthetic concerns: "We see once more that strategy, opportunism, *réclame,* mystification are primary motive forces behind the movement. A shared sense of purpose and common aesthetic principles are obviously of secondary importance." David Baguley, *Naturalist Fiction: The Entropic Vision* (Cambridge, Eng.: Cambridge University Press, 1990), 19.

4. In a document included in the preliminary notes of the dossiers, "Notes générales sur la nature de l'oeuvre," Zola writes: "Avoir surtout la logique de la déduction. Il est indifférent que le fait générateur soit reconnu comme absolument vrai; ce fait sera surtout une hypothèse scientifique, emprunté aux traités médicaux" (*Les Rougon-Macquart,* 5:1742) ("Have above all else the logic of deduction. It does not matter that the generating fact be recognized as absolutely true; this fact will be a scientific hypothesis, borrowed from medical treatises").

5. Michel Serres, *Feux et signaux de brume: Zola* (Paris: Grasset, 1975).

6. As Zola remarks in his "Notes générales sur la marche de l'oeuvre," "Mon roman eût été impossible avant 89" ("My novel would have been impossible before '89") (*Les Rougon-Macquart,* 5:1738).

7. "The description of Nana's boudoir, like that of the flowers of the Paradou, of the displays of les Halles or the stained-glass windows of *Le Rêve,* apply, in the 'equality' of their subjects, the principle of equivalence of expression. Zola, who never confronted himself with the problem of a prose poeticity, still obeys the principle of symbolicity at the heart of romanticist poetics; he makes objects speak in the same way as *Notre-Dame de Paris.* And this principle of expressivity fits seamlessly with the old style of narration, like the rhyme of the ideal in reality itself. Naturalism gives to the novel form a way of being a form of compromise: a compromise between the contradictory principles of the new poetics, and, thus, compromise between the old and new poetics, between the representative primacy of fiction and the antirepresentative principle of expression."

8. Émile Zola, *Le Roman experimental,* 4th ed. (Paris: G. Charpentier, 1880), 10.

9. Olivier Lumbroso, *Zola: La plume et le compas: Construction de l'espace dans Les Rougon-Macquart d'Émile Zola* (Paris: Honoré Champion, 2004). Likewise, for Philippe Bonnefis, "la description zolienne est cette nostalgie d'un paradis perdu des géomètres" ("description in Zola's works is this nostalgia for the lost paradise of surveyors"). Philippe Bonnefis, *L'Innomable: Essai sur l'oeuvre d'É. Zola* (Paris: SEDES, 1984), 64.

10. "Comme si le texte ne vivait que de la répétition de son geste de clôture" ("As if the text only lived by the repetition of its gesture of closure") (Bonnefis, 25).

11. Robert Lethbridge gives an excellent account of the autobiographical readings that have plagued the criticism of *L'Oeuvre,* arguing that any autobiographical value resides in the "production" or process of creation of the novel as a whole rather than in anything the final novel can reveal to the reader. Robert Lethbridge, "L'Homme et *L'Oeuvre:* Zola et la déformation romanesque," in *Lire/Dé-lire Zola,* ed. Jean-Pierre Leduc-Adine and Henri Mitterand (Paris: Nouveau Monde, 2004), 135–52.

12. "It is perhaps striking that at the moment when writing becomes an artistic search, becomes literature, the writer feels an ever greater need to keep a connection with himself. He feels disgust at giving himself over to this neutral force, formless and futureless, behind everything that is written, disgust and

apprehension revealed by the care taken by so many authors to compose what they call their *Journal.*"

Chapter 8

1. Sandy Petrey, "Stylistics and Society in *La Curée,*" *MLN: Modern Language Notes* 89, no. 4, French issue (May 1974): 630.

2. "The employee's plan for making a killing was simple and practical. . . . He knew his Paris like the back of his hand; he knew that the money shower that beat against the walls would fall harder each day. Clever people only had to open up their pockets. He put himself on the side of the clever, reading the future in the offices of the Hôtel de Ville."

3. David Bell analyzes the connection between the "universal equivalent" and political power in the *Rougon-Macquart,* arguing that the hidden origins of the gold standard function in precisely the same way as the foundation of the Second Empire: paraphrasing Marx, "gold as money can occupy a position of transcendence only if the genesis of the monetary form through four distinct phases is obscured or forgotten. Gold itself was originally a mere commodity, and only if this fact is neglected can its position of prestige and uniqueness be maintained." David Bell, *Models of Power: Politics and Economics in Zola's "Rougon-Macquart"* (Lincoln: University of Nebraska Press, 1988), 17.

4. "And with his hand spread out, open and slicing like a large knife, he made a gesture to separate the city into four parts. . . . [Speaking to his wife] 'Here, follow my hand a little. From the boulevard du Temple to the barrière du Trône, one gash; another gash from the Madeleine to Monceau; and a third gash in this direction here, another gash in that direction, a gash over here, a gash further out, gashes everywhere, Paris hacked by saber blows, its veins open, feeding a hundred thousand road workers and masons."

5. "One day, Saccard dared take the liberty of consulting, in the prefect's office, the famous map of [or plan for] Paris upon which 'an august hand' had traced in red ink the principal routes of the second network. Those bloody pen strokes cut through Paris even deeper than had the surveyor's hand."

6. "The Emperor was in a hurry to show me a map of Paris upon which He Himself had traced in blue, in red, in yellow and in green, according to the degrees of urgency, the different new roads which He proposed having constructed." Baron Haussmann, *Mémoires du Baron Haussmann: Vol. II: Préfecture de la Seine* (Paris: Victor-Havard, 1890), 53.

7. See Commission des embellissements de Paris, *Commission des embellissements de Paris: Rapport à l'empereur Napoléon III,* ed. Pierre Casselle, *Cahiers de la Rotonde,* 2001, no. 23.

8. "On the day that Haussmann took his oath of office, the Emperor handed him a map, so the legend spun by Haussmann in his *Mémoires* has it. . . . This was, according to Haussmann, the plan that he faithfully carried out (with a few extensions) over the next two decades. We now know this to be a myth." David Harvey, *Paris, Capital of Modernity* (New York: Routledge, 2003), 8. David P. Jordan, in a mostly favorable study of Haussmann's achievements, wants to take the baron at his word concerning the existence of the Emperor's

map, but concedes that "mystery" surrounds it, that its "very existence" raises questions, since it would have been destroyed along with all the other archives in the Hôtel de Ville during the bloody days of the Commune. David P. Jordan, *Transforming Paris: The Life and Labors of Baron Haussmann* (New York: Free Press, 1995), 170.

9. For a thorough study of bird's-eye views of Paris and the city in general in the first half of the nineteenth century, see Seth Graebner. "The Bird's-Eye View: Looking at the City in Paris and Algiers," *Nineteenth-Century French Studies* 36, nos. 3–4 (2008): 221–39.

10. The image can be seen at the Bibliothèque nationale de France, in the Nouvelles Acquisitions françaises, no. 10.316, folio 416.

11. "Since 1868, I stay in the grid that I have imposed for myself, the genealogical tree indicates for me the major lines, without letting me deviate right or left. I have to follow it strictly; it is at once my force and my regulator. The conclusions are ready-made. Here is what I have wanted and here is what I accomplished."

12. "It was a large sheet of yellowed paper, worn at its fold, from which rose up, drawn in bold strokes, a symbolic tree, whose outstretched, subdivided branches lined up five rows of wide leaves; and each leaf bore a name, and contained, in small handwriting, a biography, a hereditary case."

Part V
Chapter 9

1. Quotations of the *Recherche* are taken from the Pléiade editions of 1987–89. I will use the following abbreviations for convenience: *CS—Le Côté de chez Swann, JF—À l'ombre des jeunes filles en fleurs, CG—Le Côté de Guermantes, SG—Sodome et Gomorrhe, P—La Prisonnière, AD—Albertine disparue, TR—Le Temps retrouvé.* Roman numerals correspond to the Pléiade volume.

2. "A man who sleeps holds in a circle around him the thread of hours, the order of years and of worlds. He consults them instinctively upon waking and reads in a second the place on earth that he occupies, the time that has elapsed until his waking; but this order can be confused, and break . . . But it sufficed that, in my very bed, my sleep was deep and entirely relaxed my mind; then, it let go the map of the place where I had fallen asleep, and when I would wake up in the middle of the night, as I did not know where I was, I did not even know at first who I was; I only had the rudimentary sense of existence as it can quiver for an animal; I was more deprived of perception than the cave dweller; but then the memory—not yet of the place where I was, but of some of those I had inhabited and where I might have been—came to me like a salvation from above to pull me out of the nothingness which I could not escape alone; I traveled over one second over centuries of civilization and the confused images of oil-lamps, of shirts with folded-down collars, recomposed the original features of my ego."

3. Much of Proustian criticism has denied any relationship between Bergson's metaphysics and Proust's novel on the basis that they have different conceptions of duration (see Georges Poulet's *L'Espace proustien* and Julia Kristeva's

Le Temps sensible, 240 and 377). The description here of active memory, and especially later of involuntary memory in the madeleine episode, as the sensation of an "image" or "souvenir visuel" that is unanchored, rises up to the surface of consciousness, which itself is displaced and orients itself to receive the memory, is remarkably similar to Henri Bergson's concept of consciousness and pure memory, as represented in the figure of the cone (see Bergson, *Matière et mémoire,* 181; Deleuze, *Proust et les signes,* 73; and Dumoncel, 52–53).

4. "But it was no use knowing that I was not in the houses which in my unaware state of waking had for an instant if not given me a distinct image, at least made me believe the possible presence, my memory had been set in motion; generally I did not try to go back to sleep right away; I spent a good part of the night recalling our life in the old days, in Combray at my great aunt's house, in Balbec, in Paris, in Doncières, in Venice, other places still, recalling the places, the people whom I used to know, what I saw of them, what people told me about them."

5. "I put my tea cup down and I turned toward my mind. It is up to it to discover the truth. But how? Serious uncertainty, whenever the mind feels overtaken by itself; when it, the seeker, is at once the obscure country where it must search and where its baggage will be useless. To seek? More than that: to create. It is confronted with something that does not yet exist and that only it can bring about, then bring to the light."

6. In an alternative version to the beginning of *Le Côté de Guermantes,* Proust envisioned a long analysis of the "Noms de personnes" (perhaps a pun, "names of persons" or "nobody's name," since for Proust names never coincide with the people they designate). One of the versions of the "Noms de personnes," found in the "Esquisse VIII" of the second tome of the Pléiade edition, elaborates the evocative power of Names and their spatial quality (*CG II,* 1051–52). In yet another version, published in the 1954 *Contre Sainte-Beuve* (but absent from the second Pléiade), Proust is more explicit: "C'est encore aujourd'hui un des grands charmes des familles nobles qu'elles semblent situées dans un coin de terre particulier, que leur nom qui est toujours un nom de lieu . . ." (268) ("It is still one of the great charms of noble families that they seem situated in a particular corner of the land, that their name, which is always a place name . . .").

7. "La singularité supposée du nom propre répond à la singularité mythique du lieu, et la renforce" (Gérard Genette "Proust et le langage indirect" *Figures II,* 234) ("The supposed singularity of a proper name corresponds to the mythical singularity of the place, and reinforces it"). "Le charme d'un lieu tient donc, en dernière analyse, au fait qu'il est lui-même et non pas un autre, qu'il possède, à l'égal des êtres humains, cette caractéristique essentielle qui s'appelle l'unicité" (Georges Poulet, *L'espace Proustien,* 49) ("A place's charm comes from the fact that it is itself and not another, that it possesses, just like human beings, this essential characteristic called unicity").

8. Jeffrey Mehlman's reading of "Combray" in *A Structural Study of Autobiography: Proust, Leiris, Sartre, Lévi-Strauss* focuses its argument on the "failure of the paternal principle" (24).

9. Uncovering the chiasmus of critic and novelistic creation, Lawrence Kritzman argues that Barthes's work on Proust serves as an "intertext" to work through Barthes's own mourning for the death of his mother: "Ironically unlike Freud who had, seventy-five years earlier, asserted that the death of the father is the major event in a man's life, here it is not the father who is mourned, but rather the mother and, in Proust's case, by extension, the grandmother" ("Barthes's Way: *Un Amour de Proust*," 535).

10. "For there were around Combray two 'Ways' for strolling, and so opposed that we would not in fact leave our house by the same door, when we wanted to go one way or the other. . . . Since my father always spoke of the Méséglise way as comprising the most beautiful view of the plain that he knew and the Guermantes way as typical of stream scenery, I gave them, by conceiving them thus as two entities, a cohesion, a unity that only belongs to creations of our mind. . . . This habit that we had of never going both ways on the same day, enclosed them so to speak far from one another, unknowable to each other, in the sealed vessels, between which there was no communication, of different afternoons."

11. In *Proust et les signes,* Gilles Deleuze argues that the two "côtés" provide the model for other systems of "vases clos" in the *Recherche,* which are opposed to "boîtes entrouvertes" ("half-opened boxes") such as proper names, which do communicate. Deleuze resists the idea that the two "côtés" ever come together.

12. "To start, between space and place, I place a distinction that will delimit a field. A *place* is an order (whatever it may be) according to which elements are distributed in relationships of coexistence. The possibility is therefore excluded for two things to occupy the same spot. The law of the 'proper' rules there: elements are one *beside* the other, each situated in a spot 'proper' and distinct to it that defines it. A place is therefore an instantaneous configuration of positions. It implies an indication of stability."

13. "There is *space* as soon as directional vectors, quantities of speed, and the variable of time are taken into consideration . . . Space would be to place, what the written word is to the spoken word."

14. "The stone for the nave and the towers really came from the cliffs beaten by the tides. But this sea, which for those reasons I imagined as coming to die at the foot of the stained-glass window, was more than five leagues away, at Balbec-Plage, and next to its dome, this steeple, which, because I had read that it was also a harsh Norman cliff where grains were stored, where birds would whirl around, I always represented to myself as receiving at its base the last foam of the rising waves, rose up on a square at the junction of two tramway lines, opposite a café which displayed, in golden letters, the word 'Billiards'; the steeple stood out against a background of houses whose roofs mixed with no masts. And the church . . . was one with all the rest, seemed an accident."

15. "I could discern that the charm of each of the paintings consisted of a sort of metamorphosis of represented things, analogous to what in poetry is called metaphor and that if God the Father had created things by naming them, it is by taking away their name, or by giving them another that Elstir re-created

them. Names which designate things always correspond to a notion of our intellect, foreign to our true impressions and which force us to eliminate from them everything that does not relate to this notion."

16. "It is as if she told me: 'Turn left, then take the path on your right, and you will touch the intangible, you will attain the unattainable distant places that we know on earth only by the direction which leads to them, of which we know only—what I used to believe that I could know only about Guermantes, and maybe, in a sense, I was not mistaken—the 'path.'"

17. "An edifice occupying, it can be said, a space in four dimensions—the fourth being that of time—deploying through the centuries its nave [or "ship"] which, from each row of benches, from each chapel, seemed to conquer and breach not only a few meters, but successive epochs from which it emerged victorious."

18. Christie McDonald, in *The Proustian Fabric,* explains the relation between dream, text, and interpretation: "Because the fundamental structure of the novel is based on the association of ideas, Proust's equivalent to the basic rule in psychoanalysis, the entire novel calls for a kind of interpretation close to dream analysis in which associations create sense. Through their paratactic power to level hierarchies of thought, books like dreams reorganize time, space, and the sequences of experience" (40).

Chapter 10

1. Joshua Landy, in "'Les Moi en Moi': The Proustian Self in Philosophical Perspective" counts himself, Roland Barthes, and Marcel Muller among those who believe that the *Recherche* is distinct from the virtual novel of the narrator, and counts Louis Martin-Chauffier, Jean Rousset, Leo Bersani, Richard Terdiman, Roger Shattuck, and Gérard Genette among those who believe that the two works are more or less the same (Landy, 127).

2. "In fact each moment of the work is in some sort given two times: a first time in the *Recherche* as the birth of a vocation, a second time in the *Recherche* as the practice of this vocation; but these 'two times' are given to us together, and it is the reader, informed in extremis that the book he has just read remains to be written . . . that it falls upon the reader to go back all the way to the pages of the beginning . . . and that he must now reread."

3. Gérard Genette, in "Littérature et l'espace" in *Figures II,* while postulating about space in literature in general, notes four manifestations of space in Proust's *Recherche:* (1) the preponderance of spatial metaphors in language, which Genette admits was already described by Bergson; (2) the space of the plot, or as Proust calls it, the telescopic aspect of his novel; (3) metaphor, which is the space between "le signifié apparent et le signifié réel abolissant du même coup la linéarité du discours" ("the apparent signified and the real signified abolishing at the same time the linearity of discourse"), or as Genette calls it, a "figure"; and (4) the space of literary history or intertextuality, perfectly embodied by the library.

4. William C. Carter's *The Proustian Quest* studies Proust's novel in the historical, scientific, and ideological contexts of what he calls "the age of speed."

5. "I feel tremble inside me something which is moving, which would like to rise up, something that was unanchored, from a great depth; I do not know what it is, but it rises slowly; I feel resistance and I hear the rumbling of the distances traversed. Of course, what flutters within me must be the image, the visual memory, which linked to this taste, tries to follow it until it reaches me."

6. "Or, si le temps proustien prend *toujours* la forme de l'espace, c'est qu'il est d'une nature telle qu'il est directement opposé au temps bergsonien. . . . L'espace proustien est cet espace final, fait de l'ordre dans lequel se distribuent les uns par rapport aux autres les différents épisodes du roman proustien" (Poulet, 135–36) ("If Proustian time *always* takes spatial form, it is because its nature is such that it is directly opposed to Bergsonian time. . . . Proustian space is that final space, composed of the order in which the different episodes of the Proustian novel are arranged in relationship to each other").

7. "The common sensation sought to re-create around itself the former place, while the current place which occupied the spot opposed with all the inertia of its mass the immigration of a Norman beach or of a railroad embankment into a Parisian 'hôtel particulier' . . . Always, with these resurrections, the distant place engendered around the common sensation was for a moment coupled, like a wrestler, with the present place. Always the present place had come off victorious, and always the vanquished one had appeared to me the more beautiful of the two . . . And if the present place had not so soon conquered the past one, I think that I would have lost consciousness; for these resurrections of the past, in the second that they last, are so complete that they not only force our eyes to quit seeing the bedroom which is close to them in order to look at the tree-lined path or the rising tide. They force our nostrils to breathe the air of faraway places, our willpower to choose between the different projects which these places offer us, our entire person to believe itself surrounded by these places, or at least to stumble between them and the present places, in the exhilaration of an uncertainty similar to that sometimes experienced when confronting an ineffable vision, at the moment of falling asleep."

8. As I showed in chapters 2 and 4 concerning Stendhal and Nerval, Bergson proposes a model for involuntary memory that describes the consciousness occupying two places and times simultaneously, causing a hallucination (Bergson, 161). The consciousness must repress the past as memory in order to focus on immediate danger.

9. Proust's narrator also notices the analogy between his text and Nerval's. He is reassured that his discovery of the madeleine is more than simply personal, because other writers (Chateaubriand, Nerval, and Baudelaire) have preceded him (*TR IV*, 498).

10. "And now I understood what old age was—the old age that of all realities is perhaps the one for which we keep a purely abstract notion for most of our life, looking at calendars, dating our letters, seeing our friends marry, our friends' children, without understanding, either out of fear or laziness, what it means . . . I understood what death, love, the joys of the mind, of a vocation, etc. meant . . . Perhaps the cruel discovery that I had just made could only but be useful to me concerning the very material of my book. Since I had decided

that it could not be made up solely of truly full impressions, those outside of time, among the truths with which I hoped to set them, those which were connected to time, time in which people, societies, nations bathed and changed, would hold an important place."

11. Maurice Blanchot has argued that the *Recherche* as literary text cannot consist entirely of "moments bienheureux," which would lead to something of a "pure narrative," because there needs to be an articulation of emptiness between each memory that would render the intermittent character of true time. The "privileged instants" of involuntary memory are not "immobile points" but rather are in constant movement from their hidden depths to the surface and back again (*Le Livre à venir*, 34). Emptiness, conveyed by "the densest continuity" (33) of less pure everyday material and which composes the bulk of the novel, is itself in continual development and movement, turning around itself like a sphere and reflecting the more profound movement of memory (33).

12. "Like the majority of beings, moreover, was she not like the 'stars' of crossroads in the forest where paths from the most different points, as in our life as well, come to converge? The paths were numerous for me which led to Mlle de Saint-Loup and which radiated around her. And most importantly what led to her were the two great 'ways' where I had had so many walks and dreams."

WORKS CITED

Abrams, M. H. *Natural Supernaturalism: Tradition and Revolution in Romantic Literature*. New York: W. W. Norton, 1971.

Ansel, Yves. "Des usages 'prosaïques' de la biographie à la 'Vie de Henry Brulard.'" *Stendhal Club* 145 (1994): 1–8.

Augé, Marc. *Non-lieux: Introduction à une anthropologie de la surmodernité*. Paris: Seuil, 1992.

Bachelard, Gaston. *La Poétique de l'espace*. Paris: Presses Universitaires de France, 1957.

Badiou, Alain. "Logic of the Site." *Diacritics* 33, nos. 3–4 (Fall-Winter 2003): 141–50.

Baguley, David. *Critical Essays on Émile Zola*. Boston: G. K. Hall, 1986.

———. *Naturalist Fiction: The Entropic Vision*. Cambridge, Eng.: Cambridge University Press, 1990.

Balzac, Honoré de. *La Peau de chagrin. La Comédie humaine,* vol 10. Paris: Gallimard, 1979.

Barthes, Roland. "Proust et les noms." In *Le Degré zéro de l'écriture*. Paris: Seuil, 1972

Becker, Colette. *Zola: Le saut dans les étoiles*. Paris: Presses Sorbonne Nouvelle, 2002.

Beizer, Janet. "History's Life Story: *Nanon* as *Histoire de ma vie*." In *George Sand et l'empire des lettres,* edited by Anne E. McCall-Saint-Saens, 275–83. New Orleans: Presses Universitaires du Nouveau Monde, 2004.

Bell, David. *Models of Power: Politics and Economics in Zola's "Rougon-Macquart."* Lincoln: University of Nebraska Press, 1988.

Bell, Sheila M. "Stendhal's *Vie de Henry Brulard:* The Engravings—A Public or Private Matter?" *Modern Language Review* 93 (1998): 356–69.

Bender, John, and Michael Marrinan. *The Culture of Diagram*. Stanford, Calif.: Stanford University Press, 2010.

Benstock, Shari. "The Female Self Engendered: Autobiographical Writing and Theories of Selfhood." In *Women and Autobiography,* edited by Martine Watson Brownley and Allison B. Kimmich, 3–13. Wilmington, Del.: SR Books, 1999.

Bergson, Henri. *Matière et mémoire*. 1896; Paris: Presses Universitaires de France, 1999.

Bersani, Leo. *Marcel Proust: The Fictions of Life and of Art*. New York: Oxford University Press, 1965.

Biggs, Michael. “Putting the State on the Map: Cartography, Territory, and European State Formation.” *Comparative Studies in Society and History* 44, no. 2 (April 1999): 374–405.

Blanchot, Maurice. *L’Espace littéraire.* Paris: Gallimard, 1955.

———. *Le livre à venir.* Paris: Gallimard, 1959.

Blin, Georges. *Stendhal et les problèmes du roman.* Paris: Corti, 1954.

Blum, Léon. *Stendhal et le beylisme.* 1914; Paris: Albin Michel, 1947.

Bonnefis, Philippe. *L’Innomable: Essai sur l’oeuvre d’É. Zola.* Paris: SEDES, 1984.

Bourdieu, Pierre. *Les Règles de l’art: Genèse et structure du champ littéraire.* Paris: Seuil, 1992.

Bowman, Frank Paul. *La conquête de soi par l’écriture.* Orléans: Paradigme, 1997.

Brée, Germaine. “Autogynography.” In *Studies in Autobiography,* edited by James Olney, 171–79. Oxford: Oxford University Press, 1988.

Burke, Edmund. *Reflections on the Revolution in France.* London: Apollo, 1814.

Carpenter, Scott. *Acts of Fiction: Resistance and Resolution from Sade to Baudelaire.* University Park: Pennsylvania State Press, 1996.

Carter, William C. *The Proustian Quest.* New York: New York University Press, 1992.

Cellier, Léon. “De ‘Sylvie’ à *Aurélia:* Structure close et structure ouverte.” Paris: Lettres modernes, 1971.

Certeau, Michel de. *L’invention du quotidien 1. Arts de faire.* Paris: Gallimard, 1990.

Chambers, Ross. *Gérard de Nerval et la poétique de l’espace.* Paris: José Corti, 1969.

———. *Mélancolie et opposition: Les débuts du modernisme en France.* Paris: José Corti, 1987.

———. *The Writing of Melancholy: Modes of Opposition in Early French Modernism.* Translated by Mary Seidman Trouille. Chicago: University of Chicago Press, 1993.

Chotard, Loïc. *Nerval: Mémoires de la critique.* Paris: Presses de l’Université de Paris-Sorbonne, 1997.

Clark, T. J. *The Painting of Modern Life.* New York: Knopf, 1984.

Cohen, Margaret. *The Sentimental Education of the Novel.* Princeton, N.J.: Princeton University Press, 1999.

Colette. *La Naissance du jour.* 1928; Paris: Garnier-Flammarion, 1993.

Commission des embellissements de Paris. *Commission des embellissements de Paris: Rapport à l’empereur Napoléon III.* Edited by Pierre Casselle, *Cahiers de la Rotonde,* 2001, no. 23.

Conley, Tom. *The Self-Made Map: Cartographic Writing in Early Modern France.* Minneapolis: University of Minnesota Press, 1996.

———. “A Suckling of Cities: Montaigne in Paris and Rome.” *Montaigne Studies* 9, nos. 1–2 (1997): 167–86.

Cornell, Kenneth. “Zola’s City.” *Yale French Studies* 32, Paris in Literature (1964): 106–11.

Coulont-Henderson, Françoise. "Remarques sur la mémoire et les croquis dans la *Vie de Henry Brulard.*" *Stendhal Club* 102 (1984): 141–51.

Crouzet, Michel. "*La Vie de Henry Brulard:* La moins 'puante' des autobiographies?" *Stendhal Club* 132 (1991): 287–312, 133 (1991): 1–18, 135 (1992): 243–60.

Dear, Michael, et al., eds. *GeoHumanities: Art, History, Text at the Edge of Place.* London: Routledge, 2011.

Deleuze, Gilles. *Cinéma 1: L'image-mouvement.* Paris: Minuit, 1983.

———. *Critique et Clinique.* Paris: Minuit, 1993.

———. *Foucault.* Paris: Minuit, 1986.

———. *Le Pli: Leibniz et le baroque.* Paris: Minuit, 1988.

———. *Logique du sens.* Paris: Minuit, 1969.

———. *Proust et les signes.* Paris: Presses Universitaires de France, 1964.

Deleuze, Gilles, and Félix Guattari. *Mille plateaux.* Paris: Minuit, 1980.

Derrida, Jacques. *L'Écriture et la différence.* Paris: Seuil, 1967.

———. *Mal d'archive.* Paris: Galilée, 1995.

Descartes, René. *Discours de la méthode.* Paris: Bordas, 1996.

Didier, Béatrice. *Sade: Une écriture du désir.* Paris: Denoël-Gonthier, 1976.

———. *Stendhal autobiographe.* Paris: Presses Universitaires de France, 1983.

Dumoncel, Jean-Claude. *Le Symbole d'hécate: Philosophie deleuzienne et roman proustien.* Orléans: HYX, 1996.

Felman, Shoshana. *La Folie et la chose littéraire.* Paris: Seuil, 1978.

Fish, Stanley. "The Triumph of the Humanities." *New York Times.* Opinionator Blog (June 13, 2011): n.p., http://opinionator.blogs.nytimes.com/2011/06/13/the-triumph-of-the-humanities/?pagemode=print.

Fletcher, Angus. *Allegory, the Theory of a Symbolic Mode.* Ithaca, N.Y.: Cornell University Press, 1964.

Foucault, Michel. *Surveiller et punir.* Paris: Gallimard, 1975.

Genette, Gérard. *Figures I.* Paris: Seuil, 1966.

———. *Figures II.* Paris: Seuil, 1969.

———. *Figures III.* Paris: Seuil, 1972.

Goethe, Johann Wolfgang von. *Italian Journey.* Translated by W. H. Auden and Elizabeth Meyer. London: Penguin Books, 1970.

Graebner, Seth. "The Bird's-Eye View: Looking at the City in Paris and Algiers." *Nineteenth-Century French Studies* 36, nos. 3–4 (2008): 221–39.

Hamon, Philippe. *Le Personnel du roman: Le système des personnages dans les "Rougon-Macquart" d'Emile Zola.* Geneva: Droz, 1983.

Harvey, David. *The Condition of Postmodernity: An Enquiry into the Origins of Cultural Change.* Cambridge, Mass.: Blackwell, 1990.

———. *Paris, Capital of Modernity.* New York: Routledge, 2003.

Haussmann, Georges-Eugène, Baron. *Mémoires du Baron Haussmann. Vol. II: Préfecture de la Seine.* Paris: Victor-Havard, 1890.

Hiddleston, Janet. *George Sand and Autobiography.* Oxford: Legenda, Research Monographs in French Studies 5, 1999.

Holmes, Richard. *Footsteps: Adventures of a Romantic Biographer.* New York: Viking, 1985.

Jacob, Christian. *L'Empire des cartes: Approche théorique de la cartographie à travers l'histoire*. Paris: Albin Michel, 1992.

Jameson, Fredric. *The Seeds of Time*. New York: Columbia University Press, 1994.

Jefferson, Ann. *Reading Realism in Stendhal*. Cambridge, Eng.: Cambridge University Press. 1988.

Jordan, David P. *Transforming Paris: The Life and Labors of Baron Haussmann*. New York: Free Press, 1995.

Kern, Stephen. *The Culture of Time and Space: 1880–1918*. Cambridge, Mass.: Harvard University Press, 1983.

Kofman, Sarah. *Nerval: Le charme de la répétition: Lecture de "Sylvie."* Lausanne: L'Âge d'homme, 1979.

Kristeva, Julia. *Le Temps sensible: Proust et l'expérience littéraire*. Paris: Gallimard, 1994.

Kritzman, Lawrence D. "Barthes's Way: *Un Amour de Proust*." *Yale Journal of Criticism* 14, no. 2 (2001): 535–43.

Lacan, Jacques. *Écrits I & II*. Paris: Seuil, 1999.

Lampedusa, Giuseppe Tomasi di. *Il gattopardo*. Milan: Feltrinelli, 2002.

Landy, Joshua. "'Les Moi en Moi': The Proustian Self in Philosophical Perspective." *New Literary History* 32 (2001): 91–132.

Lang, Candace. "Stendhal: Une autobiographie en dérive." *MLN: Modern Language Notes*, December 1979, 1072–92.

Laplanche, L., and J.-B. Pontalis. *The Language of Psychoanalysis*. Translated by Donald Nicholson-Smith. New York: W. W. Norton, 1973.

Lefebvre, Henri. *La proclamation de la Commune*, Paris: Gallimard, 1965.

———. *La production de l'espace*. 4th edition. Paris: Anthropos, 2000.

Lejeune, Philippe. *L'autobiographie en France*. Paris: Armand Colin, 1971.

———. "L'irréel du passé." In *Autofictions & Cie.*, edited by Jacques Lecarme, Serge Doubrovsky, and Philippe Lejeune. Paris: Université Paris X, 1993.

———. *Le Pacte autobiographique*. Paris: Éditions du Seuil, 1975.

Lethbridge, Robert. "L'Homme et *L'Oeuvre:* Zola et la déformation Romanesque." In *Lire/Dé-lire Zola,* edited by Jean-Pierre Leduc-Adine and Henri Mitterand, 133–52. Paris: Nouveau Monde, 2004.

Lumbroso, Olivier. *Zola: La plume et le compas: Construction de l'espace dans "Les Rougon-Macquart" d'Émile Zola*. Paris: Honoré Champion, 2004.

Mahuzier, Brigitte. " The Graphics of Autobiography: Struggle with Description in Proust and Stendhal." *Dissertation Abstracts International* 48, no. 12 (1988): 3122A.

Marder, Elissa. *Dead Time: Temporal Disorders in the Wake of Modernity (Baudelaire and Flaubert)*. Stanford, Calif.: Stanford University Press, 2001.

Marin, Louis. "The Autobiographical Interruption: About Stendhal's *Life of Henry Brulard*." *Modern Language Notes* 93, no. 4 (1978): 597–617.

———. "Images dans le texte autobiographique: Sur le chapitre xliv de La *Vie de Henry Brulard*." *Saggi e Riccerce de Letteratura Francese* 23 (1984): 195–231.

———. *La Voix excommuniée*. Paris: Galilée, 1981.

———. "Sur un certain regard du sujet." In *Les Sujets de l'écriture*, edited by Jean Decottignies, 41–62. Lille: Presses Universitaires de Lille III, 1981.

———. *Utopiques: Jeux d'espaces*. Paris: Minuit, 1973.

McDonald, Christie. "Fractured Readers." *MLN: Modern Language Notes* 97 (May 1982): 840–48.

———. *The Proustian Fabric: Associations of Memory*. Lincoln: University of Nebraska Press, 1991.

Mehlman, Jeffrey. *A Structural Study of Autobiography: Proust, Sartre, Leiris, Lévi-Strauss*. Ithaca, N.Y.: Cornell University Press, 1971.

Melara, Miriella. "Nominal Intersections: Pseudonomity and Generic Boundaries in Stendhal's *Vie de Henry Brulard*." *Nineteenth-Century French Studies* 19, no. 2 (Winter 1991): 247–61.

Miller, Nancy K. *Subject to Change: Reading Feminist Writing*. New York: Columbia University Press, 1988.

Mitterand, Henri, and Olivier Lumbroso. *Les Manuscrits et dessins de Zola; Notes préparatoires et dessins des "Rougon-Macquart."* 3 volumes. Paris: Éditions Textuel, 2002.

Montaigne, Michel de. *Essais*. Introduction by Alexandre Micha. Paris: Flammarion, 1979.

Moretti, Franco. *Graphs, Maps, Trees: Abstract Models for a Literary History*. London: Verso, 2005.

Mossman, Carol. "Les gravures de la *Vie de Henry Brulard;* Iconographie brulardienne: Les figures de l'écriture." *Stendhal Club* 112 (1986): 339–53.

Murdoch, H. Adlai. "Ghosts in the Mirror: Colonialism and Creole Indeterminacy in Brontë and Sand." *College Literature* 29, no. 1 (Winter 2002): 1–31.

Naginski, Isabelle Hoog. *George Sand: Writing for Her Life*. New Brunswick, N.J.: Rutgers University Press, 1991.

Nerval, Gérard de. *Oeuvres*, vols. *I* and *II*. Edited by Albert Beguin and Jean Richer. Paris: Gallimard, 1961 (1978).

———. *Oeuvres complètes*, vol. *II*. Edited by Jean Guillaume and Claude Pichois. Paris: Gallimard, 1984.

Nesci, Catherine. *Le flâneur et les flâneuses: Les femmes et la ville à l'époque romantique*. Grenoble: ELLUG, 2007.

Pelletier, Monique. *La Carte des Cassini: La Science au service de l'État et des régions*. Paris: Éditions du C.T.H.S., 2002.

Perec, Georges. *Espèce d'espaces*. Paris: Galilée, 1974.

Petrey, Sandy. *In the Court of the Pear King: French Culture and the Rise of Realism*. Ithaca, N.Y.: Cornell University Press, 2005.

———. "Stylistics and Society in *La Curée*." *MLN: Modern Language Notes* 89, no. 4, French issue (May 1974): 626–40.

Poulet, Georges. *L'espace proustien*. Paris: Gallimard, 1963.

Prasad, Pratima. "Espace colonial et vérité historique dans *Indiana*." *Études littéraires* 35, nos. 2–3 (Summer-Autumn 2003): 71–85.

Prendergast, Christopher. *The Order of Mimesis: Balzac, Stendhal, Nerval, Flaubert*. Cambridge, Eng.: Cambridge University Press, 1986.

Proust, Marcel. *À la recherche du temps perdu.* Edited by Jean-Yves Tadié. 4 volumes. Paris: Gallimard, 1987–89.

———. *Contre Sainte-Beuve.* Edited by Bernard de Fallois. Paris: Gallimard, 1954. Revised edition edited by Pierre Clarac, 1971.

Rancière, Jacques. *La parole muette: Essai sur les contradictions de la littérature.* Paris: Hachette Littératures, 1998.

———. *Le Partage du sensible.* Paris: La Fabrique, 2000.

———. *Politique de la littérature.* Paris: Galilée, 2007.

Richard, Jean-Pierre. *Microlectures.* Paris: Seuil, 1979.

Richardson, Michael. "Enough Said." *Anthropology Today* 6, no. 4 (August 1990): 16–19.

Richer, Jean. *Nerval et les doctrines ésotériques.* Paris: Griffon, 1947.

———. *Nerval: Expérience vécue & Création ésotérique.* Paris: Guy Trédaniel, 1987.

Ricoeur, Paul. *Temps et récit II : La configuration dans le récit de fiction.* Paris: Seuil, 1984.

Rogers, Nancy E. "Nanon: Novel of Revolution or Revolutionary Novel?" In *The World of George Sand,* edited by Jeanne Fuchs, David A. Powell, and Natalie Datlof, 137–44. New York: Greenwood, 1987.

Ross, Kristin. *The Emergence of Social Space: Rimbaud and the Paris Commune.* Minneapolis: University of Minnesota Press, 1988.

Rousseau, Jean-Jacques. *Les Confessions.* Paris: Gallimard, 1973.

Said, Edward W. *Orientalism.* New York: Pantheon, 1978.

Sand, George. *Correspondance.* Edited by Georges Lubin. 26 volumes. Paris: Garnier, 1964–95.

———. *Histoire de ma vie II.* Edited by Damien Zanone. Paris: GF Flammarion, 2001.

———. *Indiana.* Edited by Béatrice Didier. Paris: Gallimard, 1984.

———. *Nanon.* Edited by Nicole Mozet. Saint-Cyr-sur-Loire: Christian Pirot, 2005.

Schaeffer, Gerald. *Le Voyage en Orient de Nerval: Étude des structures.* Neuchâtel: Éditions de la Baconnière, 1967.

Schehr, Lawrence. *Rendering French Realism.* Stanford, Calif.: Stanford University Press. 1997.

Schivelbusch, Wolfgang. *The Railway Journey: The Industrialization of Time and Space in the 19th Century.* Berkeley: University of California Press, 1986.

Schor, Naomi. *George Sand and Idealism.* New York: Columbia University Press, 1993.

———. "Zola: From Window to Window." *Yale French Studies* 42, "Zola" (1969): 38–51.

———. *Zola's Crowds.* Baltimore: Johns Hopkins University Press, 1978.

Serres, Michel. *Feux et signaux de brume: Zola.* Paris: Grasset, 1975.

Shattuck, Roger. *Proust's Binocular's: A Study of Memory, Time, and Recognition in "À la recherche du temps perdu."* New York: Random House, 1963.

Sheringham, Michael. *French Autobiography: Devices and Desires.* Oxford: Clarendon, 1993.

Smith, Sidonie. "Constructing Truth in Lying Mouths: Truthtelling in Women's Autobiography." In *Women and Autobiography,* edited by Martine Watson Brownley and Allison B. Kimmich, 33–52. Wilmington, Del.: SR Books, 1999.

Stanton, Domna C. "Autogynography: Is the Subject Different?" In *The Female Autograph,* edited by Domna Stanton, 3–20. Chicago: University of Chicago Press, 1987.

Stendhal. *Oeuvres intimes.* Edited by Henri Martineau. Paris: Gallimard, 1955.

———. *Oeuvres intimes I et II.* Edited by V. Del Litto. Paris: Gallimard, 1981.

———. *Promenades dans Rome.* Edited by V. Del Litto. Paris: Gallimard, 1973.

———. *Vie de Henry Brulard.* Edited by Béatrice Didier. Paris: Gallimard, 1973.

———. *Vie de Henry Brulard écrite par lui-même.* Edition diplomatique du manuscrit de la bibliothèque de Grenoble. Presented and annotated by Gérard Rannaud. 3 volumes. Grenoble: Klincksieck, 1996–98.

Sterne, Laurence. *The Life and Opinions of Tristram Shandy, Gentleman.* New York: Odyssey, 1940.

Virilio, Paul. *L'Inertie polaire.* Paris: Christian Bourgois, 1990.

Zola, Émile. *La Fabrique des Rougon-Macquart: Éditions des dossiers préparatoires.* Edited by Colette Becker and Véronique Lavielle. 4 volumes. Paris: Honoré Champion, 2003–9.

———. *Le Roman expérimental.* Paris: G. Charpentier, 1880.

———. *Les Rougon-Macquart.* Edited by Henri Mitterand. 5 volumes. Paris: Gallimard, 1960–67.

INDEX